Preface

The book titled *Mastering in Instrumentation: Questions and Answers* is designed to serve as a comprehensive resource for instrumentation engineering interviews. It covers a wide spectrum of topics relevant to the field of industrial instrumentation, providing detailed explanations supported by necessary figures and illustrations.

The content ranges from conventional pneumatic systems to the latest Foundation Fieldbus technology, ensuring readers gain a thorough understanding of both traditional and modern instrumentation concepts. The book is written in clear and simple language, making it accessible to a broad audienc

Instrumentation engineering is a multidisciplinary field that draws upon fundamentals from mechanical, electrical, electronics, and information technology. Recognizing this, the book includes essential basics from all these domains to provide a well-rounded foundation.

This book is intended not only for fresh graduates and job seekers preparing for interviews but also for experienced professionals seeking a handy reference. Additionally, it can serve as a practical handbook for working engineers and students alike.

I hope this book aids readers in mastering instrumentation concepts and helps them confidently face interviews and professional challenges in this dynamic field.

Acknowledgments

- Lessons In Industrial Instrumentation by Tony R. Kuphaldt
- Measurement and Instrumentation Principles by Alan S. Morris
- Instrumentation Reference Book by Walt Boyes
- Industrial Instrumentation and control by S.K. singh
- instrumentationtools.com
- control.com

Table of Contents

1. Units and Measurement 1–4
2. Fundamentals of Instrumentation 5–16
3. Basics of Electrical Engineering 17–24
4. Tubes and Fittings 25–31
5. Instrumentation Cable and Connectors........................32–46
6. Analog Instrumentation Signals.................................47–60
7. Pressure Measurement 61–81
8. Temperature Measurements 82–106
9. Level Measurements 107–118
10. Flow Measurements 119–143
11. Vibration Measurements 144–157
12. Discrete Process Measurements (Switches) 158–164
13. Instrumentation Documents 165–172
14. Pneumatic System 173–182
15. Valves and Actuators 183–224
16. Process Control..225–251
17. Industrial Communication System............................252–294
18. Industrial Control System 295–322
19. Safety Instrumentation 323–339
20. Gas & Fire Detection System 340–346
21. Analysers 347–353
22. Miscellaneous Industrial Instruments 354–364

Chapter: 1
Units and Measurements

1. What is the importance of unit in measurement?

Ans: Units of measurement are essential because they give us a common standard to compare things like length, weight, time, and more. Without them, it would be really confusing to share or understand measurements. Whether you're doing science experiments, building machines, or just measuring ingredients while cooking, standard units make communication clearer and more reliable.

2. What is the difference between fundamental unit & derived unit?

Ans: Fundamental units are the basic units of measurement that stand on their own, they're not formed by combining any other units. For example, the meter (for length), kilogram (for mass), and second (for time) are all fundamental units. These are the foundation of all physical measurements.

Derived units, on the other hand, are formed by combining two or more fundamental units. For instance, speed is a derived unit because it's measured in meters per second (m/s), which involves both length and time. Another example is force, measured in newtons, which comes from mass multiplied by acceleration.

3. What is absolute unit?

Ans: An absolute unit is a type of measurement that's fixed and doesn't rely on external conditions. It's based on universal constants, so its value stays the same no matter where or when it's used. A good example is the meter, which is defined based on how far light travels in a vacuum in a specific fraction of a second.

4. What is SI (System International) unit?

Ans: The SI unit, or the International System of Units, is the modern form of the metric system and is the world's most widely used system of measurement. It provides a consistent and standardized set of units for expressing various physical quantities.

5. What are the seven fundamental units?

Ans: Meter (m), Kilogram (kg), Second (s), Ampere (A), Kelvin (K), Mole (mol), Candela (cd)

6. How Seven fundamental units are defined?

Ans: Followings are the fundamental units: -

- **_Meter:_** The meter is defined as the length of the path travelled by light in a vacuum during a time interval of 1/299,792,458 of a second.
- **_Kilogram:_** A kilogram is very nearly equal (it was originally intended to be exactly equal) to the mass of 1,000 cubic cm of water at 4°C.
- **_Second:_** It is defined based on the frequency of radiation associated with a specific transition in the cesium-133 atom.
- **_Ampere:_** One ampere of current represents one coulomb of electrical charge (6.24 x 1018 charge carriers) moving past a specific point in one second.
- **_Kelvin:_** The kelvin is defined as equal to the fraction 1/273.16 of the thermodynamic temperature of the triple point of water—the point at which water, ice and water vapor co-exist in equilibrium.
- **_Mole:_** It is defined as the amount of any chemical substance that contains as many elementary entities e.g. atoms, molecules, ions, electrons or photons like atoms present in 12 gm of pure carbon with relative atomic mass 12.
- **_Candela:_** It is defined based on the luminous efficacy of monochromatic radiation.

7. How are these fundamental units relevant in the field of instrumentation engineering?

Ans: Importance of the fundamental units:

- Fundamental units provide a standardized and consistent system of measurement. This ensures that professionals in instrumentation engineering around the world use the same language of measurement, facilitating communication and collaboration.
- Instruments and devices from different manufacturers and regions can be used interchangeably because they are designed to operate within the framework of fundamental units. This allows for flexibility in choosing instrumentation components and systems.
- Calibration of instruments is based on fundamental units. Knowing the units of measurement is essential for accurate calibration, ensuring that instruments provide precise and reliable readings in real-world applications.
- In complex industrial processes, different systems and instruments need to work together seamlessly. The use of fundamental units ensures compatibility and integration between various components within an instrumentation system.

8. What are the primary and secondary standards?

Ans: Primary standards are the highest level of standards used for establishing the basic unit of measurement in a particular quantity. Main functions of the primary standards are the verification and calibration of secondary standards. They are maintained by national standard laboratories.

Secondary standards are derived from primary standards and are used for routine calibrations and everyday measurements.

9. What is IEEE standards?

Ans: The Institute of Electrical and Electronics Engineers (IEEE) is a professional association that develops standards for a wide range of industries, particularly in the field of electrical and electronics engineering. IEEE standards are documents that establish specifications and criteria for various technologies, products, and services. These standards are developed through a consensus process involving experts from industry, academia, and government.

IEEE standards are typically identified by a numerical designation. For example, the ***IEEE 802.11 standard pertains to wireless local area networks (WLANs)***.

Chapter: 2

Fundamental of Instrumentation

1. What are the functional elements of instrument system. Explain with reference to an instrument.

Ans An instrument system usually has four main functional elements. Here's how they work, using a thermocouple as an example:

- *Primary sensing element*: This is the part that first comes into contact with the quantity you want to measure. For instance, in a thermocouple, the tip of the probe senses the process temperature directly.

- *Data Conditioning Element*: After sensing, the physical input is converted into an electrical signal. In our example, the thermocouple generates a small voltage (in millivolts) corresponding to the temperature.

- *Data transmission element*: The physical quantity, once measured and converted into electrical form, needs to be transmitted to the control room for analysis and operational control. In this example, the millivolt signal from the thermocouple is transmitted via thermocouple extension cables.

- *Data Presentation element*: The information about the quantity being measured must be conveyed to the personnel handling the instrument or the system for monitoring, control, or analysis purposes. This function is performed by the data presentation element. In this example, the temperature measured by the thermocouple is displayed in a temperature scanner, temperature display unit, or on the HMI of the control system.

2.   What is the difference between Accuracy & Precision?

Ans: Accuracy means how close a measured value is to the actual or true value. For example, if you're aiming at the centre of a target and your shot lands near the bullseye, that's accurate.

Precision, on the other hand, means how consistent your results are. If you take several measurements (or shots) and they all fall close to each other, even if they're not near the true value, then your results are precise.

So, accuracy is about being correct, while precision is about being consistent.

3.   Define the terms: Repeatability, Reproducibility, Drift, Sensitivity, Resolution, Threshold, Dead time, Dead zone, Linearity, Hysteresis, Scale range & scale spam.

Ans: These are the terms use to define various characteristics of Instrumentation.

Repeatability: This refers to how consistently an instrument can reproduce the same measurement under the same conditions. For instance, if you measure the same voltage multiple times with a multimeter and get nearly identical readings each time, the device has good repeatability.

Reproducibility: This is about the instrument's ability to provide consistent results under varying conditions, such as different operators or environments. For example, if two technicians use the same thermometer in different labs and obtain similar readings, the thermometer exhibits good reproducibility.

Drift: Drift occurs when an instrument's readings change over time without any change in the measured quantity. Factors like temperature fluctuations or component aging can cause this. Regular calibration helps mitigate drift.

Sensitivity: Sensitivity indicates how much the output of an instrument changes in response to a change in the input. A highly sensitive instrument will show a noticeable change even with a slight change of input.

Resolution: The smallest increment in input which can be detected with certainty buy an instrument is called resolution. Consider a temperature sensor with a digital output. If it has a resolution of 0.1°C, it means that the sensor can distinguish between temperature values that differ by 0.1°C. If the temperature changes by less than 0.1°C, the sensor may not register a change in its output.

Threshold: The threshold is the minimum input value required to produce a detectable output change. If a pressure sensor doesn't respond until the pressure exceeds a certain point, that point is its threshold.

Dead time: This is the time delay between the application of an input and the instrument's response. Consider a temperature control system with a temperature sensor and a heater. If the temperature increases beyond a certain setpoint, the system might activate the heater to bring the temperature back to the desired level. The dead time in this system would be the time it takes for the sensor to detect the change in temperature, for the control system to process this information, and for the heater to respond and have an effect on the temperature.

Dead zone: Also known as dead band, this is a range where changes in input do not produce any change in output. Consider a pressure sensor with a dead zone. If the pressure applied falls within this dead zone range, the sensor may not register any change in its output, even though the pressure is changing. Only when the pressure exceeds the boundaries of the dead zone will the sensor respond and provide a measurable output.

Linearity: Linearity of an instrument refers to the degree to which the relationship between the input and output of the instrument follows a straight line. Linearity assesses how well an instrument's output corresponds proportionally to its input across the entire range. A linear relationship means doubling the input doubles the output.

Hysteresis: Hysteresis in the context of a measurement system refers to the phenomenon where the response of the system depends not only on the current input but also on its past history. In other words, the output of the system may vary depending on whether the input is increasing or decreasing. Consider a force measurement system with hysteresis. If a force is applied to the system, the output response may not be the same when the force is gradually increased compared to when it is gradually decreased. The output signal may follow a different path on the increasing force cycle compared to the decreasing force cycle.

Scale Range & scale span: The scale range of an instrument is the range of values that the instrument is designed to measure or display. It defines the minimum and maximum values that the instrument is calibrated to handle.

The scale span of an instrument is the difference between the maximum and minimum values on the instrument's display or measurement scale. For a thermometer designed to measure temperatures from -20°C to 120°C, the scale range is -20°C to 120°C.

4.   What is least count?

Ans: Least count is the smallest measurement that can be taken by a measuring instrument.

5.   What is the cause of drift in instrument? How to mitigate drift in the instrument?

Ans: Drift can be caused by various factors, including changes in temperature, humidity, or voltage supply, as well as component aging and wear. It is crucial to account for drift in critical measurement systems, as it can lead to inaccurate readings and compromise the reliability of the data.

To mitigate drift, regular calibration and maintenance of instruments are essential. Periodic checks and adjustments can help ensure that the measurement system remains accurate and reliable over time.

6. How sensitivity influence the performance of an instrument?

Ans: Sensitivity plays a big role in determining how well an instrument picks up on small changes. A highly sensitive instrument will respond noticeably even if the input changes just a little, this is required while measuring something that requires fine detail. For example, in lab work or medical devices, picking up tiny variations is crucial. However, too much sensitivity isn't always good, it might also react to noise or unwanted signals. So, it's important to find a balance between sensitivity, accuracy, and reliability to get the best performance.

7. What is the difference between threshold and resolution of an instrument?

Ans: Resolution is all about how finely an instrument can detect small changes in input, basically, the smallest step it can notice. Threshold, on the other hand, is the minimum amount of input needed to make the instrument react at all.

8. What are the causes of errors in the measurement system?

Ans: Following are some of the causes of error-

- *Instrumental error:* These happen because of problems within the instrument itself, like loose springs, friction in moving parts, or even wear and tear over time.
- *Environmental error:* These errors are due to conditions like temperature, humidity, pressure, or nearby magnetic fields. These can mess with readings if the instrument isn't well-protected.

9. How can errors in measurement be overcome?

Ans: Following are some of the techniques that can be utilised to mitigate errors in measurement.

- Selecting a suitable instrument for the particular measurement application.
- Applying correction factor after determining the amount of instrumental error.
- Calibrating the instrument against a standard.
- Hermetically sealing certain components in the instrument
- Use of magnetic shields.

10. What is the dynamic response in measurement system?

Ans: Measurement system in some applications like industrial, aerospace and biological are subjected to inputs which are not static but are dynamic in nature i.e. the input varies with time. The input varies from instant to instant and therefore so does the output, the behaviour of the system under such condition is described by its dynamic response.

11. Define the term Speed of response, Fidelity, lag.

Ans: *Speed of response*: it is the rapidity with which an instrument response to changes in the measured quantity.

Fidelity: It is the degree to which an instrument indicates the changes in measured variable without dynamic error.

Lag: It is a retardation or delay in the response of an instrument to changes in the measured quantity.

12. What do you mean by the term calibration?

Ans: Calibration of an instrument means to check and adjust (if necessary) the response of the instrument so the output accurately corresponds to its input throughout a specified range. Calibration is done by comparing the measurements of an instrument or device against a known standard to ensure accuracy and reliability.

13. What is ranging of an instrument?

Ans: To range an instrument means to set the lower and upper range values so it responds with the desired sensitivity to changes in input. For example, a pressure transmitter set to a range of 0 to 200 PSI (0 PSI = 4 mA output ; 200 PSI = 20 mA output) could be re-ranged to respond on a scale of 0 to 150 PSI (0 PSI = 4 mA ; 150 PSI = 20 mA).

14. Why do we need to calibrate the instrument?

Ans: Due to the aging of mechanical components and prolonged use, measurement errors may develop in an instrument. Therefore, regular calibration is required to maintain its accuracy.

15. What is zero and span adjustments?

Ans: Zero Adjustment corrects the instrument's output when the input is at its minimum (usually zero). It ensures that the device reads zero when no signal is applied. For example, in a pressure transmitter, zero adjustment ensures it reads 0 PSI when no pressure is present.

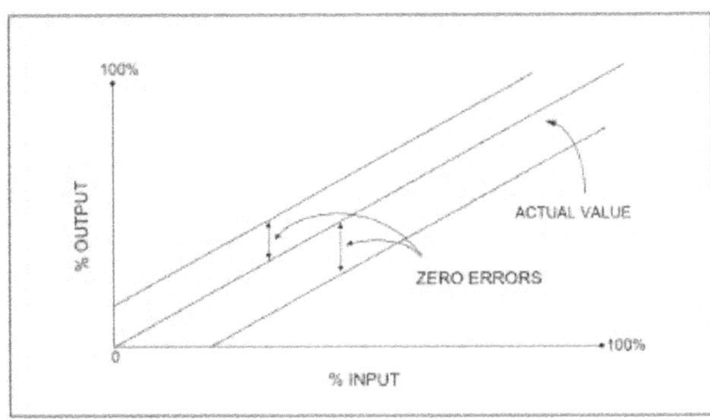

Fig 2.1- Zero adjustment

Span Adjustment modifies the instrument's response at its full-scale value. It ensures the output correctly corresponds to the maximum input. For example, if a temperature sensor measures up to 100°C, span adjustment ensures that a 100°C input gives the correct output.

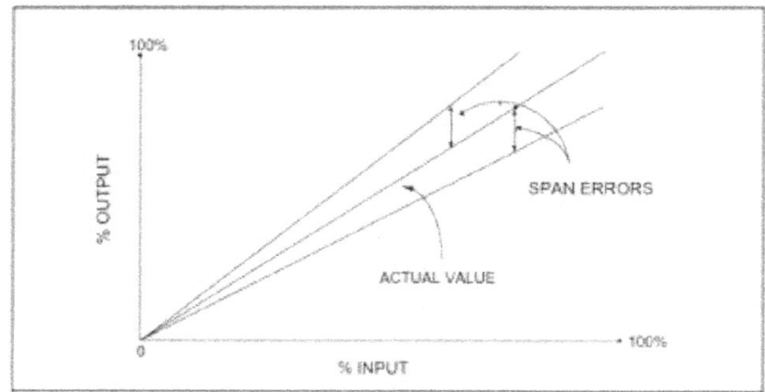

Fig 2.2- Span adjustment

For most analog instruments, zero and span adjustments are interactive. That is, adjusting one has an effect on the other. By adjusting both zero and span, the instrument may set for any range of measurement within the manufacturer's limits.

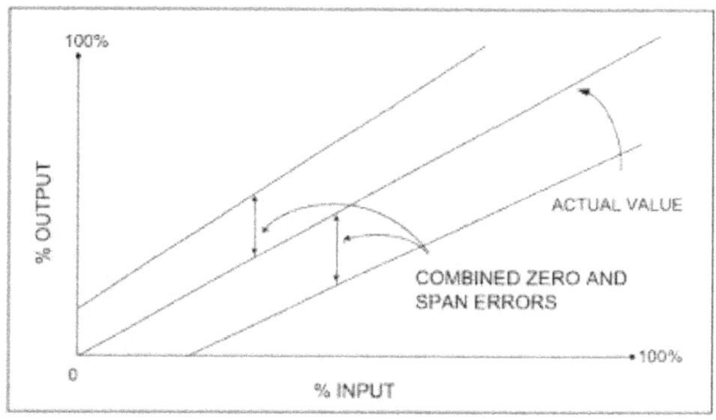

Fig 2.3- Zero & Span adjustment

16. What is single point, two point and three-point calibration?

Ans: The single-point calibration is often referred as offset adjustment, where the output of the system is forced to be zero under zero input condition.

In two-point calibration, the output of the instrument is adjusted at zero and final value.

In three-point calibration, the output of the instrument is adjusted at zero, final value and a mid-value.

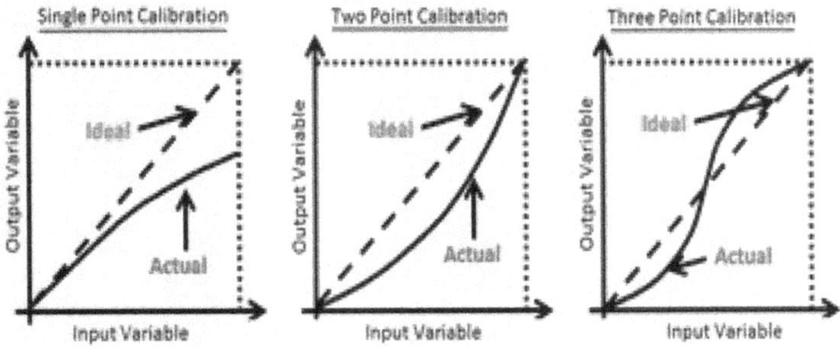

Fig 2.4 – Calibration point

17. What is calibration curve?

Ans: It is the graphical representation of input and output relationship before and after calibration of an instrument.

18. What are the different types of calibration errors?

Ans: Calibration errors occur when an instrument's output deviates from the expected or true value. The main types of calibration errors include:

- *Zero Error* – The instrument does not read zero when the input is zero. This can be corrected by adjusting the zero setting.
- *Span Error (Gain Error)* – The instrument's response is proportionally incorrect across the entire range.
- *Linearity Error* – The instrument's output does not follow a straight-line relationship with the input, causing deviations at different points in the measurement range.
- *Hysteresis Error* – A hysteresis calibration error occurs when the instrument responds differently to an increasing input compared to a decreasing input. The only way to detect this type of error is to do an up-down calibration test, checking for instrument response at the same calibration points going down as going up.

- ***Repeatability Error*** – The instrument gives different readings for the same input when measured multiple times under the same conditions.
- ***Resolution Error*** – The instrument cannot detect small changes in input, leading to quantization errors.
- ***Parallax Error*** – Occurs in analog instruments when the observer's angle affects the perceived reading.
- ***Sensitivity Error*** – The instrument does not respond correctly to small changes in input, leading to inaccurate readings.

Correcting these errors typically involves zero and span adjustments, recalibration using known standards, or replacing faulty components.

19. What is a master instrument? What are the criteria for selection of a master instrument?

Ans: A master instrument is a high-accuracy, well-calibrated reference instrument used to check, calibrate, or validate the performance of other instruments or devices.

Following are the selection criteria of a master instrument: -

- Master Instrument should cover the full range of instrument under calibration.
- To compare instrument under calibration and master Instrument, both should have the same units.
- Master Instrument should have a better least count than instrument under calibration.
- Accuracy of the Master Instrument should be at least 3 times better than instrument under calibration.
- Master Instrument should also be calibrated with higher accuracy Instrument before using has Master Instrument.

20. What is calibration certificate?

Ans: A calibration certificate is an official document issued by a certified calibration laboratory or authority after an instrument has been calibrated. It serves as proof that the instrument has been tested against known standards and meets specified accuracy requirements.

21. What is Instrument turndown? What is its significance?

Ans: Turndown is defined as the ratio of maximum allowable span to the minimum allowable span for a particular instrument. For example, a pressure transmitter has a maximum calibration range of 0 to 300 pounds per square inch (PSI), and a turndown of 20:1. This means that a technician may adjust the span anywhere between 300 PSI (e.g. range = 0 to 300 PSI) and 15 PSI (e.g. range = 0 to 15 PSI). Followings are the significance of turndown ratio:

- A higher turndown ratio means the instrument can measure a wider range of values effectively.
- It is especially important in processes with variable operating conditions (like flow, pressure, or temperature).
- Helps in cost reduction, as fewer instruments may be needed to cover a wide range.

22. What are the Uses of Screw Gauge and Vernier Callipers?

Ans: A screw gauge is a precision instrument used to measure very small lengths or thicknesses with high accuracy, typically in the range of 0.01 mm. It is commonly used for measurement of the diameter of thin wires, measurement of the thickness of small metal sheets.

A vernier callipers is a measuring instrument used to measure internal, external, and depth dimensions accurately, usually with a precision of 0.02 mm. It is commonly used for Measurement of the external dimensions of objects (like rods or pipes), and measurement of internal diameter of holes or cylinders.

23. What is the function of a Feeler Gauge?

Ans: A feeler gauge is used to measure the gap between two mating parts.

24. What is a transducer?

Ans: A transducer is a device that converts one form of energy into another. In instrumentation, transducers typically convert a physical quantity (such as pressure, temperature, force, or light) into a measurable electrical signal.

25. What is the difference between sensor and transducer?

Ans: A sensor is a device that detects or measures a physical quantity and responds with a signal, often non-electrical. A transducer, on the other hand, not only senses the physical quantity but also converts it into a usable electrical signal. For example: In a pressure transmitter, the diaphragm that senses the pressure acts as the sensor, while the transmitter as a whole function as a transducer, as it converts the sensed pressure into an equivalent electrical signal.

26. What is a smart sensor?

Ans: Smart sensors are advanced sensors that not only detect physical parameters like temperature, pressure, or flow but also include built-in signal processing, communication, and self-diagnostic capabilities. They can process data locally and communicate the information digitally to control systems.

Example: A smart temperature transmitter using a PT100 sensor not only measures the temperature but also linearizes the signal, detects sensor faults, and communicates the data over a digital protocol like HART or Foundation Fieldbus.

Chapter: 3

Basic of Electrical Engineering

1. Define voltage, current, and resistance.

Ans: Voltage, also known as electric potential difference, is the measure of electrical potential energy between two points in a circuit. It is the force that pushes electric charges through a conductor. Its unit is **volt (V)**.

Voltage, also known as electric potential difference, is the measure of electrical potential energy between two points in a circuit. Current is the force that pushes electric charges through a conductor. Its unit is **Ampere (A)**

Resistance is the opposition to the flow of electric current in a material. It determines how much a material resists the passage of current. Its unit is **Ohm**.

2. State Ohm's Law.

Ans: Ohm's Law states that the current (I) flowing through a conductor between two points is directly proportional to the voltage (V) across those points and inversely proportional to the resistance (R) of the conductor.

Mathematically, V = I X R

3. What is the unit of power?

Ans: Power is the rate at which work is done or energy is transferred per unit time. Its SI unit is Watt.

Where, 1 Watt = 1 joule per second (J/S)

1 H.P. = 746 Watt

4. What is the difference between AC and DC?

Ans: AC (Alternating Current) and DC (Direct Current) are two types of electric current that differ in the way they flow. DC flows in a

17

constant direction with a steady voltage level, making it ideal for batteries, solar panels, and electronic devices like laptops and smartphones. In contrast, AC changes direction periodically, typically following a sinusoidal wave pattern, and is used for transmitting electricity over long distances due to its efficiency.

5. What will happen if an AC device is connected to DC source and vice versa?

Ans: If an AC device is connected to a DC source or vice versa, the consequences depend on the type of device and how it operates.

Connecting an AC Device to a DC Source:

- For devices with transformers (e.g., AC motors, appliances) → The device won't work because transformers require a changing current to induce voltage.
- For resistive loads (e.g., incandescent bulbs, heating elements) → The device may work but at a lower efficiency or with overheating issues if voltage ratings don't match.
- For electronic devices with rectifiers (e.g., laptops, chargers) → Some may work if they can internally convert DC, but they may malfunction or get damaged due to improper voltage regulation.

Connecting a DC Device to an AC Source:

- For pure DC motors or circuits without rectifiers → The device may not work or could be damaged due to voltage fluctuations.
- For battery-powered devices → AC power could burn out the components unless a rectifier is used to convert AC to DC.
- For LED lights designed for DC → They may flicker, overheat, or fail immediately.

6. What is the difference between conductors, insulators, and semiconductors?

Ans: Conductors are materials that allow electricity to flow easily because they have free electrons that move freely within the material. They have low electrical resistance and are used in electrical wiring and circuits. Example: Copper, aluminium.

Insulators are materials that do not allow electricity to flow easily because their electrons are tightly bound to their atoms. They have high resistance and are used to prevent electrical conduction. Example: Rubber, Glass.

Semiconductors have electrical conductivity between conductors and insulators. Their conductivity can be controlled by adding impurities (doping) or by external conditions such as temperature and voltage. They are used in making of transistors, modern electronic chips. Example: Silicon, Germanium.

7. What is resistor, inductor, capacitor?

Ans: A resistor is a passive electrical component that opposes the flow of current by converting electrical energy into heat.

An inductor is a coil of wire that stores energy in a magnetic field when current flows through it. It opposes changes in current due to electromagnetic induction.

A capacitor is a device that stores electrical energy in an electric field between its plates. It resists changes in voltage and can discharge energy when needed.

8. What is the difference between a fuse and a circuit breaker?

Ans: A fuse and a circuit breaker both serve the purpose of protecting electrical circuits from overcurrent and short circuits, but they operate differently.

A fuse is a one-time protective device that consists of a thin wire or strip of metal that melts when excessive current flows through it, breaking the circuit.

A circuit breaker is a resettable protective device that automatically trips (opens) a circuit when excessive current flows. It can be manually or automatically reset after a fault is cleared.

9. What is the function of a diode?

Ans: A diode is a semiconductor device that allows current to flow in one direction only while blocking it in the opposite direction. It acts as an electrical one-way valve and is primarily used for rectification, protection, and signal processing.

10. What are active, reactive, and apparent power?

Ans: *Real Power (P)* – Measured in watts (W), it represents the actual power consumed by the load to perform useful work (e.g., heating, lighting, motors).

Reactive Power (Q) – Measured in volt-amperes reactive (VAR), it represents the power used to maintain magnetic and electric fields in inductors and capacitors. It does no useful work but is essential for AC circuits.

Apparent Power (S) – Measured in volt-amperes (VA), it is the total power supplied to the circuit, combining both real and reactive power.

11. What is a power triangle?

Ans: A power triangle is a graphical representation of the relationship between real power (P), reactive power (Q), and apparent power (S) in an AC circuit. It helps visualize how power is distributed in electrical systems.

12. What is the power factor. What is its significance in electrical circuit?

Ans: Power factor (PF) is the ratio of active power (P) to apparent power (S) in an AC circuit. It indicates how efficiently electrical power is being converted into useful work.

Following is the significance of power factor:

- A high-power factor (≈ 1) means more of the supplied power is converted into useful work. A low power factor means more reactive power is present, leading to wasted energy.
- A low power factor causes higher current flow, increasing resistive losses (I^2R losses) in transmission lines. A high-power factor reduces these losses, improving system efficiency.
- Industries and businesses are often charged penalties for operating at a low power factor. Improving PF reduces demand charges and energy costs.

13. What is a megger used for?

Ans: A Megger (Megohmmeter) is a specialized instrument used to measure high insulation resistance in electrical systems. It is commonly used for testing insulation in cables, motors, transformers, and electrical installations to ensure safety and prevent electrical failures.

14. What is an earthing system?

Ans: An earthing system (or grounding system) is a safety mechanism used in electrical installations to connect electrical equipment and systems to the Earth. It helps prevent electric shocks, protects equipment from faults, and ensures a safe path for fault currents.

15. What are the different types of earthing?

Ans: The different types of earthing are:

- ➢ ***Neutral Earthing:*** Connects the neutral of electrical systems (like transformers and generators) to the Earth.
- ➢ ***Equipment Earthing:*** Connects metallic parts of electrical equipment to the ground. Ensures that if a live wire touches

metal casing, the fault current is safely discharged.

16. What is an MCB and MCCB?

Ans: Both MCB (Miniature Circuit Breaker) and MCCB (Molded Case Circuit Breaker) are protective devices used in electrical circuits, but they differ in terms of capacity, application, and protection features.

An MCB is a small automatic electrical switch that protects circuits from overcurrent and short circuits in low-power applications. When current exceeds the rated limit, a bimetallic strip inside heats up and bends, tripping the switch. Current rating: up to 125A

An MCCB is a larger and more powerful circuit breaker used for higher currents and industrial applications. Up to 100A to 2500A.

17. What is an ELCB and RCCB?

Ans: An ELCB is a type of leakage protection device that detects leakage current through the earthing system. It is used to disconnect power when leakage current flows through the ground wire. If a fault occurs and current leaks to the earth wire, the ELCB detects the voltage rise and trips the circuit. It requires a good earthing system to function properly.

An RCCB is a modern and more effective safety device that detects imbalance in live (phase) and neutral currents. It trips the circuit if a leakage current flows through a person or an unintended path. It continuously monitors the current entering (live) and leaving (neutral) a circuit. If there is a difference (leakage current), it assumes electricity is leaking (e.g., through a human body) and immediately trips the power.

18. What is a battery? What are the main components of a battery?

Ans: A battery is an electrochemical device that stores and provides electrical energy by converting chemical energy into electrical energy.

A battery consists of: Anode, Cathode and Electrolyte. A battery works based on electrochemical reactions. During discharge, the anode releases electrons, which travel through an external circuit to the cathode. During charging, the process is reversed.

19. What is the difference between primary and secondary batteries?

Ans: A primary battery is a non-rechargeable battery that is designed for single-use only. Once discharged, it cannot be reused and must be replaced. Example: Alkaline Battery (Used in remote controls, flashlights), Zinc-Carbon Battery (Used in clocks, radios).

A secondary battery is a rechargeable battery that can be used multiple times by recharging with an electric current. Example: Lithium-ion Battery (Used in smartphones, laptops, EVs), Lead-Acid Battery (Used in cars, UPS systems).

20. What is battery capacity?

Ans: Battery capacity is the amount of charge a battery can store, measured in Ampere-hours (Ah) or milliampere-hours (mAh).

21. What is thermal runaway in batteries?

Ans: Thermal runaway is an uncontrollable reaction where overheating causes the battery to break down, releasing gases and possibly leading to fire or explosion.

22. What is a trickle charge and boost charge?

Ans: A trickle charge is a low-current, continuous charging method used to keep a battery fully charged without overcharging. A boost charge is a high-current, fast charging method used to quickly restore a discharged battery to an operational level.

23. How to Test a Diode with a Multimeter?

Ans: A diode can be tested by using a digital multimeter by setting to the diode test mode to check whether it conducts current in one direction (forward-biased) and blocks it in the other (reverse-biased).

At first Identify the Diode Terminals: The Anode (A) is the positive side and the Cathode (K) is the negative side. Then, connect the red lead of multimeter to the anode and the black lead to the cathode. A good diode will show a voltage drop of approximately 0.6 to 0.7V. Next, rreverse the leads: black to anode, red to cathode. A good diode should show OL (over-limit), meaning no conduction.

If the diode shows voltage in both directions, it indicates diode is shorted and if the diode shows OL in both directions, it indicates diode is open circuit.

24. How will you test a transistor with a multimeter?

Ans: To test a bipolar junction transistor (BJT) using a multimeter, first set the multimeter to the diode test mode. For an NPN transistor, connect the red lead to the base and the black lead to the emitter; the display should show a forward voltage drop of approximately 0.6 to 0.7 volts. Reversing the leads should result in an open line (OL) reading, indicating no conduction. Similarly, connect the red lead to the base and the black lead to the collector; it should again show around 0.6 to 0.7 volts, and reversing the leads should show OL. Then test between the collector and emitter in both directions; in a good transistor, this should show OL in both directions, indicating no conduction between these terminals without base current. For a PNP transistor, the procedure is the same, but the multimeter leads are reversed—black lead to base and red lead to emitter or collector.

A transistor is considered good if both junctions (base-emitter and base-collector) conduct in one direction and block in the other. If either junction conducts in both directions or fails to conduct in any direction, the transistor is faulty.

Chapter: 4
Tubes & fittings

1. What is the difference between tube and pipe?

Ans: Tubes are used in precision applications where high accuracy and reliability are crucial, such as instrumentation, whereas Pipes are used for the transport of high-pressure fluids and gases over long distances, in various industrial applications.

2. What is the difference in tube and pipe connection?

Ans: The fundamental differences between tube and pipe are that tube is never threaded at the end to form a connection. Instead, a device called a tube fitting must be used to couple a section of tube to another tube.

3. How tube fittings are done?

Ans: Tube fittings are assembled by placing the tube into the fitting body. A nut and ferrule(s) are then added. As the nut is tightened, the ferrule compresses against the tube's outer surface, creating a pressure-tight seal. This action also slightly crimps the tube, locking the ferrules in place to ensure a secure connection. This type of fittings is called compression-style fit.

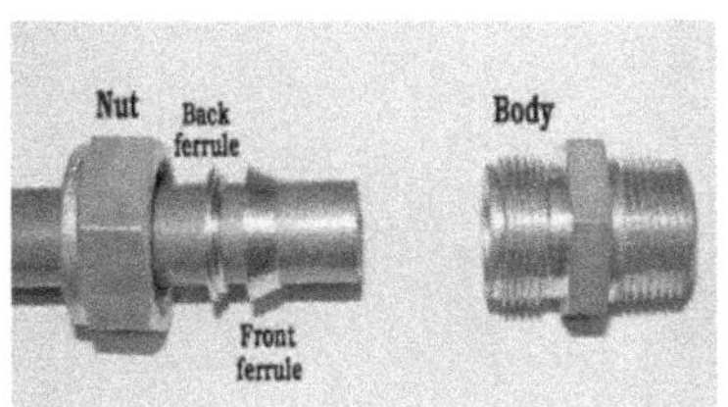

Fig 4.1- Fittings & ferrules

4. What are the purposes of front and back ferrule in tube fittings?

Ans: The front ferrule is responsible for creating a seal on the tube's outer surface, preventing fluid leakage. It provides mechanical support to the tube, preventing it from being pushed into the fitting.

The back ferrule grips the tube's outer surface, preventing it from being pulled out of the fitting. It provides extra mechanical support to the tube, reinforcing the connection.

5. What are the different types of adaptors used in Industry for tube fittings?

Ans: Adaptors connect a smaller tube to a larger tube or vice versa. Different types of adaptors are:

- Reducers (reduce tube size)
- Enlargers (increase tube size)
- Nipples (connect two male threads)
- Couplings (connect two female threads)
- Tees (connect three tubes at a 90-degree angle)
- Elbows (connect two tubes at a 90-degree angle)
- Crosses (connect four tubes at 90-degree angles)

Fig 4.2- Different types of connectors

6. What are male and female adaptors?

Ans: Male adaptor has a projecting thread or a protruding connection, designed to insert into a female connection and typically has a threaded or tapered end that screws into a female counterpart.

Female adaptor has a recessed connection or a socket, designed to receive a male connection and typically has a threaded or tapered interior that accepts a male counterpart.

When connecting two tubes or components, a male adaptor is screwed into a female adaptor, creating a secure, leak-tight seal.

Fig 4.3- Male & Female Connectors

7. What do you know about NPT and BSF?

Ans: NPT and BSF are two thread connection standards used for pipes and fittings. NPT (National Pipe Taper) a standardized thread connection used in North America. NPT has a tapered thread and commonly used for general-purpose piping or tubing.

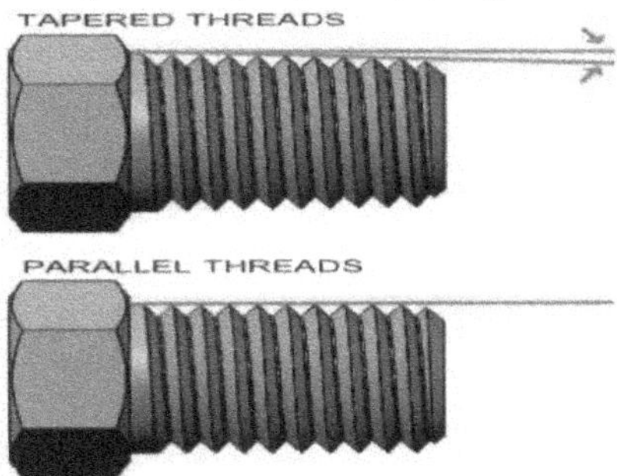

Fig 3.4- NPT & BSF connectors

BSF (British Standard Fine) a standardized thread connection used in the United Kingdom and other countries. BSF has parallel threads and is used for precision applications.

8. What is pitch of thread and thread angle?

Ans: The pitch of a thread is the distance between two consecutive threads, measured along the thread axis. A smaller pitch means a finer thread, while a larger pitch means a coarser thread.

The thread angle is the angle between the flanks of a thread, measured from the axis of the thread. It's the angle formed by the two sides of the thread. The thread angle is typically measured in degrees.

60° for NPT (National Pipe Taper) threads and 55° for BSF (British Standard Fine) threads

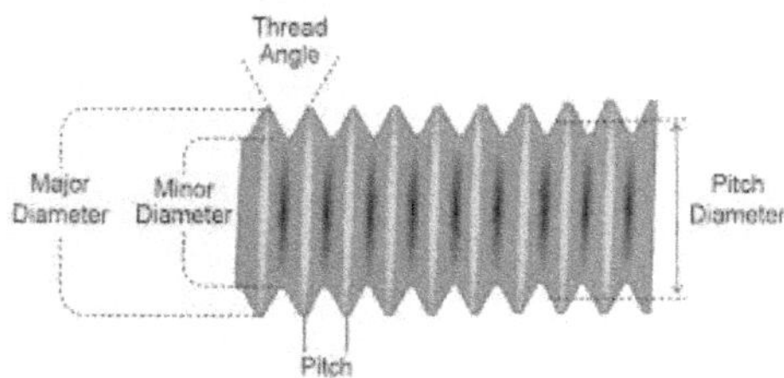

Fig 4.5- Thread angle

9. What do you mean by the specification ½" NPT connection?

Ans: ½" NPT connection refers to the nominal diameter of the thread.

10. What is a thread gauge?

Ans: A thread gauge is a tool used to measure the pitch (threads per inch) and diameter of a thread. It typically consists of a set of blades or leaves with different thread pitches and diameters.

Fig 4.6- Thread Gauge

11. What is the vibration loop in tubing?

Ans: If an instrument tube connect between a stationary object and a vibrating object, a straight (square) run of tube is actually not desirable, since it will not have much flexibility to absorb the vibration. Instead, a loop should be made in the tube, giving it the necessary elasticity to tolerate the vibrational stresses. This loop is called vibration loop.

12. When it comes to instrumentation tubing, which material is preferred: stainless steel (SS) or copper?

Ans: Stainless steel (SS) tubing is generally preferred in instrumentation applications due to its:

- Excellent corrosion resistance in harsh environments
- Higher pressure rating and durability
- Lower risk of contamination or reaction with process fluids
- Ease of installation and maintenance

13. In instrumentation fittings, what is role of teflon tape?

Ans: Teflon tape creates a tight, leak-proof seal on threaded connections, preventing fluid leakage and reduces friction between threads, making it easier to assemble and disassemble fittings.

14. In what direction, Teflon tape should be wrapped?

Ans: Teflon tape is used in instrumentation fittings by wrapping it around the male thread in clockwise direction of a connection before assembling it to the female thread.

If Teflon tape is wrapped anti-clockwise (instead of clockwise) on a male thread, the tape may unravel or come loose during assembly.

15. What is "no-go gap gauge" used in tube fittings?

Ans: No-go gap gauge is a special tool used to measure proper ferrule compression during the assembly process. The design of the gauge is such that its thickness will fit between the nut and fitting shoulder if the nut is insufficiently tightened, but will not fit if it is sufficiently tightened. Thus, the gauge has the ability to reveal an under-tightened fitting, but not an overtightened fitting.

16. What is the use of an O-Ring?

Ans: An O-ring is a mechanical gasket in the shape of a looped elastomer (rubber-like material) with a circular cross-section, designed to be seated in a groove and compressed during assembly between two or more parts. Its primary function is to prevent the passage of liquids or gases, acting as a seal.

It is used in instrumentation fittings, transmitters, pressure gauges manifolds to prevent fluid or gas leaks in Hydraulic and Pneumatic system.

17. What is a push in connector in Instrumentation fittings?

Ans: A push-in connector is a type of quick-connect fitting used in instrumentation to join pneumatic or hydraulic tubing easily without the need for tools.

Fig 3.7- Push in Connector

It works by simply pushing the tube into the connector, where an internal gripping holds the tube securely and creates a leak-tight seal. Push-in connectors are widely used because they speed up installation, allow easy disconnection, and ensure reliable, vibration-resistant connections, pneumatic systems, and instrumentation manifolds.

Chapter: 5

Instrumentation Cables and Connectors

1. What is terminal block in electric connection?

Ans: A terminal block is a modular, insulated block that secures two or more wires together in an electrical system. It provides a safe and organized method to connect, separate, or terminate electrical wires.

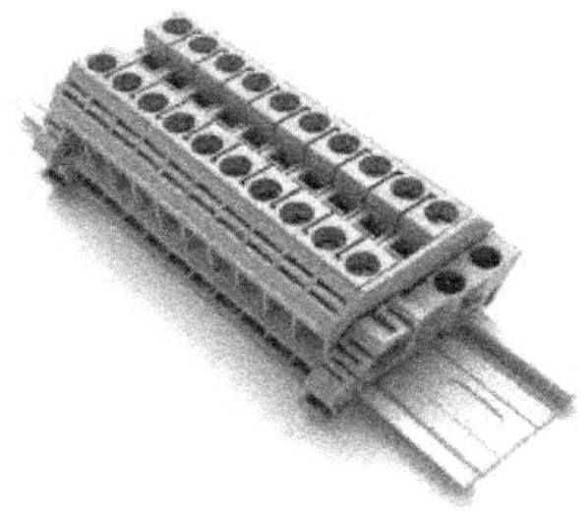

Fig 5.1 Terminal Block

2. What is the use of lugs in electric connection?

Ans: Electrical lugs are mechanical connectors used to securely connect wires or cables to electrical devices, terminals, or other cables.

Lugs help avoid damage to stranded wire ends, which can fray or break if directly clamped under a terminal. They allow for easier disconnection and reconnection during maintenance or replacement work.

Types of electric lugs are:

- **Ring lugs** – Circular end; fits over a stud or bolt.
- **Fork lugs** – Open-ended; easy to install or remove.
- **Pin lugs** – Solid pin end; used with clamp-type terminals.
- **Compression lugs** – Crimped or compressed onto the cable using a crimping tool.

- **Solder lugs** – Require soldering to attach to the conductor.

3. What is DIN rail?

Ans: A DIN rail is a standardized metal rail used for mounting electrical and industrial control equipment inside equipment racks, control panels, and enclosures.

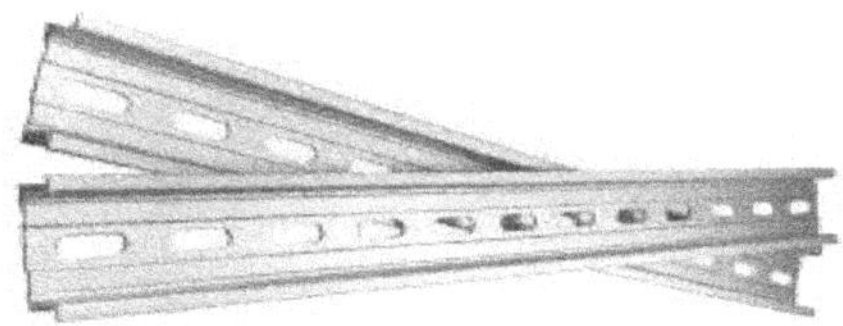

Fig 5.2- DIN rail

4. What is electrical conduit?

Ans: An electrical conduit is a protective tube or pipe used to route and shield electrical wiring in buildings, machines, or industrial installations. It provides a safe pathway for electrical conductors and protects them from mechanical damage, moisture, chemicals, and other environmental hazards.

5. What are the utilities of metal conduit and plastic conduit?

Ans: Metal conduit naturally forms a continuously-grounded enclosure for conductors which not only provides a measure of protection against electrical shock (all enclosures and devices attached to the conduit become safely grounded through the conduit) but also shields against electrostatic interference. This is especially important for power wiring to and from devices such as rectifiers and variable-frequency motor drive (VFD) units, which have a tendency to broadcast large amounts of electromagnetic noise.

Plastic conduit, of course, provides no electrical grounding or shielding because plastic is a non-conductor of electricity. However, it is superior to metal conduit with regard to chemical corrosion resistance, which is why it is used to route wires in areas containing water, acids, caustics, and other wet chemicals.

6. What is a cable tray? What are the advantages of perforated cable tray?

Ans: A cable tray is a structural system used to support and route electrical cables and wires in industrial, commercial, or residential settings. It acts like a bridge for safely carrying electrical and data cables across open spaces, walls, or ceilings.

Perforated cable trays have multiple holes or slots in their base and sometimes sides. These holes serve several important purposes:

- It allows air to circulate around the cables, which helps in heat dissipation and thus Prevents overheating.
- Reduces the overall weight of the tray, making it easier to handle and install.
- Holes provide points for tying cables down or attaching cable clamps, keeping cables secure and organized.
- In case of moisture or condensation, the holes allow water to drain out, preventing corrosion or damage to cables.

7. What is a cable gland?

Ans: A cable gland is a small but important mechanical fitting used to secure and seal the end of a cable where it enters an electrical enclosure, like a control panel or junction box. Its main job is to hold the cable firmly in place so it doesn't get pulled out or damaged.

Besides providing strain relief, a cable gland also helps protect against dust, water, and other environmental factors. Depending on the type, it can also help with grounding (for electrical safety) or insulation. In short, it ensures that the cable connection is secure, safe, and protected—especially in industrial or outdoor settings.

8. How to select the Cable Gland?

Ans: Gland should be selected on following Points:
- Type of Cable
- Gland Size
- Entry Type/Thread Specification of application
- Ingress Protection required.
- Material

9. What are the types of Cable Glands?

Ans: Following are the types of glands:
- Brass Indoor Type Gland
- Brass Outdoor Type Gland
- Brass Straitening Unarmoured Cable Gland
- Brass Weather Proof Gland
- PG Threaded Gland
- Industrial Type Gland

10. How is cable gland used for unarmoured and armoured cable?

Ans: For unarmoured cables, the gland mainly provides a tight seal around the outer sheath of the cable. This helps protect against dust, moisture, and other environmental factors. Since unarmoured cables don't have a metal layer for extra grip, the gland must firmly hold the outer jacket to keep the cable from slipping out.

For armoured cables, the gland must include a clamping mechanism designed to terminate the armour both mechanically and electrically. This ensures proper mechanical retention, as well as the establishment of electrical continuity for grounding. The gland effectively anchors the cable while connecting the metallic armour to the system ground.

11. What is an Instrument Cable?

Ans: An instrument cable is thinner in size and can handle only a smaller amount of voltage and current (typically up to 24VDC and

20 mA). For automation and instrumentation control, this type of cable is used.

12. What is the common size of the conductor of Instrumentation cable?

Ans: 0.5mm2 to 1mm2.

13. What are the different components of cable?

Ans: Components of cable are:

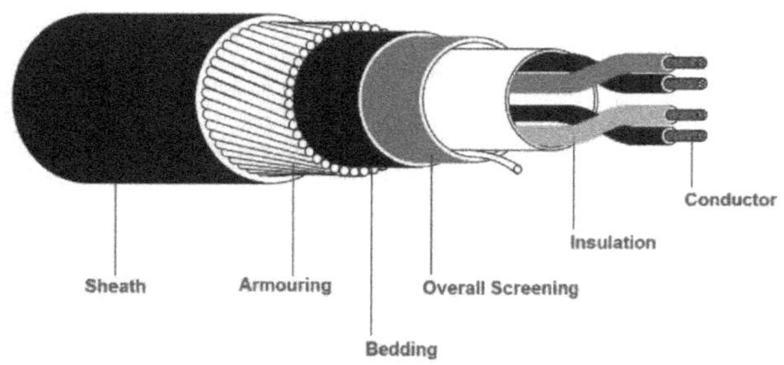

Fig 5.3- Components of cable

- **Sheath:** A protective layer around the cable's inner components, shielding them from physical damage such as abrasion, cuts, and impacts during installation and use.
- **Armour:** The armour increases cable life thus improves the performance, reliability, and safety of the cable core. The cable with an outside layer or layers of armour wired or tapes to provide tensile strength during the cable laying operation, and protection while resting underground.
- **Bedding:** The bedding in a cable serves as an intermediate layer that provides additional protection and support to the cable's internal components, particularly the conductors and insulation layers. It can also contribute to the overall insulation properties of the cable by providing an additional barrier between the conductors and the external environment.

- **Screen:** The presence of large machines, welders and other processes in industrial environments create a lot of electrical interference (noise). This noise has the potential to distort the clarity of signals that are transmitted between equipment, which may lead to false readings. A metallic screen will shield the cores of a cable from interference, thus improving the clarity of a signal.
- **Insulation**: The insulation around each conductor ensures that the current flows through the conductor without leaking into other conductors or external surfaces.
- **Conductor:** The conductor in a cable is the core component responsible for carrying electrical current or transmitting signals from one point to another.

14. What are the different types of Instrumentation cable?

Ans: The types of instrumentation cables include are:
- Signal cables
- Control cables
- Instrumentation Power cables
- Thermocouple Extension, Compensating cables
- RTD Cables

15. what is the difference between signal cable & control cable?

Ans: Following are the differences between signal cable a& control cable.

Aspect	Signal Cable	Control Cable
Purpose	Transmits low-voltage electrical signals for communication or data transfer.	Carries control signals for operation and automation of equipment and machinery.

Aspect	Signal Cable	Control Cable
Construction	Often consists of twisted pairs, coaxial structures, or shielded configurations.	Typically includes multiple conductors with robust insulation.
Applications	Data transmission systems, telecommunications, audio/video equipment, instrumentation.	Industrial environments, machinery, conveyor systems, automated systems.
Shielding	Frequently shielded to protect against EMI and RFI.	May or may not be shielded, depending on the application.
Voltage Rating	Designed for low-voltage applications.	Can handle a broader range of voltages, often up to several hundred volts.

16. What are the materials used for cable sheath?

Ans: Rubber, Silicone, Polyethylene, PVC, the selection of cable sheaths are different for high-voltage, high-current, fire resistant, fire retardant applications etc.

17. What are the Common Materials used in Instrumentation Cables?

Ans: Common materials used in Instrumentation cable are:

- *PVC:* Polyvinylchloride (PVC) is used as either an insulation material or as a sheathing material. It is good for medium mechanical stress and it offers good resistance to different chemicals.
- *Polyethylene (PE)* is used as either an insulation or

sheathing material. It has excellent chemical resistance, including oils, and extremely low water absorption. It also has superior mechanical strengths and good low-temperature resistance.

- **Cross-linking PE** improves the performance of the cable, increasing the temperature and chemical resistance. XLPE material is used mainly as an insulation material.

- **Low smoke zero halogen (LSZH)** materials are used in place of PVC materials where there is a significant risk to life and equipment in fire situations. These cables do not produce halogen acid gases when they burn and do not release the significant levels of dense black smoke that the PVC equivalent materials would in the event of a fire.

18. What is a Flame-Resistant Cable?

Ans: A flame-resistant cable is one that will continue to operate and not burn in case of fire. Without melting, it will resist high temperatures and prevent itself from burning. Typically, it can survive temperatures of up to 300 ° C.

19. What is a Flame-Retardant Cable?

Ans: A flame-retardant cable is one that will continue to operate in case of fire; but it will burn slowly and prevent the fire from spreading by reducing the amount of heat released from a fire and the potential for a fire to spread. Thus, they inhibit or suppress the combustion process. These cables either self-distinguish themselves or burn slowly; thus, preventing the fire from spreading to other areas.

20. What are the Differences between Cable Jackets & Insulations?

Ans: A jacket is an outer sheath that protects the wire or cable core from mechanical, moisture and chemical issues. Jackets help with flame resistance, protect against sunlight and facilitate installation. Jackets come in a variety of types and styles and are mainly plastic or rubber based.

Insulation is a coating that is extruded or taped onto bare wire to separate conductors from each other electrically and physically. There are a variety of insulation types for different applications.

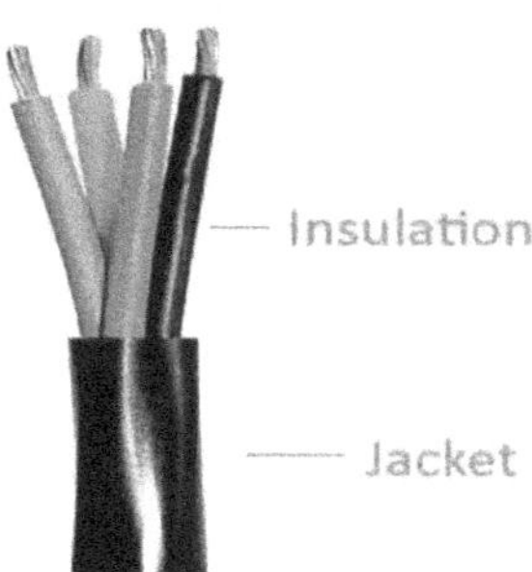

Fig 5.4- Cable cover

21. What are the different testing standards of cable?

Ans: Followings are the cable testing standard

Standard	Description
IS 8130	Annealing test for conductors, Wrapping test for conductors, Persulphate test for tinned copper conductors, Conductor resistance test for copper conductors.
ANSI MC 96.1	Thermo-emf performance test for thermocouple cables, Loop resistance test for thermocouple cables.
IS 5831	Insulation and sheath thickness test, Tensile strength of insulation and sheath, Elongation test for insulation and sheath, Shrinkage test for insulation and sheath, Loss of mass test for insulation and sheath, Ageing test for insulation and sheath, Heat shock test for insulation and sheath, Bleaching and blooming test for insulation

Standard	Description
	and sheath, Insulation resistance test for insulation and sheath, Flammability test for cable.
IS 3975	Tensile strength of armour material, Elongation test for armour material, Zinc coating test on GI armour wire.
IS 1554	Tensile strength for insulation and sheath, Elongation strength for insulation and sheath, High voltage test for insulation and sheath.
IS 694	Spark test for insulation and sheath, HV test for insulation and sheath.
IEEE 383	Flame resistance test.
ASTM-D-2863	Limiting Oxygen Index test, Temperature Index Test.
ASTM-D-2843	Smoke density test.
IEC 332-1 and 3	Flammability test.
IEC 754-1	HCl gas emission test.
SS-424-14-75 (F-3)	Flame retardancy test (Swedish chimney test), Noise rejection ratio test, and Rodent & termite resistance chemical test.

22. What is single Strand and Multistrand cable?

Ans: A single-strand cable, also known as a solid conductor cable, consists of a single, solid piece of wire. Single-strand cables are more rigid and durable for fixed installations and are cost-effective. They offer slightly better signal quality due to the continuous nature of the conductor, with lower resistance and less signal loss over long distances. Mainly used in the internal wiring of electronic devices where flexibility is not required.

A multistrand cable consists of multiple smaller wires twisted or braided together to form a single conductor. Multistrand cables are highly flexible and can withstand bending, twisting, and movement without breaking, making them ideal for dynamic applications. Commonly used in power cords for appliances and electronic devices where flexibility is necessary.

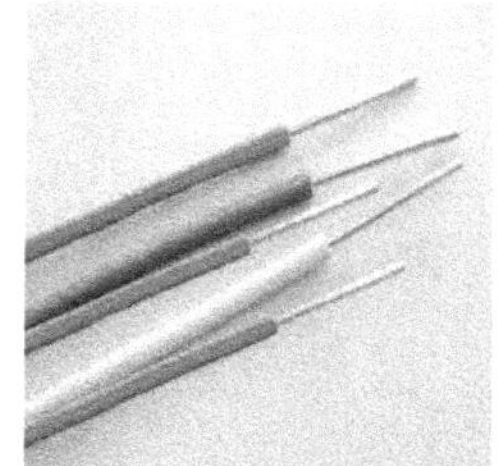

Fig 5.5 – Single & Multistrand cable

23. In instrumentation applications, which type of cable is mostly preferred, Copper or Aluminum?

Ans: In instrumentation applications, copper cables are predominantly preferred over aluminum cables, due to following reasons:

- Copper has significantly higher electrical conductivity than aluminum, meaning it can transmit electrical signals with less resistance and voltage drop. This is crucial in instrumentation, where accurate signal transmission is vital for precise measurements and control.
- Copper cables are less prone to electrical interference and provide better shielding properties, which is important in environments with high electromagnetic interference.
- Copper wires are more flexible and durable than aluminum wires, making them easier to handle, install, and maintain. This is particularly important in instrumentation, where cables often need to be routed through complex and confined spaces.

- Copper is more resistant to corrosion than aluminum, especially in environments where humidity, chemicals, or other corrosive agents are present. This makes copper cables more durable and reliable over time.

24. What is the normal size of thermocouple cable?

Ans: For Single pair – 16 AWG (1.295 mm dia) and for Multi pair – 20 AWG (0.813 mm dia).

25. What is AWG?

Ans: AWG stands for American Wire Gauge, is a standard system for measuring the diameter of electrical conductors in the United States, where a lower gauge number indicates a thicker wire with higher current-carrying capacity.

The diameter d of a wire in inches can be calculated using the following formula for any given AWG number n:

$$d_n = 0.005 \times 92^{(36-n)/39}$$

Where:
- dn is the diameter of the wire in inches.
- n is the AWG number.

26. What do you mean by signal coupling between cables?

Ans: When AC power cables and low-level instrumentation signal cables (such as thermocouple cables) are routed in close proximity to one another, there is a significant risk of induced noise in the instrumentation signal. This can result in distorted or inaccurate process values at the receiving instrument. This interference occurs due to electromagnetic coupling, specifically through capacitive and inductive coupling between the conductors:

Capacitive Coupling: Capacitance is an inherent property of any two conductors separated by a dielectric (insulating material). It allows energy to be stored in the electric field created by the voltage between the wires. The natural capacitance between mutually insulated wires can act as a "bridge" for AC signals, enabling unwanted signal transfer between them.

Inductive Coupling: Inductance is a property of any current-carrying conductor, where energy is stored in the magnetic field created by the flow of current. When two conductors run parallel, mutual inductance allows a varying current in one conductor (e.g., an AC power cable) to induce a voltage in the adjacent conductor (e.g., a signal cable), especially when both are unshielded or improperly separated.

As a result of these coupling effects, the instrumentation signal becomes "noisy," leading to inaccurate readings. The magnitude of the induced noise is directly proportional to both the voltage level and the frequency of the nearby AC power signal.

27. Why is electric power conductors and instrumentation cable never route through same path?

Ans: Electrical power conductors and instrument signal cables are almost never found in the same conduit or in the same ductwork together to avoid capacitance and inductance coupling.

28. What is the recommended angle for a signal cable to cross a power cable path, when crossing is unavoidable?

Ans: It is recommended to orient signal cable and power conductors perpendicular to each other, when crossing is unavoidable.

Perpendicular conductor orientation reduces both inter-conductor capacitance and mutual inductance by two mechanisms. Capacitance between conductors is reduced by means of minimizing overlapping area resulting from the perpendicular crossing. Mutual inductance is reduced by decreasing the coupling coefficient (k) to nearly zero since the magnetic field generated perpendicular to the current-carrying wire will be parallel and not perpendicular to the "receiving" wire.

29. How can capacitance coupling between electric conductors and instrumentation cable be minimized?

Ans: Capacitive coupling happens when an electric field from one conductor affects a nearby signal cable, introducing unwanted noise. To prevent this, instrumentation cables are usually designed with a metallic shield, like a foil wrap or braided wire, that surrounds the signal wires inside.

This shield acts like a barrier that blocks external electric fields from reaching the signal wires. When this shield is properly connected to the ground, any stray electric energy is safely redirected, instead of interfering with the signal.

So, by using shielded cables and grounding the shield, we can significantly reduce capacitive coupling and keep the signal clean and accurate.

30. Why are instrumentation cables shielded?

Ans: To avoid capacitance coupling.

31. How can inductance coupling between electric conductors and instrumentation cable be minimized?

Ans: Inductive coupling happens when a magnetic field from a nearby power cable creates unwanted voltage in a signal cable. One simple and effective way to reduce this is by twisting the signal wires together tightly.

Because when wires are twisted, each loop reverses the direction of the magnetic influence. So, any voltage that's induced in one part of the twist tends to get cancelled out by the next one. This helps keep magnetic interference from building up in the cable.

That's why most instrumentation cables are made as twisted shielded pairs. The twisting helps fight off magnetic interference (inductive coupling), and the shielding (usually a grounded metal braid or foil) protects against electric field interference (capacitive coupling).

32. Why the Cable Screen shall not be Grounded at instrument field device?

Ans: Cable screen protects the signal carried on the conductor from external interference. Cable screen blocks the external interference and noise, then directs it to the ground. Screen shall only be grounded at one source. The grounding is usually made in equipment panel or cabinet while field device point is left ungrounded and insulated.

This is to eliminate the ground-loop current that may arise if screen is grounded at both ends. Ground loop provides a path for current to flow through the cable's shield resulting from differences in Earth potential at the cable ends. Not only can ground loops induce noise in a cable's conductor(s), but in severe cases it can even overheat the cable.

Chapter: 6

Analog Instrumentation Signal

1. What are the common analog electronic instrumentation signal used in control system?

Ans: Current signal (4-20 mA) and voltage signal (1-5 V) used for control and signal processing in the industry.

2. What is live zero and dead zero?

Ans: A "live zero" refers to a signal range where the zero point of the measured parameter is represented by a nonzero signal value. For e.g. 4–20 mA: 4 mA represents the zero point (minimum value), while 20 mA represents the maximum value.

A "dead zero" refers to a signal range where the zero point of the measured parameter is represented by a true zero value. For e.g. 0–20 mA: 0 mA represents the zero point, and 20mA represents the maximum value.

3. Why 4-20 mA signal is used in instrumentation instead of 0-20 mA?

Ans: The 4–20 mA signal is used because it makes it easier to detect faults in the system. In this range, 4 mA represents the lowest value of the measurement (like 0 pressure or 0 flow), and 20 mA represents the maximum. If the signal ever drops below 4 mA, it usually means there's a problem like a broken wire or a sensor failure. This makes it easier for the system to spot faults quickly.

With a 0–20 mA signal, it is impossible to distinguish between a real zero (like 0 pressure) and a fault condition. Both would give 0 mA, which could be confusing. So, using 4 mA as the "live zero" avoids this issue and keeps the system more reliable.

Moreover, the minimum current of 4 mA can be used to power the field devices (e.g., sensors or transmitters) in a two-wire system. This eliminates the need for additional power wiring. But, at 0 mA, the device cannot be powered, making it unsuitable for two-wire devices that rely on loop power.

4. Why current signal is preferred over voltage signal?

Ans: Current loops (e.g., 4–20 mA) can transmit signals reliably over long distances, often up to thousands of feet, without significant signal degradation. Whereas, voltage signals degrade significantly over long distances due to wire resistance, which makes them less suitable for remote sensing or control.

Current signals are less affected by electromagnetic interference (EMI) and electrical noise whereas, Voltage signals are more susceptible to EMI, which can distort the signal and cause measurement errors.

Current loops can power field devices (e.g., sensors or transmitters) with the same current used for signaling, simplifying wiring by eliminating the need for an external power source. But Voltage signals usually require separate power supplies for devices, increasing complexity and wiring costs.

5. How to wire a 4 to 20 mA system?

Ans: The components of the 4 to 20 mA system get wired in series, one after the other. Connect the devices together so that the "+" power terminal of the power supply goes to the "+" terminal on the first device, the "-" terminal of the first device to the "+" terminal of the second device, the "-" terminal of the second device to the "+" terminal of the third device, and so on and so on until one wires back to the "-" terminal of the power supply.

Because the wiring starts at the power supply and goes from one device to another, the 4/20mA system is commonly called a 4 to 20 mA loop.

6. **How can you calculate percentage value (output or input devices) from corresponding 4-20 mA value?**

Ans: By using the following equation: -

$$y = \frac{20-4}{URV-LRV}x + 4$$

Where: y represents milliamp

x represents corresponding percentage value

URV represents Upper range value and LRV represents lower range value.

7. **An electronic loop controller outputs a signal of 8.55 mA to a direct-responding control valve (where 4mA is shut and 20 mA is wide open). How far open should the control valve be at this signal level?**

Ans: For percentage of stem travel (x) at 8.55 milliamps of signal current (y)-

$$y = \frac{20-4}{100-0}x + 4$$
$$=> 8.55 = \frac{16}{100}x + 4$$
$$=> 4.55 = \frac{16}{100}x$$
$$=> x = 28.4$$

Therefore, the valve to be 28.4% open at an applied signal of 8.55 milliamps.

8. **A pressure transmitter is ranged 0 to 10 kgf, 4-20 mA output, direct-responding. Calculate the current signal value at a pressure of 6 kgf.**

Ans: According to question, x = 6kgf, y=?

$$y = \frac{20-4}{10-0}x + 4 = \frac{16}{10} * 6 + 4 = 13.6$$

Therefore, the transmitter should output a signal of 13.6 mA at a pressure of 6 kgf.

9. **How can you calculate percentage value (output or input devices) from corresponding 4-20 mA value for reverse acting**

transducer?

Ans: By using the following equation: -

$$y = \frac{20-4}{URV-LRV}x + 4$$

Where: y represents milliamp

x represents corresponding percentage value

URV represents Upper range value and LRV represents lower range value.

10. How 4 wire transmitters work in current loops?

Ans: in 4 wire transmitters, it has two terminals for the 4-20 mA signal wires to connect, and two more terminals where a power source connects. These transmitters are called "4-wire" or "self-powered" units. The current signal from the transmitter connects to the process variable input terminals of the controller to complete the loop.

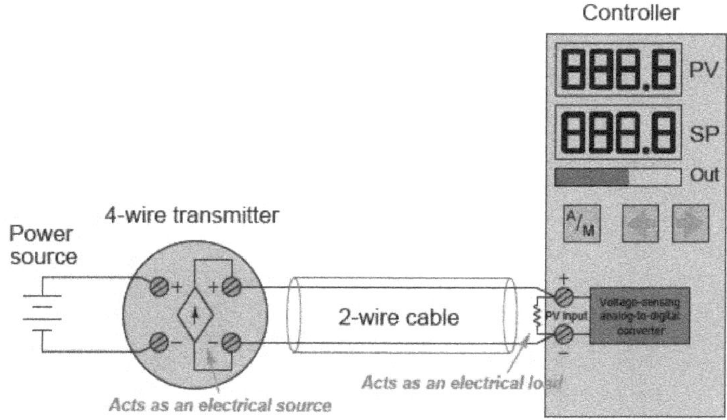

Fig 6.1- 4 wire transmitter

11. How 2 wire transmitters work in current loops?

Ans: 2 wire transmitter connects to a process controller with only two wires, which is why such transmitters are known as 2-wire transmitters or loop powered transmitters. 2-wire transmitter's circuitry is designed to act as a current regulator, limiting current in the series loop to a value representing the process measurement. A loop-powered transmitter gets its operating power from the minimum terminal voltage and current available at its two terminals.

With the typical source voltage being 24 volts DC, and the maximum voltage dropped across the controller's 250-ohm resistor being 5 volts DC, the transmitter should always have at least 19 volts available at its terminals. Given the lower end of the 4-20 mA signal range, the transmitter should always have at least 4 mA of current to function on. Thus, the transmitter will always have a certain minimum amount of electrical power available on which to operate, while regulating current to signal the process measurement to the receiving instrument.

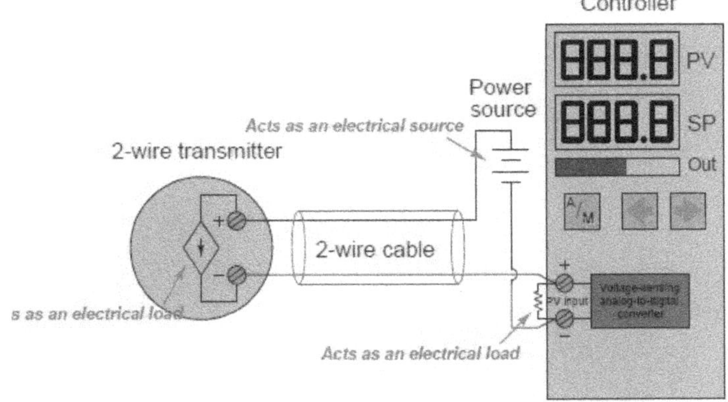

Fig 6.2 – 2 Wire transmitter

12. Why 250-ohm resistor used in 4-20 mA current loop?

Ans: Some process controllers are not equipped to directly accept milliamp input signals, but rather can only interpret DC voltage signals. In such cases we must connect a precision resistor across the controller's input terminals to convert the 4-20 mA transmitter signal into a standardized analog voltage signal the controller can understand. If the voltage range is 1-5 volts and the current range is 4-20 mA, the precision resistor value must be 250 ohms according to Ohm's Law.

13. What would happen if a resistor higher or lower than 250 Ohms is used in a 4-20 mA current loop?

Ans: If a resistor higher than 250 Ohms is used, the corresponding voltage drops across the load resistance will be higher, and as a result, the controller or display will receive a higher process value than the actual process value. Conversely, if a resistor lower than 250 Ohms is used, the corresponding voltage drops across the load resistance will be lower, and the controller or display will receive a lower process value than the actual process value.

For example, if a 275 Ohm resistor is used for a pressure transmitter with a range of 0–25 kgf, then for a 12.5 kgf process value, the current will be 12 mA (using calculations shown in the previous question). The corresponding voltage drops across the load resistance (for a 275 Ohm resistor) will be 3.3 V instead of 3 V. The controller will interpret this as 13.2 mA and the corresponding process value as 14.37 kgf instead of 12.5 kgf.

14. How can you measure current in a loop?

Ans: By using milliammeter meter or clamp on meter. To the use of a milliammeter, the circuit must be "broken" at some point or terminal to connect the meter in series with the current. Clamp on meter using Hall-effect sensors have been completely non-intrusive because they merely clamp around the wire, to measure current in the loop.

15. What is the main problem of measuring loop current by milliammeter in live condition? How this problem can be addressed?

Ans: Measuring loop current in a live system using a milliammeter poses a significant challenge because the meter must be connected in series with the circuit. This requires temporarily breaking the current loop to insert the instrument. The moment the loop is opened, the current flow drops to zero, which disrupts the signal being transmitted. Since current loops in instrumentation typically carry process information or control signals, this interruption can cause unintended consequences, such as control system instability, false alarms, or even an unplanned shutdown.

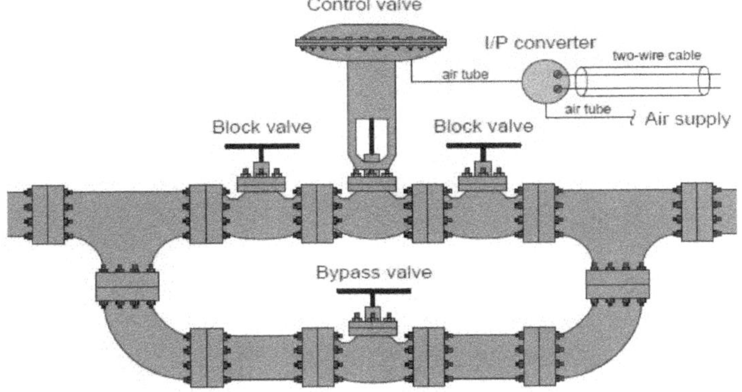

Fig 6.3- Bypass control valve

To address this issue, certain precautions must be taken. Before breaking the loop, it is essential to inform the relevant personnel about the planned interruption, as the system will momentarily lose signal. If the signal originates from a process transmitter to a controller, the controller should be switched to manual mode to prevent automatic responses that might disturb the process. In systems using PLCs or DCS, the affected process value can be forced to a safe and constant value to maintain operational stability.

When the loop carries a control signal to a final control element, such as a valve, it becomes necessary to manually override the control element or divert the flow through a bypass arrangement. Typically, this involves opening a bypass valve and closing at least one block valve to isolate the main control valve. During this time, a trained operator is required to manually adjust the bypass valve to maintain process conditions.

By following these careful steps, the impact of measuring loop current during live operation can be minimized, ensuring both process safety and measurement accuracy.

16. How "test" diode is used to measure loop current?

Ans: To measure a 4-20 mA signal without interrupting it involves the use of a rectifying diode, originally installed in the loop circuit when it was commissioned. A "test" diode may be placed anywhere in series within the loop in such a way that it will be forward-biased. During normal operation, the diode will drop approximately 0.7 volts, The following schematic diagram shows such a diode installed in a 2-wire transmitter loop circuit:

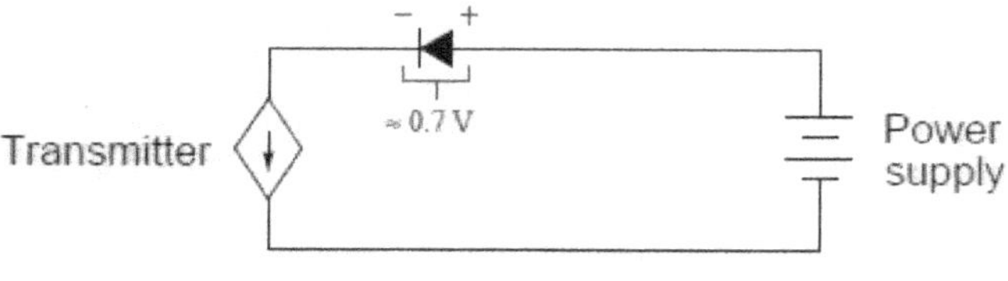

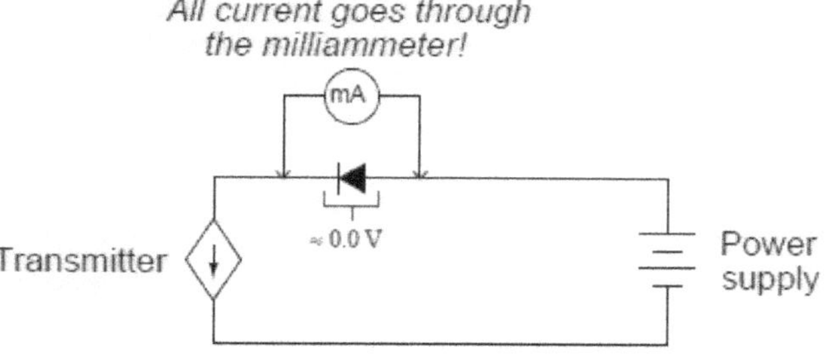

Fig 6.4 – Transmitter test diode

If a milliammeter connects in parallel with this diode, the very low input resistance of the ammeters "shorts past" the diode and prevents any substantial voltage drop from forming across it. Without the necessary forward voltage drop, the diode effectively turns off and conducts 0 mA, leaving the entire loop current to pass through the ammeter. When the milliammeter is disconnected, the requisite 0.7 volt drop appears to turn on the diode, and all loop current flows through the diode again. At no time is the loop current ever interrupted, which means current measurements can be done without disturbing the process.

17. What is the use of test terminal point of the transmitter?

Ans: The "test" terminals serve as points to connect the milliammeter across, for measurement of current within the loop. A diode installed in the transmitter itself (connection in series within the loop). Connecting an ammeter to these two test points allows for direct measurement of the 4-20 mA current signal without having to un-do any wire connections in the circuit.

18. What is the difference between Analog and Smart transmitter?

Ans: Following are the differences between Analog and Smart transmitter:

Feature	Analog Transmitter	Smart transmitter
Signal Output	4–20 mA	4–20 mA signal plus digital communication (e.g., HART protocol).
Internal Components	Uses analog circuitry only	Has a built-in microprocessor
Calibration and Configuration	Calibration is done manually using zero/span screws	Calibration (Sensor Trim and Output Trim) can be done digitally using a communicator
Diagnostics	Not available	Built-in self-diagnostics
Communication	One-way	Two-way (read/write)

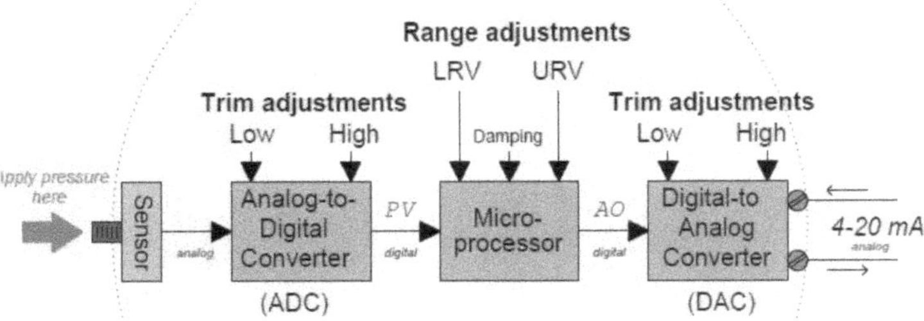

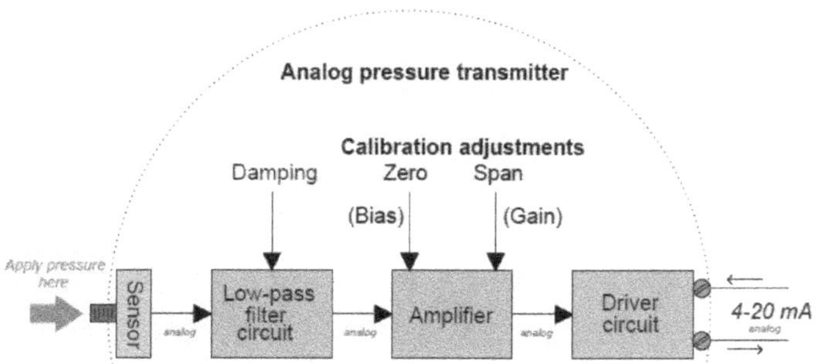

Fig 6.5- Smart vs Analog transmitter

19. What is Sensor Trim and output trim in SMART Transmitters?

Ans: Sensor Trim adjusts the internal measurement system of the transmitter based on a known, accurate reference. Sensor trim is used when the actual process variable (e.g., pressure, temperature) is known precisely from a standard calibrator, and the transmitter's sensor reading needs to match this. Example: If a high-accuracy pressure calibrator applies 100 psi, but the transmitter shows 98 psi, sensor trim is used to align the transmitter's internal sensor reading with the known 100 psi.

Output Trim adjusts the analog (usually 4–20 mA) output signal of the transmitter to ensure it matches the internal digital value. Output trim is used when the transmitter's digital reading is correct, but the current output is not accurate. Example: If the transmitter is correctly reading 50% of the range, but the output current is 11.8 mA instead of 12.0 mA, output trim corrects this discrepancy.

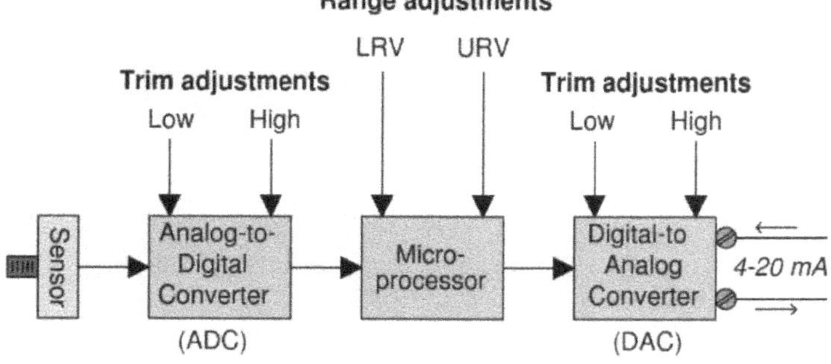

Fig 6.6 – Smart transmitter range adjustments

20. What is upper range value (URV) and lower range value (LRV) adjustments in Smart transmitter?

Ans: LRV is the minimum value of the process variable that corresponds to 4 mA output. Example: If LRV is set to 0 psi, then when the pressure is 0 psi, the transmitter will output 4 mA.

URV is the maximum value of the process variable that corresponds to 20 mA output. Example: If URV is set to 100 psi, then when the pressure is 100 psi, the transmitter will output 20 mA.

21. What if the power supply connections to a two-wire transmitter get interchanged? What signal will go to DCS?

Ans: Usually there is a blocking diode to protect the transmitter against supply reversal and almost zero current signal should be transmitted.

22. What happens if transmitter wires get shorted?

Ans: The barrier if installed limits electrical energy flowing into hazardous area. If there is no barrier, typically a fuse in the power distribution system will blow.

23. What is loop calibrator?

Ans: A loop calibrator is a portable electronic device used in industrial instrumentation to measure, test, calibrate, and troubleshoot current loops, typically 4–20 mA loops.

It generates a precise 4–20 mA current to test and verify the operation of devices like transmitters, controllers, and indicators without requiring a live process. And also acts as a transmitter by sourcing current or voltage to verify the operation of the receiving device, such as a PLC or DCS.

24. What is NAMUR signal level?

Ans: NAMUR signal levels refer to standardized electrical signal levels defined by the NAMUR organization. These signal levels are primarily used in industrial automation for sensors and field devices, particularly in hazardous areas. NAMUR-compliant transmitters are designed to limit their output signals *between **3.8 mA and less than 21 mA*** when functioning properly. Signals lying outside this range indicate some form of failure has occurred within the transmitter or the circuit wiring.

25. What are Sinking and Sourcing Circuits?

Ans: Sinking and sourcing circuits describe the direction of current flow in an electronic circuit, particularly in relation to input and output devices. These concepts are commonly used in industrial automation and control systems to explain how sensors, controllers, and actuators interact with each other in terms of power and signal transmission.

A sourcing circuit supplies (or "sources") current to the load and it provides the positive side of the circuit. The load (e.g., sensor, actuator, or input device) "sinks" the current by completing the circuit to the negative side (ground).

A sinking circuit allows current to flow through it to ground, thereby "sinking" the current and it provides the negative side of the circuit. The load must "source" current by providing the positive connection. A 2-wire transmitter is a passive device and thus "sinks" current. A 4-wire transmitter operates on an external power source and thus "sources" or provides power to the circuit.

26. How PLC or DCS card be wired based on Sourcing or sinking device?

Ans: PLC or DCS's input cards connect internally to power or ground. This switching between sinking and sourcing in input cards can be done by changing jumper settings in card hardware. An input card wired internally to ground is typically regarded as a sinking input card. A sinking input card requires power to be sourced to the input to turn it "on". For 4-wire transmitter that operates on an external power source and thus "sources" or provides power to the circuit, DCS input cards are wired to ground. If the input card connects internally to power, it is typically regarded as a sourcing card. A sourcing card input requires a ground connection to turn it "on". For A 2-wire transmitter which is a passive device and "sinks" current, input cards wired to source.

27. What is HART Communicator?

Ans: A HART communicator is a handheld device used to interface with field instruments that operate on the HART (Highway Addressable Remote Transducer) protocol. It allows technicians to configure, calibrate, monitor, and troubleshoot smart field devices over 4-20mA analog wiring in industrial automation systems.

Key feature:

- Configure parameters such as measurement range, zero/span adjustments, damping, and engineering units.
- Perform calibration tasks by adjusting the device to ensure it outputs correct signals for specific conditions.
- Check the health of the device, such as identifying faults, errors, or warnings related to the instrument.
- Store configuration data, diagnostics, and operational history for analysis.

28. What is loop checking? How loop checking is performed?

Ans: Loop checking is a process in industrial instrumentation and control systems used to verify that the components within a control loop are properly installed, configured, and functioning as intended. Loop checking involves testing the entire control loop from the field device (e.g., sensor or transmitter) through the wiring and signal processing to the final control element or monitoring system (e.g., PLC, DCS, or actuator).

Loop checking involves several steps:

- To ensure that all components in the loop are installed, powered, and wired correctly.
- To check for proper cable routing, terminations, and labelling.
- Continuity test to verify that there are no breaks or shorts in the wiring.
- To ensure the power supply voltage is correct and stable (e.g., 24 V DC for most instrumentation loops).
- Use a loop calibrator to inject a known signal (e.g., 4 mA, 12 mA, 20 mA) into the loop. Verify that the corresponding signal is received at the control system (PLC/DCS) or display device.
- To check the calibration of sensors, transmitters, and final control elements (e.g., valves) and adjust settings to match the required accuracy.

Chapter:7

Pressure Measurements

1. Define Pressure.

Ans: Pressure is defined as the amount of force applied to a surface or distributed over it and is measured as force per unit area.

2. Define atmospheric pressure.

Ans: Atmospheric pressure is the force exerted by the weight of the Earth's atmosphere against a surface.

3. Express atmospheric pressure in PSI or and in mm of liquid column.

Ans: The atmospheric pressure is 14.696 psi or (1kg/cm2),

In terms of liquid column, atmospheric pressure is 760mm (or 29.92 inches)

4. What is the full form of PSI?

Ans: Pound square inch

5. What are the different types of pressure?

Ans: Gauge pressure, Absolute pressure, vacuum Pressure

In the fig, P_g represents gauge pressure, a gauge that represents zero at atmospheric pressure measures the difference between actual and atmospheric pressure. This difference is called gauge pressure.

In the fig, P_{abs} represents absolute pressure, it is actual total pressure (including atmospheric pressure) acting on a surface.

In the fig, P_{vac} represents vaccum pressure, it is the measurement of the pressure of a fluid in a space where the pressure is lower than atmospheric pressure.

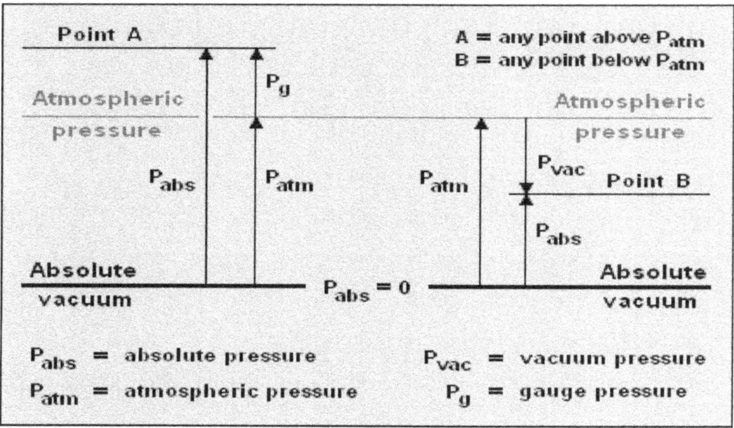

Fig 7.1- Different types of pressure

Gauges that indicate absolute pressure cannot indicate pressure below zero because zero is a perfect vaccum.

6. Explain the working principle of U- tube manometer.

Ans: When the pressure at one end of the U-tube differs from the pressure at the other end, it causes a height difference in the liquid levels in the two arms of the U-tube. The pressure difference is directly proportional to the difference in the heights of the liquid columns in the two arms of the U-tube.

To measure pressure, one end of the U-tube is connected to the point where pressure is to be measured (such as a pipe or container). The other end is left open to the atmosphere or connected to a reference pressure point. The difference in the liquid levels in the two arms of the U-tube is then used to calculate the pressure difference.

7. Which liquids are used in mercury?

Ans: Generally, water or mercury is used as fluid as they do not sick to the tube. When manometer is used to measure low pressure then water is used as liquid, and when it is used to measure high pressure then mercury is used as the liquid. Mercury is almost 14 times as heavier as water. Therefore, the difference in levels in a mercury filled manometer is about 1/14 of what it would be if water were in the tube.

8. What are the errors in pressure measurement by manometer?
Ans:Following are the errorsin Pressure measurement by manometer:

- *Effect of temperature*: Due to change in temperature, density of the liquid in manometer increase or decrease resulting in variation of the reading as fluid expands or shrinks.
- *Effect of variable meniscus*: The crescent shaped top surface of a liquid column is called meniscus. Due to high surface tension of liquid makes meniscus slightly convex and low surface tension makes slighthly concave. To avoid error, reading should be taken from the indication of the center of the meniscus.

9. What are the advantages & disadvantages of manometer?
   Ans: *Advantages*
   - They are Simple & low cost.
   - They have high accuracy & sensitivity.
   - They are suitable for low pressure & low differential Pressure application.
   Disdavantages
   - They are large & bulky
   - They need proper levelling
   - They are vulnerable to environmental change.

10. What is the working principle of bourdon type pressure gauge?
Ans: The Bourdon tube pressure gauge is a mechanical device used to measure the pressure of a fluid or gas in a system.

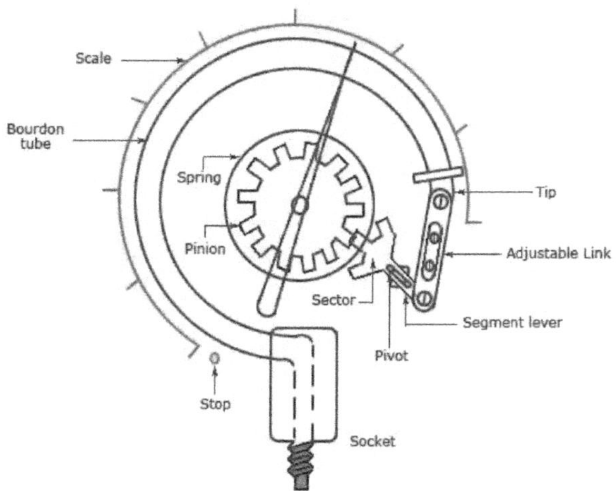

Fig 7.2- Bourdon type pressure gauge

The primary component of a Bourdon-type pressure gauge is the Bourdon tube, which is a curved, hollow tube typically made of metal. The tube is oval or elliptical in cross-section and is closed at one end while the other end is fixed and connected to the connected to the system where pressure needs to be measured. When pressure is applied, it enters the open end of the tube, causing the curved shape to attempt to straighten out. This happens because the internal pressure tries to push the walls of the tube outward, and due to the tube's elasticity, it begins to uncoil slightly. The degree to which the tube straightens is directly related to the pressure being applied.

This movement, although small, is mechanically linked to a gear and lever system that converts the tube's motion into a rotating movement. That rotation moves a pointer across a dial, which is marked with pressure values in units like psi, bar, or kPa. When there is no pressure in the system, the tube springs back to its original shape, and the pointer returns to zero.

11. Which metal is used to make bourdon tube?

Ans: Bronze or stainless steel.

12. What are the different shapes in which bourdon tube available?

Ans: C-type, Helical Type, and spiral type.

13. What are the advantages and disadvantages of bourdon tube?

Ans: <u>Advantages:</u>

- They are low cost and simple in construction.
- These tubes are available in a wide variety of ranges.
  <u>Disadvantages:</u>
- They are susceptible to shock & vibration
- They are susceptible to hysteresis.

14. What is the working principle of Diaphragm type pressure measuring element?

Ans: Diaphragm widely used in pressure measurement, particularly in very low ranges. The primary component is a flexible diaphragm, which is a thin, circular membrane made of a flexible material such as metal, or composite materials. When pressure is applied to the process side of the diaphragm, it causes the diaphragm to deform or flex. The extent of the deformation is proportional to the pressure applied As the diaphragm deforms, this motion is mechanically transmitted through linkages or sensing mechanisms to move a pointer across a calibrated scale. This allows the pressure to be read easily. They are commonly found in pressure transmitters, pressure switches, and other pressure measurement devices.

15. What is the working principle of Bellows type pressure measuring element?

Ans: The bellow type gauges are used for the measurement of absolute pressure and is more sensitive than bourdan tube gauges and generally used for the low range. The bellows are made of an alloy which is ductile, has high strength and retains its properties over long use. The bellows is sealed at one end and open at the other. The sealed end is often fixed, while the open end is connected to the pressure source. When pressure is applied to the open end of the bellows, it causes the bellows to expand or contract. The deformation of the bellows is directly proportional to the applied pressure. The deformation of the bellows is transferred to a mechanism that translates the mechanical motion into a measurable parameter.

16. How bellow is used in the measurement of differential pressure?

Ans: In the differential pressure measurement arrangement, one pressure is applied to the inside of one sealed bellow while the other pressure is applied to the inside of another sealed bellow. By suitable linkage and calibration of the scale, the pressure difference is indicated by apointer on the scale.

17. What is a pressure switch, and how does it function in an industrial setting?

Ans: A pressure switch is a device that monitors pressure levels in a system and opens or closes an electrical circuit based on predefined pressure setpoint.

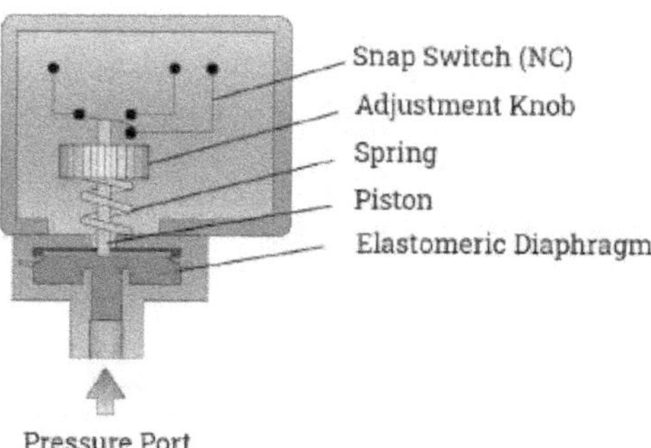

Fig 7.3 – Pressure Switch

It typically consists of a sensing element, a setpoint adjustment, and electrical contacts. When pressure reaches set value, the contact plate touches contact point, thus closing an electrical circuit.

18. What are the different types of pressure switches available in the market?

Ans: Types of pressure switches include electromechanical, solid-state, and smart/digital pressure switches.

19. Can you provide examples of industries or applications where pressure switches are commonly used?

Ans: Pressure Switches are used in industries to limit pressure in process within a prescribed set point. Consider an example, where discharge pressure of a pump is to be maintained below 5kgf. When discharge pressure of the pump exceeds set pressure 5kgf, pressure switch will act and open the circuit thereby tripping the pump due to high discharge.

20. How is a pressure switch calibrated?

Ans: Pressure switch calibration procedure-

- First we connect the pressure gauge and Pressure switch to the hand pump.
- Then we need to measure the present status (NO/NC) of electrical output of the switch with the multimeter. Put multimeter in Continuity mode.
- Lets take the example of normally open (NO) pressure switch. So when you connect the multimeter before calibration we have default Normally Open (NO) signal as output.
- With our connections complete, we are ready to perform the calibration. We do this by increasing pressure until we detect a change in the switch.
- Now increase the pressure with the help of hand pump.

- When we see the switch change state from open to close, we record the result.
- Next, we decrease the pressure till we see the switch reset (change from close to open) and record the results.
- Also record the dead band.
- Lastly, we would repeat this test at least once to determine repeatability. The difference between set point and rest pressures is the dead band. The dead band must be within the range. The deadband & setpoint of pressure switch available on nameplate of pressure switch.

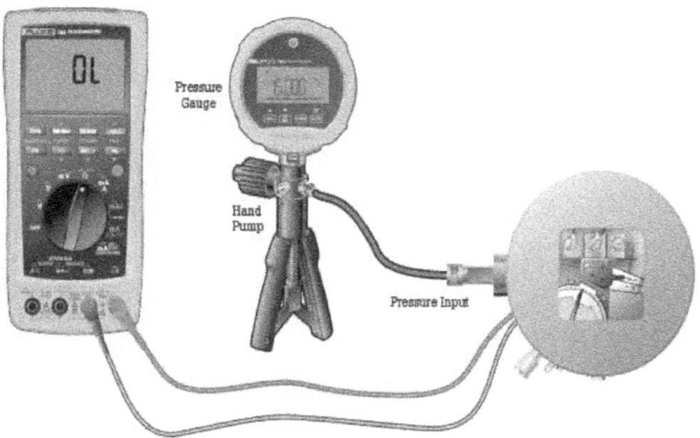

Fig 7.4 – Pressure calibration setup

21. What are the factors that can affect the accuracy of a pressure switch over time, and how can they be mitigated?

Ans: Factors affecting accuracy include wear, aging, and environmental conditions.

Regular calibration is crucial for maintaining accuracy over time. Regular maintenance includes checking for leaks, cleaning contacts, and ensuring proper electrical connections.

22. What are some common failure modes of pressure switches, and how would you troubleshoot them?

Ans: Common failures include contacts sticking, drifting setpoints, or failure to trip at the designated pressure. Troubleshooting involves checking electrical connections, inspecting the sensing element, and recalibrating if necessary.

23. What is the dead band in pressure switch?

Ans: Dead band in the pressure switch is the pressure difference between the change-of-states. (i.e. OPEN to CLOSE or CLOSE to OPEN).

24. What is the trip type in pressure switch?

Ans: This is the direction to which the change-of state should happen. If the trip type is low, this means the change-of-state happens when the pressure is falling. If the trip type is high, this means the change-of-state happens when the pressure is rising.

25. What is NO & NC Contact in pressure switch?

Ans: In a pressure switch with a NO contact configuration, the electrical circuit is open (non-conductive) when there is no pressure applied or the pressure is below the set threshold. When the pressure rises and reaches the predetermined setpoint, the NO contact closes (becomes conductive), completing the electrical circuit and allowing current to flow.

In a pressure switch with an NC contact configuration, the electrical circuit is normally closed (conductive) when there is no pressure applied or the pressure is below the set threshold. As the pressure increases and reaches the predetermined setpoint, the NC contact opens (becomes non-conductive), breaking the electrical circuit and interrupting the current flow.

26. When will you use NO/NC Contact in pressure switch?

Ans: NO contacts are commonly used in applications where the electrical circuit needs to be closed or activated when the pressure rises above a certain level. NC contacts are often employed in applications where the electrical circuit needs to be open or deactivated when the pressure rises above a certain level.

27. What is impulse piping?

Ans: Impulse piping serves as a conduit for the transfer of process pressure to the pressure-sensing element of a pressure transmitter or gauge.

28. How should Instrument be installed in impulse line for Liquid/gas/steam?

Ans: If the process fluid is liquid, the transmitter should be placed lower than the taps. If the process fluid is gas, the transmitter should be placed higher than the taps.

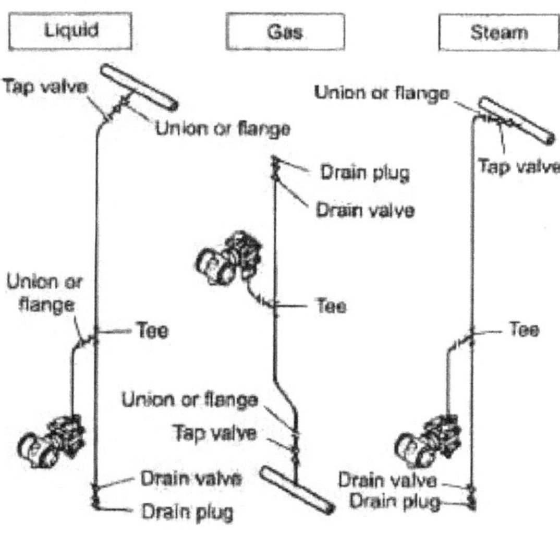

Fig 7.5 -Impulse line

If the process fluid is steam, it has more chances to vaporize, so condensate pot should be used, and the transmitter should be placed at lower level than the taps.

29. What is condensate pot?

Ans: Condensate pots find application in scenarios where steam is present in the process line. Positioned between the process line and the differential pressure transmitter, these pots serve a crucial role. A pool of water resides between the condensate pot and the transmitter, offering a dual-purpose solution.

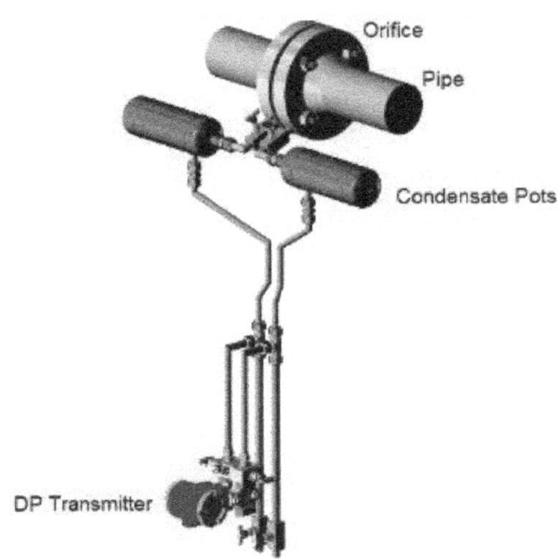

Fig 7.6 – Condensate Pot

Firstly, this configuration eradicates potential measurement errors arising from a mixture of liquid and vapor at the measurement device. Secondly, it acts as a barrier, preventing direct contact between the steam and the sensitive components of the transmitter. This design ensures accurate and reliable pressure measurements, safeguarding the integrity of the differential pressure transmitter in steam-containing industrial processes.

30. What is 3 valve manifold and 5 valve manifolds?
Ans: A three-valve manifold is a device that is used in differential pressure transmitter. It also allows isolation of the transmitter from the process loop.

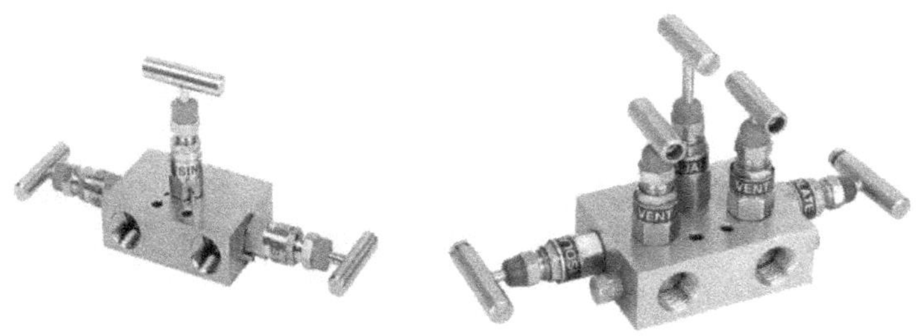

Fig 7.7- Manifolds

It consists of two block valves – high pressure and low-pressure block valve – and an equalizing valve. Two block valves provide instrument isolation, and one equalize valve is positioned between the high and low transmitter process connections to provide equal pressures on both sides. 5 valve manifolds is similar to 3 valve manifolds, while 5 valve manifolds have two vent valves in both HP & LP process line.

31. How will you put a DP transmitter in service and make out of service by using 3 valve manifold?

Ans: To valve a DP transmitter into service an operator would perform the following steps:

- Check all valves are closed.
- Open the equalizing valve – this ensures that the same pressure will be applied to both sides of the transmitter, i.e., zero differential pressure.
- Open the High Pressure block valve slowly, check for leakage from both the high pressure and low-pressure side of the transmitter.
- Close the equalizing valve – this locks the pressure on both sides of the transmitter.

- Open the low-pressure block valve to apply process pressure to the low-pressure side of the transmitter and establish the working differential pressure.
- The Transmitter is now in service.

Reversal of the above steps allows the DP transmitter to be removed from service:

- Close the low-pressure block valve.
- Open the equalizing valve.
- Close the high-pressure block valve.
- The transmitter is now out of service

32. Why is slopping required in the impulse line?

Ans: The slope of impulse lines is a critical factor in their design. For gas or steam applications, impulse lines should slope upwards from the process connection to the transmitter. This allows any condensate to drain back into the process.

Conversely, for liquid applications, impulse lines should slope downwards from the process connection to the transmitter. This allows any trapped gas to be carried back into the process.

33. What is the minimum slopping required in impulse line?

Ans: Normally 80 mm/m is standard. For liquid services, level, etc., the slope should be down from the source point to the instrument, whereas for air and gas services it should be upward from the source point to the instrument.

The slope should never be less than 20 mm/m. Impulse lines connecting to the transmitter should be as short as possible to prevent errors.

34. What postioning should be considered while installing impulse line for Flow & Level measurement?

Ans: For flow measurements, impulse lines should be connected at the same horizontal level to avoid measurement errors due to the head of fluid in the lines.

For level measurements, they should be connected at different vertical levels corresponding to the high and low points of the tank.

35. How would you select a pressure gauge for a process?

Ans: While selecting a pressure gauge for a process, consider the following points:

- Characteristic of the process (corrosive or non-corrosive)
- Operating pressure
- Maximum process pressure

The gauge range should be a minimum of twice the process operating pressure.

36. What type of pressure gauge should use for corrosive liquid?

Ans: Diaphragm seals are often used with pressure gauges for measuring corrosive liquids.

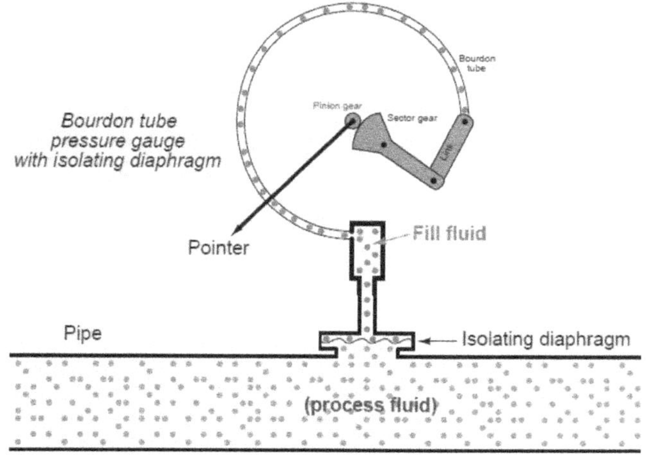

Fig 7.8 – Pressure gauge for corrosive liquid

These seals act as a barrier between the corrosive fluid and the internal components of the pressure gauge. The diaphragm seal is filled with a compatible incompressible fluid that transmits the pressure from the process to the gauge, protecting the gauge internals from direct contact with the corrosive liquid.

37. What type of gauges should be used for pulsating media?
Ans: For pulsating media, pressure gauges filled with liquid (Glycerine) are used.

38. What is gauge siphons?
Ans: Gauge Syphons are used to protect the pressure gauge from the effect of hot pressure media such as steam and also to reduce the effect of rapid pressure surges. The syphon allows condensate to form and be collected inside the syphon, preventing the hot media (hot vapors, not just steam) from coming in direct contact with the pressure sensors.

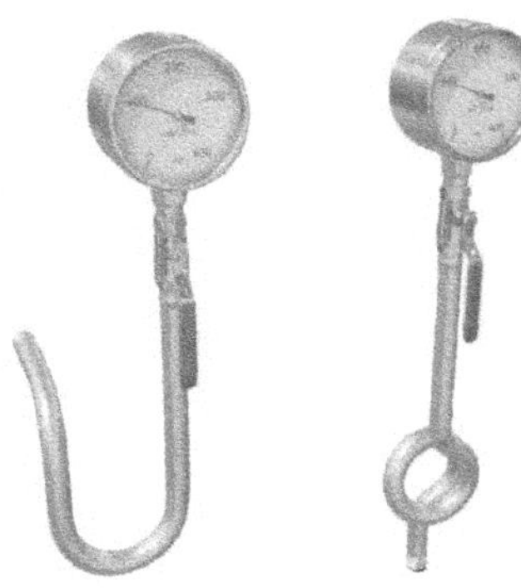

Fig 7.9 – Gauge Siphon

There are two types of syphons:
Coil syphon: used for vertical installation
U type syphon: used for horizontal installation

39. How to isolate pressure transmitter from direct contact with the process fluid?
Ans: Pressure transmitter can be isolate by filling the impulse line with some other fluids.

40. Which type of fluid used in impulse line?

Ans: Generally, Glycerine is used in impulse line. As, Glycerine freezes below the freezing point of water in cold conditions. And the greater density of glycerine keeps it placed in the impulse line, below the process water line.

41. How to protect pressure gauge from pressure pulsations?
Ans:

Snubber

Fig 7.10 – Snubber

The Snubber (Pulsation Dampener) protects the pressure instruments from pressure pulsations / rapid pressure fluctuation. Ideal for instruments which undergo severe pressure pulsations like those located at the pump discharge.

42. What is the purpose of capillary tubing pressure gauge?
Ans: Capillary tubing is used to separate the direct connection between the measuring instrument and the process tapping point.

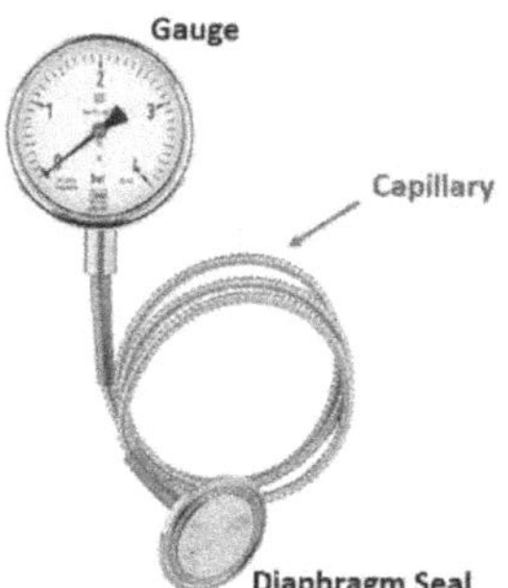

Fig 7.11 – Capillary gauge

76

Capillary tubes also serves as the purpose of a cooling element as the distance between the process tapping and the instrument will be more than the direct type installation.

The instrument can be installed as per convenience and easy access for the maintenance.

43. What is dead weight tester?

Ans: A dead weight tester is a calibration instrument used to calibrate pressure measuring devices, such as pressure gauges, transmitters, and sensors. The dead weight tester operates on the principle of balancing a known force (the weight of a mass) against the pressure in a fluid, creating equilibrium and allowing for accurate pressure calibration.

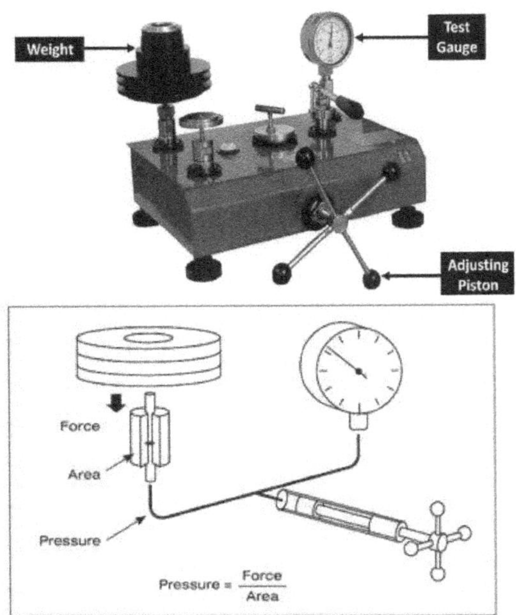

Fig 7.12 – Dead weight tester

A Dead Weight Tester is made up of a piston-cylinder assembly, known weights, and a pressure source (like a hand pump or screw press). The piston sits inside the cylinder, and weights are placed on top of the piston. To test a pressure gauge, pressure is applied to the system. As the pressure increases, it pushes the piston upward. The pressure is adjusted until the upward force of the pressure balances the downward force of the weights. At this point, the piston starts to float steadily, which is why it's called a "dead weight" tester. Since the pressure is directly related to the weight and the area of the piston, the applied pressure is known and accurate. The pressure reading from the device under test is then compared to the known pressure from the Dead weight tester.

44. What is the difference between dead weight tester and gauge comparator?

Ans: Dead weight tester is used for calibrating a test gauge. It works on the hydraulic principle, where a test gauge is compared with the standard dead weights.

Gauge comparator is used for calibrating a pressure gauge against a test gauge. Calibration procedure is simple and quicker.

45. What is the working principle of strain gauge in pressure measurement?

Ans: In pressure measurement, strain gauges are used to detect how a material deforms when pressure is applied. The basic idea is to convert mechanical strain (stretching or compressing) into an electrical signal.

When pressure is applied to a sensing element like a diaphragm or Bourdon tube, it deforms slightly. A strain gauge, which is a thin piece of wire or foil, is attached to this element. As the pressure changes, the element expands or contracts, and the strain gauge stretches or compresses with it.

This change in shape causes a small change in the electrical resistance of the strain gauge. To measure this change accurately, strain gauges are usually arranged in a Wheatstone bridge circuit. When the resistance changes, the bridge becomes unbalanced and produces a voltage signal that's proportional to the amount of strain and therefore, to the applied pressure.

The system is calibrated so that this voltage can be directly related to a pressure reading.

46. What is the working principle of capacitive type sensor in pressure measurement?

Ans: In capacitive type pressure measurement, a diaphragm or membrane undergoes deflection due to applied pressure. This deflection alters the separation distance between two capacitive plates, forming a capacitor. The change in capacitance resulting from the varying separation distance is directly proportional to the applied pressure. This capacitance variation is then converted into an electrical signal, enabling accurate and precise pressure measurement.

47. What is the working principle of Piezoelectric sensor in pressure measurement?

Ans: In piezoelectric pressure measurement, pressure-induced mechanical deformation causes a piezoelectric crystal to generate an electric charge. The crystal's response to pressure is directly proportional to the applied force, resulting in an electrical signal. This signal is then translated into a pressure reading, making piezoelectric sensors suitable for dynamic and high-frequency pressure measurements.

48. Explain the working principles of SMART Pressure Transmitter?

Ans: A SMART pressure transmitter measures pressure and converts it into a usable electronic signal, typically a 4–20 mA output. It also includes onboard digital electronics for added functions like self-diagnostics and remote communication.

At its core, the transmitter has a pressure-sensing element, usually a diaphragm, that deforms slightly when pressure is applied.

This mechanical deformation is detected using a strain gauge setup, often configured in a Wheatstone bridge circuit. As pressure changes, the resistance in the bridge changes, producing a small voltage signal.

This raw signal is weak, so it's first amplified and filtered to remove noise. Next, an Analog-to-Digital Converter (ADC) turns this analog signal into a digital one. A microprocessor then processes the signal and performs tasks like calibration, temperature compensation, and signal linearization to ensure the final reading is accurate.

SMART transmitters also have memory to store configuration and calibration data. They support digital communication protocols like HART or Fieldbus, allowing technicians to configure or troubleshoot the device remotely.

Finally, the processed value is converted into a standard output signal usually 4–20 mA and sent to the control system. The transmitter typically operates on a 24V DC power supply.

49. What is the working principle of DP type pressure transmitter?
Ans: A DP (Differential Pressure) type pressure transmitter is an instrument designed to measure the difference in pressure between two points in a process. It typically consists of a pressure-sensing element, two pressure ports for high and low pressure, and circuitry that converts the pressure difference into an electrical signal. The transmitter is commonly used in industrial applications where accurate monitoring of pressure differentials is essential, such as flow measurements, level measurements, and filtration processes.

50. How would the pressure transmitter respond if equal pressures applied to both "H" and "L" ports?
Ans: when equal pressure applied at both H & L ports, pressure difference will be zero and hence output will yield zero Value.

51. How is DP Transmitter used for filtration monitoring?

Ans: A differential pressure (DP) transmitter is commonly used to monitor the condition of filters in both liquid and gas systems. It works by measuring the pressure difference across the filter from the inlet (upstream) side to the outlet (downstream) side.

The high-pressure side of the transmitter is connected before the filter, where the fluid or gas enters. The low-pressure side is connected after the filter, where the cleaned media exits. When the filter is clean, there is very little resistance to flow, so the pressure drop across the filter is small, often close to zero.

As the filter begins to clog with contaminants, the flow becomes restricted, and the pressure on the downstream side drops. This increases the differential pressure. The DP transmitter senses this change and provides a signal that increases linearly with the pressure difference.

By monitoring this signal, operators can determine when the filter is getting clogged and needs cleaning or replacement, helping to maintain system efficiency and prevent damage.

52. What is Damping Adjustment in a Pressure Transmitter?

Ans: While measuring pump discharge pressure, turbulence at the pump outlet can cause rapid pressure fluctuations, leading to noisy signals that disturb control system performance. Most modern pressure transmitters (analog and digital) have a damping feature that acts as a low-pass filter to smooth out these fluctuations. High-frequency noise is attenuated, reducing its impact on the output signal. In analog transmitters, damping is adjusted by changing resistance (R) or capacitance (C) in an RC circuit. In digital transmitters, damping is set through software configuration. Pneumatic transmitters achieve damping mechanically by adding volume or viscous elements. Proper damping ensures stable and accurate control responses.

Chapter: 8
Temperature Measurements

1. Define temperature.

Ans: Temperature is a measure of the average kinetic energy of the particles in a substance. It indicates the degree of hotness of the body.

2. What are the lower fixed point and upper fixed point in temperature scale?

Ans: The lower fixed point (also called ice point or freezing point) is the temperature of ice when melting under a pressure of 760mm of Hg. The upper fixed point (also called steam point or boiling point) is the temperature of steam from pure water boiling under a pressure of 760mm of Hg.

3. How freezing point and boiling point of water is defined in Fahrenheit, Centigrade, Kelvin, Rankine and Reaumur scale?

Ans: In Fahrenheit scale, freezing point of water defined as 32°F and boiling point of water is defined as *212°C* at standard atmospheric pressure.

In Centigrade scale, freezing point of water defined as 0°C and boiling point of water is defined as *100°C* at standard atmospheric pressure.

In Kelvin scale, freezing point of water defined as 273.15°K and boiling point of water is defined as **373.15°K** at standard atmospheric pressure.

In Rankine scale, freezing point of water defined as 491.7°R and boiling point of water is defined as *671.7°R* at standard atmospheric pressure.

In Reaumur scale, freezing point of water defined as 0°R' and boiling point of water is defined as 80°R' at standard atmospheric pressure.

4. What is the scale of divisions between two fixed points in each of Fahrenheit, Centigrade, Kelvin and Rankine scale?

Ans: Fahrenheit Scale: 180 divisions

Centigrade Scale: 100 divisions

Kelvin Scale: 100 divisions

Rankine Scale: 180 divisions

5. What do you mean by absolute zero temperature?

Ans: Absolute zero is the theoretical temperature at which all particle motion ceases, meaning the particles have minimal vibrational motion, essentially possessing zero kinetic energy. It represents the lowest possible temperature in the universe.

In the Kelvin scale, absolute zero is defined as 0 K, which is equivalent to:

- **-273.15°C** in the Celsius scale.
- **-459.67°F** in the Fahrenheit scale.

6. What is the working principle of bimetallic thermometer?

Ans: Bimetallic Thermometer is made by bonding two thin strips of different metals together having different co-efficient of thermal expansion. When the temperature changes, the two metals expand or contract at different rates. This causes the bimetallic strip to bend or curve because one metal expands or contracts more than the other. The bending of the bimetallic strip is converted into a rotational movement, typically using a pointer attached to the strip. The pointer moves across a calibrated scale that shows the temperature.

7. Which liquid is used in glass thermometer for measurement of low temperature?

Ans: Alcohol, as it freezes in very low temperature.

8. How bimetallic strips work in temperature gauge?

Ans: A bi-metallic strip is twisted over a long length, and it will tend to un-twist as it heats up. This twisting motion may be used to directly drive the needle of a temperature gauge.

9. How liquid in glass thermometer used for temperature measurement?

Ans: It consists of a sealed glass tube with a thin capillary bore. Inside the tube, a liquid (such as mercury or alcohol) is used. The tube has a temperature scale marked on it. When the temperature increases, the liquid inside the thermometer expands and rises in the capillary tube and when the temperature decreases, the liquid contracts and moves down. The level of the liquid corresponds to a calibrated temperature scale, allowing temperature measurement.

10. How Does a Temperature Gauge Work?

Ans: Temperature gauge consists of a coiled Bourdon tube filled with a temperature-sensitive liquid or gas. When temperature increases, the liquid or gas expands, causing the tube to straighten slightly. This movement is transferred to a pointer on a calibrated dial, indicating temperature.

Some temperature gauge consists of a bimetallic strip. When temperature changes, the strip bends due to differential expansion. This bending motion moves a pointer on the dial, indicating the temperature.

11. What is a capillary type temperature gauge?

Ans: A capillary type temperature gauge operates on the principle of thermal expansion of a liquid or gas enclosed within a sealed system. It consists of a bulb (sensing element), a capillary tube, and a Bourdon tube with a dial indicator. When temperature increases, the liquid or gas in the bulb expands, increasing pressure inside the capillary tube. This pressure change is transmitted to the Bourdon tube, causing it to move and rotate the pointer on the dial, displaying the temperature.

Fig 8.1 – Capillary type temperature gauge

The advantages of capillary tube temperature gauge are: it can measure temperature from far-off locations and prevents the gauge from high vibrations.

12. What is Resistance temperature detector (RTD)?

Ans: A Resistance Temperature Detector (RTD) is a special temperature-sensing element made of fine metal wire, the electrical resistance of which changes with temperature. The resistance of the RTD changes according to the equation:

$$R_T = R_{ref}\left[1 + \alpha(T - T_{ref})\right]$$

Where,

R_T = Resistance of RTD at given temperature T (ohms)

R_{ref} = Resistance of RTD at the reference temperature T_{ref} (ohms)

α = Temperature coefficient of resistance (ohms per ohm/degree)

13. How is RTD used in temperature measurement?

Ans: To measure temperature, the RTD is inserted into the medium whose temperature is to be measured and is connected by leads to a Wheatstone bridge. The principle of the Wheatstone bridge states that, under normal conditions, no current flows through the galvanometer connected to it. As the temperature changes, the resistance of the RTD also changes, resulting in a change in the current through the bridge. This change in current is calibrated to measure the temperature using the RTD.

14. What material is used in RTD?

Ans: Normally, platinum or nickel is used.

15. What is Pt100 and Pt1000 ?

Ans: Pt100 and Pt1000 are two types of Platinum Resistance Temperature Detectors (RTDs) used for temperature measurement. The difference between them lies in their nominal resistance at 0°C. The resistance of Pt100 at 0°C is 100 ohm and Pt1000 is 1000 ohm.

Pt1000 has 10 times higher resistance than Pt100, making it more sensitive to temperature changes. Pt100 is used in industrial temperature measurement and Pt1000 is used in precise instrument like medical drives.

16. What are the problems in two wire RTD connection?

Ans: The wire resistance adds to the sensing element's resistance to create a larger total circuit resistance which will be interpreted by the receiving instrument (ohmmeter) as a falsely high temperature reading.

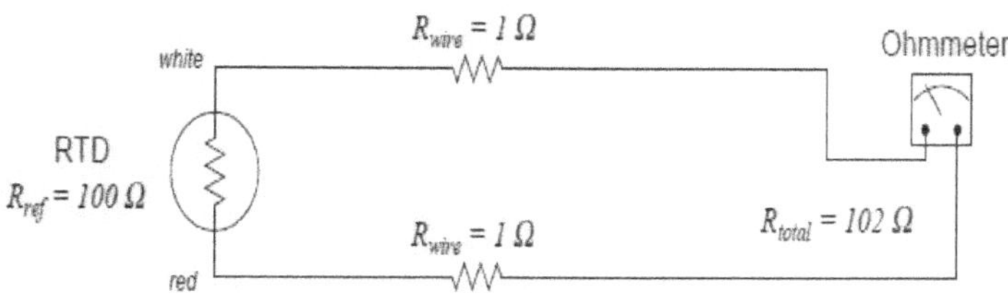

Fig 8.2 – Two wire RTD

17. What are the 3 -wire and 4-wire connections of RTD?

Ans: A 3-wire and 4-wire RTD measurement is a technique used to compensate for lead wire resistance in resistance temperature detectors (RTDs).

In 3 wire RTD, two wires are on one side of the RTD element, and the third wire is on the opposite side. A Wheatstone bridge circuit measures the resistance. The bridge assumes that both lead wires have equal resistance and subtracts their effect from the measurement, compensating for lead wire resistance.

A 4-wire RTD measurement is the most accurate method for measuring resistance in RTDs. It completely eliminates lead wire resistance errors by using four separate wires—two for carrying the excitation current and two for measuring the voltage drop across the RTD element. A precision measuring instrument calculates resistance and converts it to temperature.

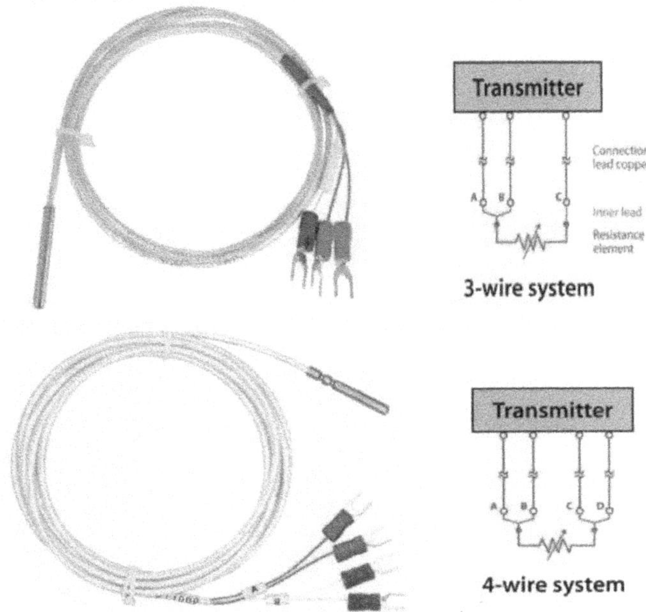

Fig 8.3 – 3-wire and 4-wire RTD

18. How are RTDs constructed?

Ans: An RTD (Resistance Temperature Detector) is made up of a few key components. At the heart of it is a sensing element, usually made from platinum wire or film (like Pt100 or Pt1000), though sometimes nickel or copper is used. This material changes resistance as the temperature changes, which is how the RTD measures temperature.

The sensing element is carefully insulated, often with materials like glass, ceramic, or mica, to protect it from electrical interference or short circuits. This core is then housed inside a protective sheath, typically made of stainless steel or ceramic, to guard against physical damage and harsh environmental conditions.

Wires made of copper, nickel, or silver connect the sensing element to the measuring device, ensuring that the signal can be transmitted accurately. Finally, the whole assembly is sealed to keep out moisture and other contaminants, which helps the RTD stay stable and reliable over time, especially in industrial settings.

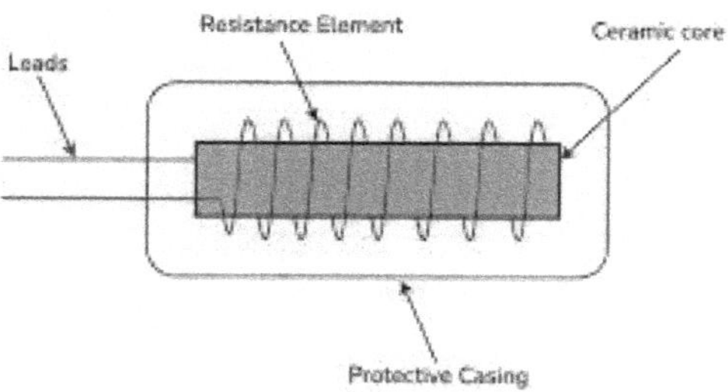

Fig 8.4 – RTD construction

19. How will you check the healthiness of RTD?

Ans: _To check the healthiness of a 3-wire RTD:_

- Check the continuity of the wire with the common colour using a multimeter. If there is continuity, the RTD is healthy; if it is open, the RTD is faulty.
- Measure the resistance between the two wires of different colours at room temperature and compare the value with the

RTD chart or RTD calculator.

- Insert the RTD into a temperature bath and check the resistance at different temperature points.
  To check the healthiness of a 4-wire RTD:
- Check the continuity between both the common pair of colour wire. If there is continuity, the RTD is healthy; if it is open, the RTD is faulty.
- Measure the resistance between the two wires of different colours at room temperature and compare the value with the RTD chart or RTD calculator.
- Insert the RTD into a temperature bath and check the resistance at different temperature points.

20. How will you connect a 2-wire RTD to a 3- wire transmitter or how will you convert a 2 wire RTD to 3 -wire RTD?

Ans: For connecting a 2-wire RTD to a 3-wire transmitter, a junction must be made on one of the RTD wires as close to the sensor as possible. The junction should not be made at or near the transmitter.

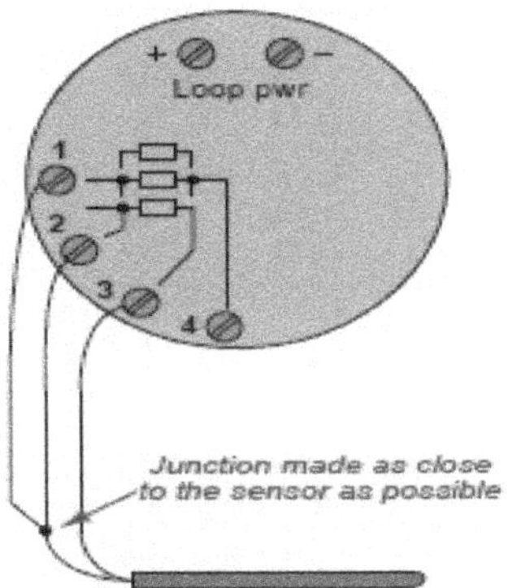

Fig 8.5 – 2-wire RTD to 3-wire transmitter

21. How will you connect a 2-wire RTD to a 4- wire transmitter?

Ans: For connecting a 2-wire RTD to a 3-wire transmitter, junctions must be made on both RTD wires as close to the sensor as possible.

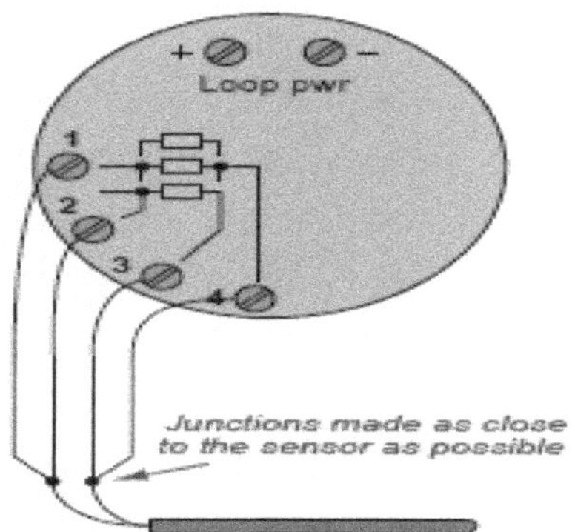

Fig 8.6 – 2-wire RTD to 4- wire transmitter

22. What is Thermistor?

Ans: Thermistors are devices made of metal oxide which either increase in resistance with increasing temperature (a positive temperature coefficient) or decrease in resistance with increasing temperature (a negative temperature coefficient).

23. What is the major difference between RTD and thermistor?

Ans: The major difference between thermistors and RTDs are linearity and sensitivity. Thermistors are highly sensitive and nonlinear, whereas RTDs are relatively insensitive but very linear.

24. What are the major applications of thermistor?

Ans: Thermistors are mainly used in HVAC (Heating, Ventilation, and Air Conditioning) systems, electronic components etc, where the temperature measurement range is relatively narrow, the nonlinearity of thermistors is not a serious concern.

25. What is RTD tolerance?

Ans: RTD (Resistance Temperature Detector) tolerance refers to the allowable deviation between the actual resistance value of the RTD and the ideal resistance value at a given temperature. It determines the accuracy of the RTD sensor.

26. What are the different tolerance classes of RTD?

Ans: RTDs are classified into different tolerance classes based on their precision. The most common standard is IEC 60751, which defines RTD accuracy as follows:

Class A: $\pm(0.15 + 0.002 \times t°C)$

Class B: $\pm(0.30 + 0.005 \times t°C)$

Class AA: $\pm(0.10 + 0.0017 \times t°C)$

Class C: $\pm(0.60 + 0.01 \times t°C)$

Example: for Class B RTD at 100°C, tolerance = 0.30+(0.005*100) =±0.80°C

27. How to Choose the Right RTD Tolerance Class?

Ans: Based on application right RTD tolerance class can be choose as:

- **Class AA (1/3 DIN):** High-precision applications (laboratories, calibration setups).
- **Class A:** Industrial process control where moderate accuracy is required.
- **Class B:** General-purpose applications where cost is a factor.
- **Class C:** Suitable for applications where accuracy is not critical.

28. What is the working principle of thermocouple?

Ans: A thermocouple works on the Seebeck effect, which states that when two dissimilar metals are joined at two different temperatures, a voltage (thermoelectric EMF) is generated, which is proportional to the temperature difference.

A thermocouple consists of two different metal wires joined at one end (hot junction). And the other ends (cold/reference junction) are connected to a measuring device. When there is a temperature difference between the hot and cold junctions, a small voltage (mV range) is generated. This voltage is proportional to the temperature difference and is used to determine the temperature at the hot junction. The Measuring Instrument converts the generated voltage into temperature using standard thermocouple tables or calibration formulas.

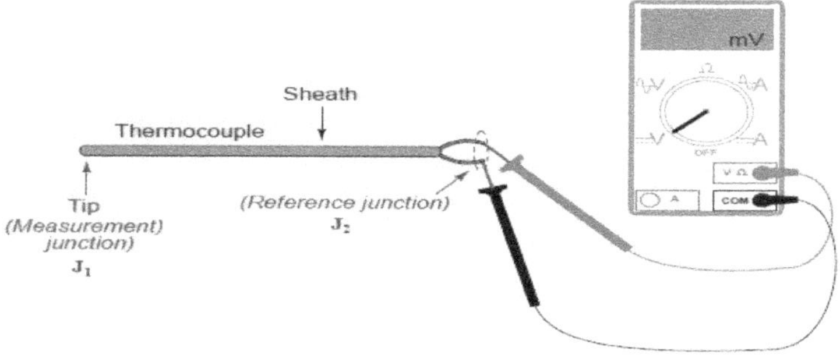

Fig 8.7- Thermocouple Connection

29. Mention the different types of thermocouples with colour codes.

Ans: Here are the thermocouple list:

Type	Metal used	Colour code	Temp range
T	Copper / Constantan	Blue-Red	-200°C to 350°C
J	Iron / Constantan	White-Red	-40°C to 750°C
E	Chromel/Constantan	Violet-Red	0°C to 870°C
K	Chromel/Alumel	Yellow-Red	-200°C to 1,250°C
S	Platinum/Rohdium	Black-Red	0°C to 1,600°C

30. How will you identify the type of thermocouple?
Ans: By colour code.

31. What are the different tips of thermocouple used in industry?

Ans: The different tips of thermocouple used are: Exposed tip, Grounded tip and Ungrounded tip.

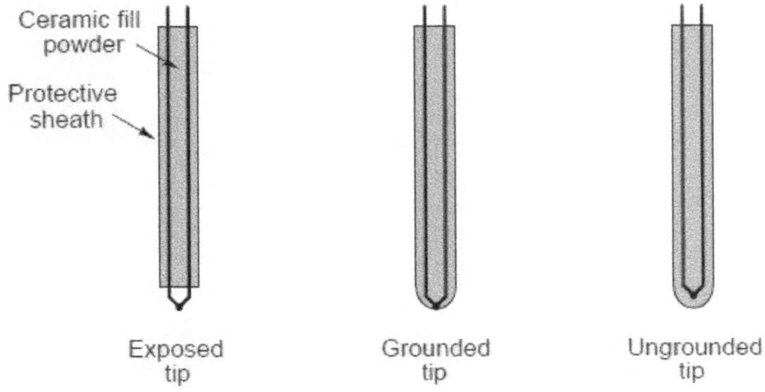

Fig 8.8- Thermocouple tips

For maximum sensitivity and fastest response, the dissimilar-metal junction may be unsheathed (bare). This design, however, makes the thermocouple more fragile.

Sheathed tips are typical for industrial applications, available in either grounded or ungrounded forms. Grounded-tip thermocouples exhibit faster response times and greater sensitivity than ungrounded-tip thermocouples, but they are vulnerable to ground loops. In order to avoid this potentially troublesome effect, most industrial thermocouples are of the ungrounded design.

32. What is reference junction compensation in thermocouple?

Ans: A thermocouple measures temperature based on the temperature difference between the hot junction (measurement point) and cold junction (reference point). The generated voltage depends upon the temperature of both the junctions. If the cold junction is not at 0°C, the output voltage will not directly correspond to the actual hot junction temperature. To get an accurate temperature reading, the cold junction temperature must be known and compensated for.

33. How is reference junction compensation of thermocouple done?

Ans: One method is to keep the reference junction at a constant temperature, usually 0°C (32°F), by submerging it in an ice bath. Since thermocouple voltage tables assume a cold junction at 0°C, no additional compensation is needed.

In modern thermocouple instruments, a cold junction sensor (e.g., RTD or thermistor) measures the cold junction temperature. The instrument calculates the true hot junction temperature using correction formulas or thermocouple tables.

$$T_{hot} = T_{measured} + T_{cold}$$

Where,

T_{hot} - Actual temperature at the hot junction

$T_{measured}$ - Temperature from the thermocouple voltage

T_{cold} - Measured temperature at the cold junction

34. What is the Law of Intermediate Metals in thermocouples?

Ans: The Law of Intermediate Metals states that inserting a third metal into a thermocouple circuit will not affect the generated thermoelectric voltage as long as the junctions remain at the same temperature.

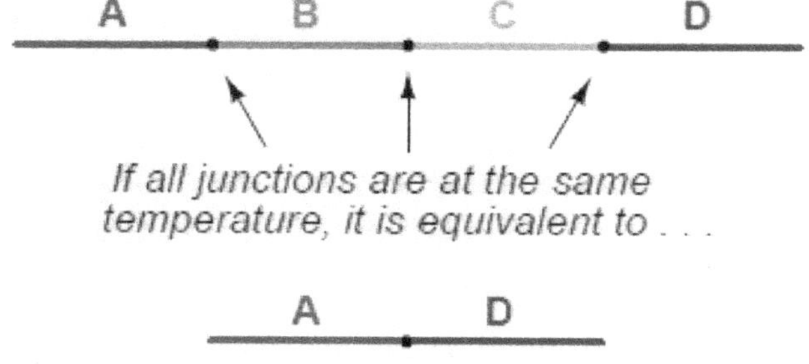

Fig 8.9 – Law of intermediate metals

35. What are the practical applications of law of intermediate metal?

Ans: Reference junctions in measuring instruments often use copper wiring for thermocouple connections. The law ensures that as long as the connections are at the same temperature, measurement accuracy is maintained.

For e.g. a Type K thermocouple (Chromel-Alumel) is connected to a copper measuring circuit, the copper does not affect the voltage because both Copper Chromel and Copper Alumel connections are at the same temperature. However, if one connection heats up while the other stays cool, an unwanted voltage is introduced, leading to measurement errors.

36. What type of cable is used as an extension wire for thermocouples?

Ans: When using an extension cable for long-distance thermocouple measurement, the reference junction shifts to a new location. This new location is likely to be at a different temperature than the panel-mounted indicator, meaning the indicator's reference junction compensation will compensate for the wrong temperature.

If an extension wire is used for remote monitoring, the best approach is to use thermocouple wire of the same type as the installed thermocouple. This prevents the formation of another dissimilar-metal junction at the thermocouple head and ensures that the junction forms only at the receiving instrument.

However, using an extension cable made of the same material as the thermocouple increases the potential expense of thermocouple-grade cable. A more economical alternative is to use extension-grade wire to connect the thermocouple to the receiving instrument.

Extension-grade thermocouple wire is less expensive than full thermocouple-grade wire because it is made from metal alloys that have similar thermoelectric characteristics to the actual thermocouple wires but within a limited temperature range.

Extension-grade cable is denoted by the letter "X" following the thermocouple type. For example, in a Type K thermocouple system, the appropriate extension cable would be labelled as "KX.

37. What will happen if thermocouple wires get shorted?

Ans: A cold junction compensated instrument will typically indicate temperature of the location where the T/C wires are shorted.

38. What is skin type thermocouple?

Ans: A skin type thermocouple is a thermocouple sensor that measures the surface temperature of a pipe or tank. The thermocouple junction is placed in direct contact with the surface. The temperature difference between the measurement point (hot junction) and reference junction generates a millivolt signal.

Fig 8.10 – Skin type thermocouple

39. What is temperature transmitter?

Ans: A temperature transmitter is a device that converts a temperature sensor's signal (such as from an RTD or thermocouple) into a standardized output signal, typically 4-20 mA.

40. How temperature transmitter performs cold junction compensation of thermocouple?

Ans: Smart transmitter contains microprocessor, which is programmed with look-up tables relating voltage values to temperature values.

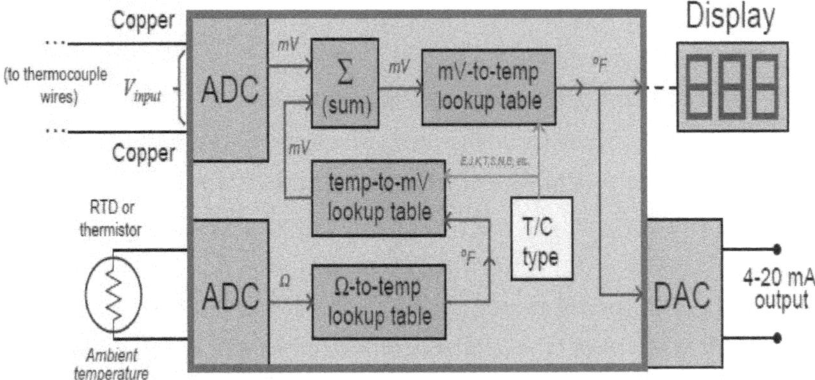

Fig 8.11 – Cold junction compensation at Temperature transmitter

For reference junction compensation, an RTD or thermistor is used. The smart transmitter converts the measured resistance into the corresponding temperature and then converts this temperature into the equivalent thermocouple millivolt signal. The transmitter then adds this calculated millivolt value to the millivolt signal from the thermocouple wires. The resultant millivolt signal is converted into the temperature measured by the thermocouple. This temperature is further converted into a 4-20 mA current signal for long-distance transmission.

41. What will be the result when +ve and -ve terminals of thermocouple transmitter is shorted?

Ans: With the input short-circuited, the transmitter "sees" no voltage at all from the thermocouple circuit. There is no measurement junction nor a reference junction to compensate for, just a piece of wire making both input terminals electrically common. However, the transmitter does not "know" it is no longer connected to the thermocouple, so the compensation keeps on working even though it has nothing to compensate for. Hence, it will display ambient temperature only.

42. How do you check if a thermocouple is working properly?

Ans: The health of a thermocouple can be checked using the following methods:

Disconnect the thermocouple from the circuit and measure resistance between the two thermocouple wires. If very high resistance or OL (Open Line), then thermocouple is faulty and if low resistance (below 40 ohm), then thermocouple is likely to be healthy.

Heat the thermocouple tip using a heat source and measure the voltage across the thermocouple wires. Compare the measured millivolt value with the thermocouple voltage-temperature chart. If it shows correct mV reading, then thermocouple is healthy and for no or incorrect mV reading, thermocouple may be considered faulty.

43. What is Thermocouples Green Rot Effect? How it can be avoided?

Ans: Whenever, a reducing gas (such as hydrogen) is present, a reducing atmosphere can come in contact with the wires of thermocouple. Under these conditions, with only a very small amount of oxygen present, the chromium in the chromel alloy of type K thermocouple oxidizes. This reduces the emf output and the thermocouple reads low temperature reading. This phenomenon is known as "green rot," due to the color of the affected alloy.

To overcome this problem, a "purged" thermowell is used. Here, a flow of air is brought down through a small tube inside the thermowell to sweep out any hydrogen which has entered the well.

44. What is a thermopile?

Ans: A thermopile is a temperature-sensing device that consists of multiple thermocouples connected in series or parallel to increase the output voltage. It is used for non-contact temperature measurement, heat sensing, and infrared radiation detection.

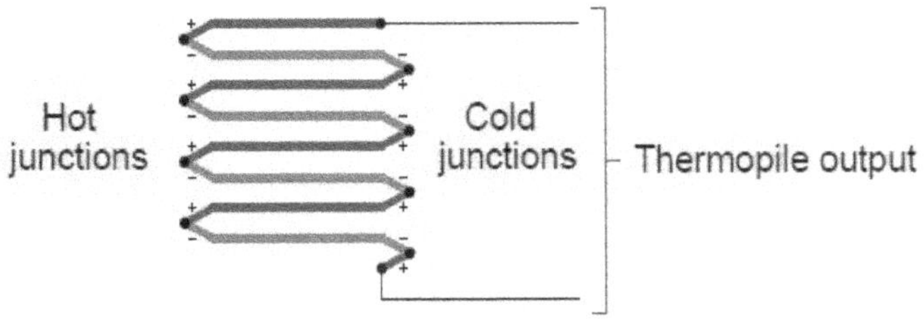

Fig 8.12 – Thermopile

45. How do you select between RTD and thermocouple for a process temperature measurement?

Ans: The selection of RTD and thermocouple for a process connection can be done based on following criteria:

Parameter/Criteria	Thermocouple	RTD
Measurement Range	-250°C to 2300 °C	-250°C to 600°C
Interchangeability	Good	Excellent
Long term stability	Poor to fair	Excellent
Accuracy	Medium	High
Repeatability	Poor to fair	Excellent
Sensitivity	Low	Good
Response	Medium to fast	Good
Linearity	Fair	Good
Cost	Inexpensive	Marginally higher cost

46. What is thermowell? What are the different types of thermowell?

Ans: A thermowell is a protective sheath used to shield temperature sensors (such as thermocouples and RTDs) from harsh process conditions like high pressure, corrosive media, or mechanical stress. It allows the sensor to be inserted and removed without disrupting the process. Most thermowells are formed out of either metal (stainless steel or other alloy) or ceramic materials.

Based on process thermowell are classified as: Threaded Thermowell, Flanged Thermowell, Weld-in Thermowell.

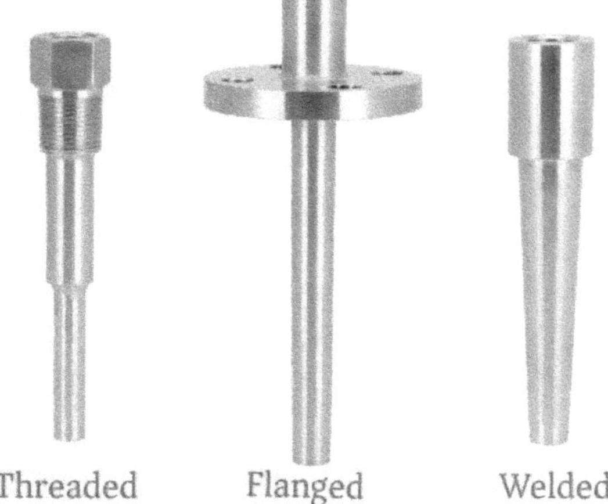

Fig 8.13 – different types of thermowell

47. What are the basic components of a thermowell?

Ans: Following are the basic components of thermowell:

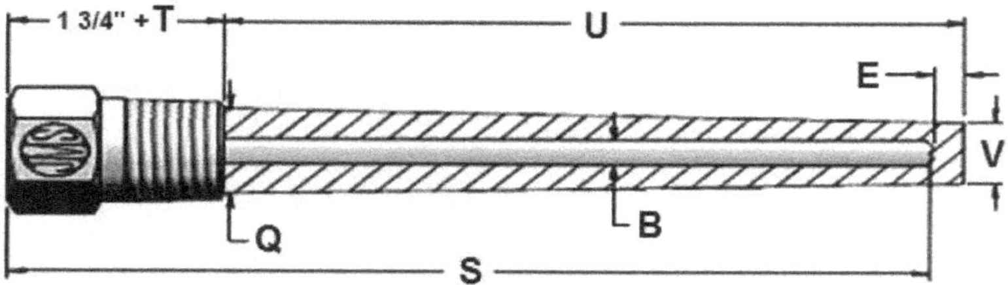

Fig 8.14 – Thermowell basic components

- **Bore Diameter (B):** This is the inside diameter of the Thermowell.
- **Bore Depth (S):** Total length of the bore.
- **Insertion length (U):** Thermowell immersion lengths are often called the "U" length which is the measurement of the Thermowell from the bottom of the process connection to the top portion of the Thermowell.

- ***Lagging extension length (T)***: The lagging extension commonly referred to as the "T" length is located on the cold side of the process connection and is usually an extension of the hex length.

- ***Base Diameter dimension (Q):*** This is the outside dimension of the Thermowell shank and is densest part because the outside surface area is exposed to the hazardous materials of the process.

- ***Tip thickness (E):*** Thickness of the bottom portion of thermowell.

- ***Tip diameter (V):*** Thermowell end Diameter.

48. What are the different types of thermowell based on shank construction?

Ans: The thermowell shank is the portion of the thermowell that immersed into the process fluid. It is of three types: straight, step or tapered.

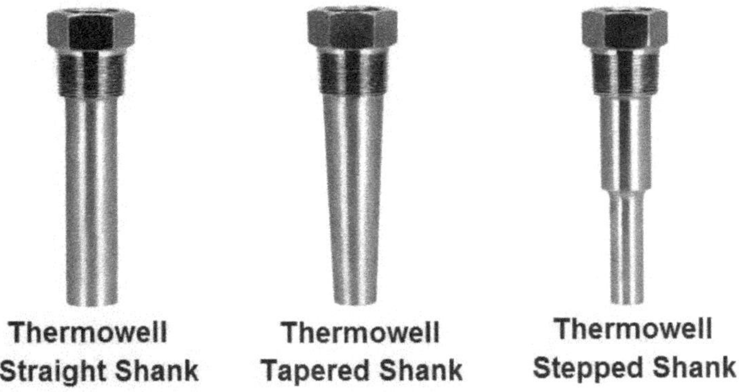

Fig 8.15- Thermowell shank

- ***Straight Shank:*** It has uniform diameter from the base to the tip. For general purpose, where additional strength is not required, the straight shank or stem is used, best for low-flow and low-pressure applications. It is More prone to vibration and wake frequency issues in high-velocity flows.

- ***Tapered Shank:*** It gradually reduces in diameter from the base to the tip and thus enhances strength while reducing wake frequency effects. It is recommended for high-flow and high-pressure applications.
- ***Stepped Shank:*** It has a larger diameter at the base and a reduced diameter near the tip. It is suitable for moderate-pressure and moderate-flow applications.

49. What are the factors for selecting a thermowell?

Ans: Following factors are to be considered for selecting a thermowell:

- ***Process Temperature & Pressure*** → Choose materials that withstand the conditions.
- ***Fluid Velocity*** → High-velocity flow requires stronger thermowells.
- ***Insertion Length*** → The well must be long enough for accurate sensing.
- ***Response Time*** → Thicker wells slow down response time.

50. What is thermowell wake frequency?

Ans: When a thermowell is placed in a flowing fluid (such as gas, steam, or liquid), vortices form alternately on either side of the thermowell. The frequency at which vortex shedding occurs around a thermowell when fluid flows past it, is known as wake frequency. The vortex shedding frequency (or Wake frequency) is linear with flow velocity and inversely proportional to thermowell tip diameter.

If the wake frequency matches or exceeds the natural frequency of the thermowell, resonance can occur, leading to vibration, fatigue, and potential failure of the thermowell.

51. How are thermowells designed based on wake frequency?

Ans: The ASME PTC 19.3 TW standard provides guidelines for evaluating wake frequency ratio (WFR) to ensure thermowell safety.

WFR = Wake Frequency / Natural Frequency

If **WFR < 0.8** → Safe design

If **0.8 ≤ WFR < 1.0** → Requires detailed analysis

If **WFR ≥ 1.0** → **Unsafe, thermowell redesign needed.**

52. How to Avoid Wake Frequency Issues?

Ans: Following process ca be adopted to avoid wake frequency issue:

- *Shorter Thermowell Length* – It reduces vibration and increases natural frequency.
- *Increased Thermowell Diameter* - It reduces vibration and increases natural frequency.
- *Proper Installation Angle* – Proper angled placement reduces wake formation.

53. How to Install a Thermowell on an Elbow?

Ans: When thermowell is installed at a 90° angle to the flow direction, it ensures maximum immersion in the fluid stream but may experience higher wake frequency effects.

If the thermowell is installed at an angled position (typically 45° or 60°) on the elbow, it reduces wake frequency effects, minimizing vibration and fatigue failure and provides better fluid contact while reducing stress on the thermowell.

54. Why use a temperature transmitter instead of direct wiring from sensors?

Ans: A temperature transmitter converts the sensor signal (RTD or thermocouple) into a standardized 4-20 mA signal. Following are the advantages:

- Direct wiring of RTDs or thermocouples over long distances can lead to voltage drop and signal degradation. The 4-20 mA current signal is less susceptible to electromagnetic interference (EMI) than a low-voltage thermocouple signal.

- The direct wiring of thermocouples to a control system requires the use of thermocouple extension wires. Extension wire can cost several times more than common shielded copper wire used for a temperature transmitter's 4-20 mA signal. The longer the wire run, the greater the potential savings.

- Temperature transmitters provide standardized signals (4-20 mA, HART, or digital protocols like Modbus/Profibus), making them easy to connect to PLCs, DCS, systems. It reduces the cost of additional input card (thermocouple/RTD cards) for PLC or DCS. Smart transmitters support HART, Foundation Fieldbus, allowing remote calibration and diagnostics.

55. What is pyrometry?

Ans: Pyrometry is a technique for measuring temperature without physical contact. It depends upon the relationship between the temperature of a hot body and the electromagnetic radiation emitted by the body.

56. What is the working principle of a pyrometer?

Ans: A pyrometer is a non-contact temperature measurement device that detects the thermal radiation emitted by an object and converts it into a temperature reading. It is widely used for measuring high temperatures in furnaces, kilns, and metal processing industries.

A pyrometer operates based on Planck's Law of Blackbody Radiation, which states that all objects emit thermal radiation depending on their temperature. The pyrometer captures this radiation and determines the object's temperature using one of the following methods:

Radiation Pyrometers: The pyrometer detects infrared radiation emitted by the object. A lens system focuses this radiation onto a detector. The detector consists of a thermopile which converts the radiation into an electrical signal proportional to the temperature. The signal is processed and displayed as temperature.

Optical Pyrometers: The pyrometer focuses the emitted radiation from a hot object onto a filament (usually tungsten). The filament's brightness is adjusted by changing the current passing through it. When the filament's brightness matches the object's brightness, the temperature is read from the calibrated scale.

57. What is the working principle of thermal imager?

Ans: A thermal imager works by detecting and converting infrared radiation (heat) emitted by objects into a visible image, called a thermogram. This allows users to see temperature variations across a surface without physical contact.

Every object emits infrared radiation proportional to its temperature. A special infrared lens focuses the emitted radiation onto a thermal sensor array. The sensor (microbolometer) absorbs the infrared radiation and converts it into an electrical signal. The camera processes these signals and applies a colour scale to represent different temperatures. The final thermal image (thermogram) is displayed, where warmer areas appear in red/yellow and cooler areas in blue/purple.

58. What types of primary elements are used to measure the compressor or turbine bearing temperature?

Ans: RTD is generally used to measure compressor or turbine bearing temperature. As, bearing temperature measurement normally falls in the range of 25°C to 150°C and RTD is more accurate and linear in measuring temperature between the range -200 °C to +200 °C. Hence, RTD is preferred.

59. What is a temperature scanner?

Ans: A Temperature Scanner is a device that measures at more than one temperature points. It is a multi-channel indicator that measures and displays signals of each channel one-by-one up to last channel and then returns to first channel and continues the process cyclically.

By using a temperature scanner, temperature of multiple points can be measured in a single unit thus saving cost and space. It is capable of measuring temperature from resistance temperature sensors like RTD Pt100 or from different types of thermocouples like J, K, R, S, T, B, E and N. It is mostly used in motor or generator winding temperature measurement from the sensor at different winding locations.

60. What is a duplex sensor?

Ans: A duplex sensor is a temperature sensor that consists of two independent sensing elements within a single probe. These elements can be two thermocouples, two RTDs, or a combination of both, allowing for redundancy, accuracy, and reliability in critical applications.

61. What is a Temperature Bath?

Ans: A temperature bath, also known as a calibration bath or thermal bath, is a controlled liquid or dry medium used to maintain a stable temperature for testing, calibrating, or conditioning of temperature sensors. The sensor or device under test is immersed in the bath, allowing for accurate calibration by comparing its readings to a reference standard.

It is of two types: Liquid bath and Dry bath. In a liquid bath, the fluid (water or oil) is used to provide stable temperatures. In a dry block bath, a metal block is heated or cooled to maintain the required temperature.

Chapter: 9

Level Measurements

1. What is Pascal's principle?

Ans: Any changes in fluid pressure are transmitted evenly throughout an enclosed fluid volume. Relevant to pressure measurement, as fluid pressure in all parts of an enclosed system will experience the same changes in pressure.

2. What is hydrostatic pressure?

Ans: The fluids having substantial weight generate pressure proportional to their density and to their vertical height ($P = \rho g h$).

3. What is Archimede's principle?

Ans: The buoyant force experienced by an object submerged in liquid is equal to the weight of the fluid that object displaces, which is equal to the volume displaced multiplied by the weight density of the fluid.

4. How slight glass or gauge glass is used for level measurement?

Ans: A slight glass instrument consists of a graduated tube of glass which is connected to the interior of the tank at the bottom. As the level of liquid in the tank rises and falls, the level in the sight glass also rises and falls accordingly. Thus, by measuring the level in the sight glass, the level of liquid in tank is measured.

5. How is the slight glass connected in open tank and closed pressurised tank for level measurement?

Ans: In open tank, the slight glass is connected to the bottom of the tank and top of the glass tube is kept open to atmosphere.

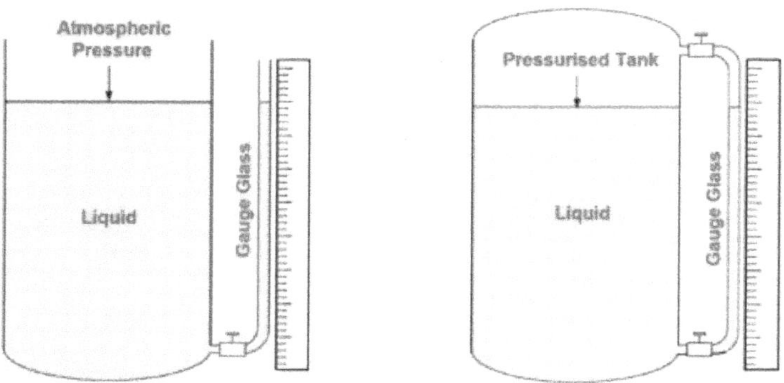

Fig 9.1 – Open and closed tank for level measurement

In closed tank, the slight glass is connected to both the top and bottom of the tank.

6. Why is the slight glass required to connected to both the top and bottom of the tank in a closed vessel for level measurement?

Ans: In a closed vessel, the pressure at the top of the tank may be different from atmospheric pressure. Connecting the top of the sight glass to the top of the tank ensures that the pressure in the sight glass matches the pressure inside the tank, preventing erroneous readings due to pressure differences.

The liquid level in the sight glass follows the hydrostatic principle, meaning it will naturally align with the level inside the tank due to gravity. If only the bottom were connected, the liquid might not rise properly, especially if there is pressure at the top of the tank.

7. What are the limitations of slight glass?

Ans: Following are the limitations of slight glass:

- It is read only where the tank is located, which is not always convenient.
- Accuracy and readability depend on the cleanliness of glass and fluid.

8. What are transparent level gauge and reflex level gauge?

Ans: The transparent level gauge seen the actual liquid level through the flat glass. While the reflex level gauge uses a prismatic groove as a device to reflect the light if there is a liquid-filled in the chamber. If liquid is colourless, then it recommends using a reflex type level gauge so that the light will not be reflected back to the viewer and the chamber becomes dark.

9. How is float type level indicator used for level measurement?

Ans: The float, which is made of a lightweight, rests on the liquid surface and moves up and down as the liquid level changes. This movement is then mechanically, or electrically transmitted to an indicator.

A float is connected to a counterweight via a cable or a pulley system. As the liquid level rises or falls, the float moves accordingly, pulling the counterweight. The movement is displayed on a scale to indicate the liquid level.

10. How are displacer type level detectors used for level measurement?

Ans: The displacer type level detectors work on the Archimedes' principle which states that a body, wholly or partially immersed in fluid, is buoyed up by a force which is equal to the weight of the fluid displaced.

A displacer (a cylindrical or rod-shaped object) is suspended in the liquid inside a tank using a spring. When the liquid level rises, more of the displacer gets submerged, reducing the effective weight of the displacer due to the increased buoyant force. When the liquid level falls, the buoyant force decreases, and the displacer's weight increases. This weight change is detected by a force-sensing mechanism. The change in force is converted into a level measurement, which can be displayed locally.

11. How can a pressure gauge be used in level measurement? What is the limitation of this method of measurement?

Ans: This method of level measurement is based on the equation that,

Pressure, P = Liquid density x gravity x height of liquid,

Where, density and gravity is constant.

A vertical column of fluid generates a pressure at the bottom of the column owing to the action of gravity on that fluid. The greater the vertical height of the fluid, the greater the pressure, all other factors being equal. This principle allows us to infer the level (height) of liquid in a vessel by pressure measurement. Thus, by connecting a pressure gauge at the lowest level of tank, the level of liquid can be measured.

The instrument must be mounted at same level as the minimum level in the tank. This is often inconvenient, as a tank may be located at certain height above the measuring point or control room. In this case, the level indicator in the measuring point would show an error equivalent to the height of the tank from the measuring point.

12. Explain level measurement by capacitance level indicator.

Ans: The principle of operation of capacitance level indicator is based on the capacitance equation of a parallel plate capacitor given by:

$$C = K\frac{A}{D},$$

Where, K = dielectric constant, A= Area of plate, D= distance between two plates

Therefore, it is seen from the above equation that if A and D are constant, then the capacitance of a capacitor is directly proportional to the dielectric constant, and this principle is utilized in the capacitance level indicator.

It consists of an insulated capacitance probe (which is a metal electrode) firmly fixed near and parallel to the metal wall of the tank. The capacitance probe and the tank wall form the plates of a parallel plate capacitor and liquid in between them acts as the dielectric. If liquid is conductive, the capacitance probe and liquid form the plates of the capacitor and the insulation of the probe acts as the dielectric. A capacitance measuring device is connected with the probe and the tank wall, which is calibrated in terms of the level of liquid in the tank.

When liquid level changes, the capacitance changes accordingly. This increase or decrease in the capacitance is measured and displayed on the indicator calibrated in terms of liquid level.

13. How is radiation level detector work?

Ans: A radiation level detector is a non-contact level measurement device that uses gamma rays or X-rays to detect the level of liquids or solids in a tank or vessel. A sealed source of gamma radiation is mounted on one side of the vessel. A radiation detector is placed on the opposite side of the vessel. The sensor detects the radiation passing through the vessel and converts it into an electrical signal. When the vessel is empty or partially filled, more radiation reaches the detector. When the level rises, the material in the tank absorbs or scatters some of the radiation, reducing the amount reaching the detector. The detector measures the intensity of the radiation received and converts this information into a level reading.

14. How are radar level detector works?

Ans: A radar level detector is a non-contact level measurement device that uses radio waves (microwaves) to determine the level of liquids or solids in a tank. A radar level detector operates on the principle of time-of-flight measurement, where electromagnetic waves are transmitted, reflected, and received. A radar sensor emits high-frequency microwave signals which travels at the speed of light toward the surface of the measured material. When the radar waves hit the surface of the liquid or solid, they are partially reflected back to the sensor. The amount of reflection depends on the dielectric constant of the material. The radar sensor detects the returning signals and calculates the time delay between transmission and reception. Using this time delay and the speed of light, the sensor determines the distance to the surface of the material. The level is calculated as tank height minus measured distance.

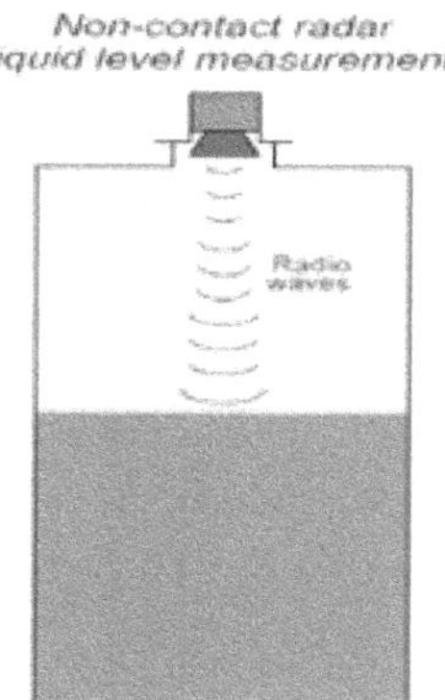

Fig 9.2 – Radar level detector

15. How are ultrasonic level detector works?

Ans: An ultrasonic level detector is a non-contact level measurement device that uses sound waves to determine the level of liquids or solids in a tank. Ultrasonic level detectors operate based on the time-of-flight principle, similar to radar sensors but using sound waves instead of microwaves. The ultrasonic sensor emits high-frequency sound pulses (typically 20 kHz to several MHz) toward the material surface. When the sound waves hit the surface of the liquid or solid, they reflect back toward the sensor. The sensor detects the returning echo and measures the time delay between transmission and reception. Using the known speed of sound in air, the sensor calculates the distance to the surface of the material: **Distance = (speed of sound x Time delay)/2**. The level is calculated as tank height minus measured distance.

16. How to install ultrasonic level transmitters?

Ans: Ultrasonic transmitter should install perpendicular to the liquid. And for solid tank level measurement the transmitter must point to the tank outlet. The transmitter should not be mounted too close to the tank wall, the build-up on the tank wall causes false echoes.

17. What is the advantage of using guide tube for ultrasonic level transmitters?

Ans: The transmitter can be mounted on the top of guide tube to prevent the false echoes from turbulence and foam.

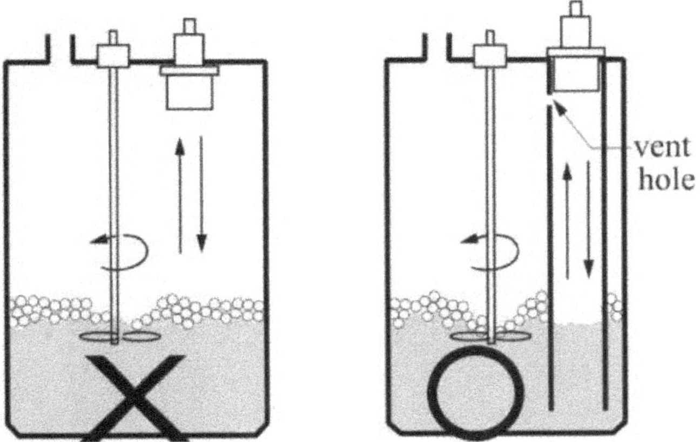

Fig 9.3 – Guided ultrasonic level transmitter

18. How is a differential type pressure transmitter used for level measurement?

Ans: A DP transmitter measures the difference between two pressure points:

High-Pressure Side (HP): Connected to the bottom of the tank, where the liquid pressure is highest. Low-Pressure Side (LP): Connected to the top of the tank (for pressurized tanks) or left open to atmospheric pressure (for open tanks). The level is determined using the hydrostatic pressure equation:

Pressure, P = Liquid density x gravity x height of liquid,

Since the density and gravity are known, the DP transmitter calculates the liquid height from the measured pressure difference.

19. What is dry leg and wet leg in DP type level measurement?

Ans: A dry leg is when the LP side of the DP transmitter is left filled with gas or vapor and remains dry (i.e., it does not contain liquid). It is used in in open tanks where the LP side is vented to the atmosphere and in pressurized tanks with gases that do not condense.

A wet leg is when the LP side of the DP transmitter is intentionally filled with a reference liquid to prevent gas condensation effects. It is used in condensing vapours like steam, where condensation could cause fluctuating pressure readings and in pressurized tanks where the LP side needs to be at a stable reference pressure.

20. What is zero suppression and zero elevation in DP transmitter level measurement?

Ans: In differential pressure (DP) level measurement, the transmitter measures the pressure difference between the high-pressure (HP) side (bottom of the tank) and the low-pressure (LP) side (top of the tank or reference leg). The DP transmitter is calibrated based on the position of the transmitter relative to the tank. When the transmitter is not at the same height as the tank bottom or reference point, zero suppression or zero elevation is required to adjust the transmitter's zero point.

Zero suppression is applied when the DP transmitter is installed below the bottom of the tank. When the tank is empty, the liquid in the HP impulse line still exerts some pressure on the DP transmitter. This creates a false positive reading, so the transmitter's zero point must be adjusted downward (suppressed) to compensate. The zero point is suppressed by subtracting the static pressure due to the height of the HP impulse line.

Zero elevation is applied when the DP transmitter is installed above the bottom of the tank. When the tank is empty, the wet leg still applies pressure on the LP side of the DP transmitter. This creates a false negative reading, so the transmitter's zero point must be elevated (raised) to compensate. The zero point is elevated by adding the static pressure due to the wet leg height.

21. How will you calculate LRV and URV of DP transmitter for level measurement in open tank and closed tank?

Ans: *For open tank*,

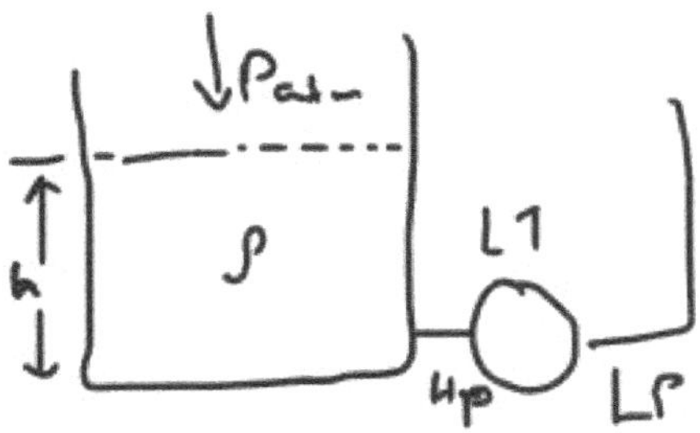

For, water of height h and density ρ

At 0% level,

HP= P_{atm} , LP = P_{atm}

LRV = HP- LP = P_{atm} - P_{atm} = 0,

At 100% level,

HP= P_{atm} + ρhg , LP = P_{atm}

HRV = HP − LP = P_{atm} + ρhg - P_{atm} = ρhg,

Thus, by HART communicator LRV and URV can be set to 0 and ρhg respectively.

***For Closed tank*,**

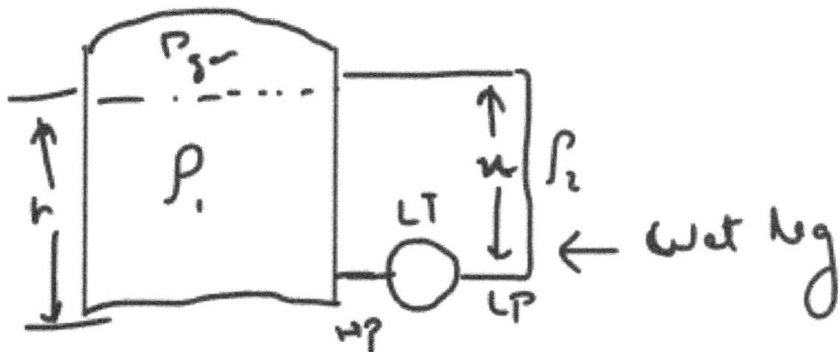

Density of liquid in tank is ρ_1 and maximum height is h

Density of liquid in wet leg is ρ_2 and height is x

P_{gas} is the vapour pressure formed in the tank

At 0% level,

HP= P_{gas}, LP = P_{gas} + $\rho_2 gx$

LRV = HP $-$ LP = P_{gas} - P_{gas} + $\rho_2 gx$ = - $\rho_2 gx$

At 100% level,

HP = P_{gas} + $\rho_1 gh$, LP = P_{gas} + $\rho_2 gx$

URV = HP $-$ LP = P_{gas} + $\rho_1 gh$ - P_{gas} + $\rho_2 gx$ = $\rho_1 gh$ - $\rho_2 xh$

Thus, by HART communicator LRV and URV can be set to - $\rho_2 gx$ and $\rho_1 gh$ - $\rho_2 xh$ respectively.

If both in wet lag and in tank have same liquid then, $\rho_1 = \rho_2$

For e.g, consider an open tank filled with water of maximum height 10 meter.

Conversion of pressure due to 1 meter height of water in mm Water column is 1000mmWC.

LRV = 0,

URV = 10 * 10000 = 100000 mmWC

Range: 0 to 100000 mmWC and span 100000 mmWc

For closed tank, consider a tank filed with water of maximum height 10 meter and wet leg   filled with water of height 15 meter.

LRV = -15*10000 = -150000 mmWC

URV= 10*10000 -15*10000 =-50000 mmWC

Range: -150000 mmWc to -50000 mmWc and Span =100000 mmWC

22. Find the LRV and URV of a DP transmitter for level measurement installed for boiler drum level measurement? Maximum drum level = 1 meter, transmitter installed at 2 meters below HP measuring point and height of wet leg 3 meter.

Ans:

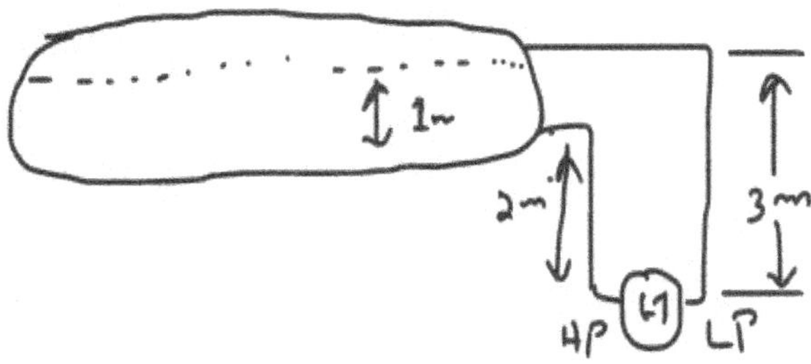

At 0%,

HP= 2*10000 mmWC = 20000 mmWC

LP = 3*10000 mmWC = 30000 mmWC

LRV = HP -LP = -10000 mmWC

At 100%,

HP= 1*10000 + 2*10000 =30000 mmWC

LP = 3*10000 mmWC = 30000 mmWC

HRV = HP -LP = 0

Range: -10000 mmWc to 0 mmWc and Span =10000 mmWC

23. Which level measuring instrument is suitable for highly viscous liquids?

Ans: Radar level transmitter.

24. What type of level measuring device uses the time-of-flight principle?

Ans: Ultrasonic level sensor

25. Which type of level gauge is best for colourless liquids?

Ans: Reflex level gauge.

Chapter: 10

Flow Measurements

1. What is laminar flow and turbulent flow?

Ans: Laminar flow is a condition where fluid particles move smoothly in parallel layers with minimal mixing. In laminar flow, velocity at any point remains constant over time. For e.g. Flow of oil in pipelines.

Turbulent flow is a chaotic, irregular flow where fluid particles move in random directions, causing mixing. For e.g. water flow in rivers.

2. What is Bernoulli's principle?

Ans: Bernoulli's principle states that in an ideal fluid (incompressible and frictionless), the total mechanical energy (pressure energy, kinetic energy, and potential energy) remains constant along a streamline.

Bernoulli's equation:

$$P + \frac{1}{2}\rho v^2 + \rho gh = \text{constant}$$

This equation shows that as a fluid moves, the sum of its pressure energy (P), kinetic energy ($\frac{1}{2}\rho v^2$), and potential energy (ρgh) remains constant.

3. What are the implications of Bernoulli's theorem?

Ans: Following are the key implication of Bernoulli's theorem:

- It provides pressure-velocity relationship: If the fluid speed increases, the pressure decreases.
- In a vertical column of fluid, higher elevation (h) means lower pressure (e.g., water flows faster from a higher tank).

4. What is Reynolds Number?

Ans: Reynolds Number (Re) is a dimensionless number used in fluid mechanics to predict the type of flow (laminar, turbulent, or transitional) in a pipe or over a surface. It is the ratio of inertial forces to viscous forces within a fluid and helps determine whether the flow is smooth (laminar) or chaotic (turbulent).

For Re<2000, flow is laminar and for RE>4000, flow is turbulent.

5. What are the different types of flowmeters use for flow measurement?

Ans: The different types of flowmeters are: Differential pressure flowmeter, Rotameter, Magnetic flowmeter, Turbine flowmeter, Target flowmeter, Thermal flowmeter, Vortex flowmeter, Ultrasonic flowmeter, Positive displacement flowmeter, Coriolis flowmeter.

6. What is the working principle of a differential pressure flowmeter?

Ans: A differential pressure (DP) flowmeter measures the flow rate of a fluid by detecting the pressure drop across a restriction in the flow path. It works based on Bernoulli's principle, which states that an increase in fluid velocity leads to a decrease in pressure.

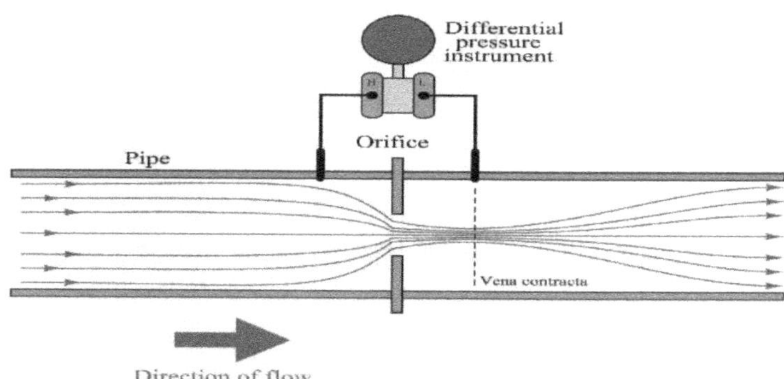

Fig 10.1 – Differential pressure flowmeter

A primary element (such as an orifice plate, Venturi tube, or flow nozzle) is placed in the pipeline, creating a restriction. As fluid flows through the restriction, it speeds up, causing a drop in pressure on the downstream side. This pressure difference is proportional to the flow rate. A differential pressure transmitter measures the high pressure (upstream) and low pressure (downstream) and calculate the flow rate.

Flow rate calculation:

$$Q=C\sqrt{\Delta P}$$

Where,

Q- Flow rate,

C - Flow coefficient

ΔP - Differential pressure

7. What are the limitations of differential pressure flowmeter?

Ans: Following are the limitations: -

- It is difficult to use for slurry services, small openings (orifice plates) can clog with debris in dirty fluids.
- Low flow rates are not easily measured with these meters.
- It exhibits a square root relationship between head sand flow rate, rather than linear characteristics, which required additional calculation.

8. What are the parts of a differential flowmeter?

Ans: A differential flowmeter basically consists of two parts: i) primary elements and ii) secondary elements.

Primary elements are the part of the meter used to restrict the fluid flow in pipe line in order to produce a differential pressure. They are: Orifice Plates, Venturi tubes, Flow nozzles, Dall tubes, Pitot tubes, Annubar tubes, Elbow tapes, Weir and Flume.

Secondary elements are those which measure the differential pressure produced by the primary element and convert them to usable signals.

9. What is Orifice plate? What are the different types of orifice plates used in industry?

Ans: An orifice plate is a thin, flat plate with a hole (or orifice) in the centre used as a primary element in differential pressure (DP) flow measurement. It restricts fluid flow, creating a pressure drop that is proportional to the flow rate. It is usually made up of stainless steel.

Different types of orifice plates are:

- **Concentric Orifice Plate:** It has a circular hole (orifice) in the middle, and is installed in the pipe line with the hole concentric to the pipe. It is used for clean liquids, gases, and steam.

- **Eccentric Orifice Plate:** It has hole which is off-centre (not at the middle). It is used for slurries, viscous fluids, and dirty gases. The eccentric orifice plate is used where liquid fluid contains a relatively high percentage of dissolved gases, and is installed with the bore tangential to the upper surface of the pipe when the flowing material is liquid, and tangential to the lower surface of the pipe when the fluid is a gas.

- **Segmental Orifice Plate:** It has a semi-circular hole at the bottom and allows solids to pass, reducing clogging.

- **Quadrant Edge Orifice Plate:** It has a rounded edge instead of a sharp hole and is suitable for viscous and low Reynolds number fluids (e.g., crude oil, syrups).

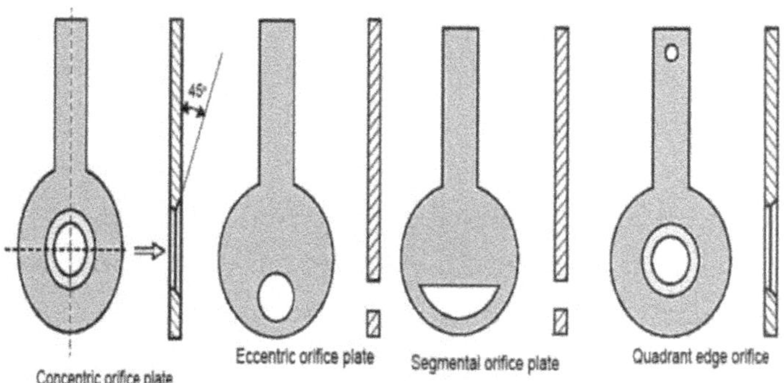

Fig 10.2 – Different types of orifice plate

10. What is vena contracta?

Ans: The point where the fluid flow profile constricts to a minimum cross-sectional area after flowing through the orifice is called the vena contracta. And it is the area of minimum fluid pressure.

11. What is the purpose of vent hole and drain hole in the orifice plate?

Ans: A drain hole is a small hole that is provided in the lower region of the orifice plate. A drain hole is required in gas flow service to pass liquid droplets or solids.

The vent hole is a small hole that is provided in the upper region of the orifice plate. The vent hole is required in liquid flow service to pass vapor bubbles.

12. What is orifice beta?

Ans: Orifice beta is the ratio of inner diameter of orifice (bore of orifice) to the outer diameter of orifice (inner dia of pipe).

$$\beta = \frac{\text{I.D. (Bore of Orifice)}}{\text{O.D. of Orifice (I.D. of Pipe)}}$$

Orifice plate designed in the orifice beta range in between 0.3 to 0.7. Below 0.3 beta, pressure drop is maximum which affects process flow and above 0.7 beta, pressure drop is minimum which affects flow measurement.

13. How much maximum and minimum orifice 'd' (orifice diameter) is permitted in a pipeline?

Ans: 'd' – the Orifice diameter should be in-between 0.25 and 0.75 of the pipeline 'D' diameters.

14. What is a venturi tubes?

Ans: A Venturi tube is a flow measurement device that operates on Bernoulli's principle. It consists of a gradually narrowing throat, which causes an increase in velocity and a decrease in pressure, followed by a gradual expansion to recover pressure. A differential pressure transmitter measures the pressure difference between the inlet and throat and thus calculate flow rate.

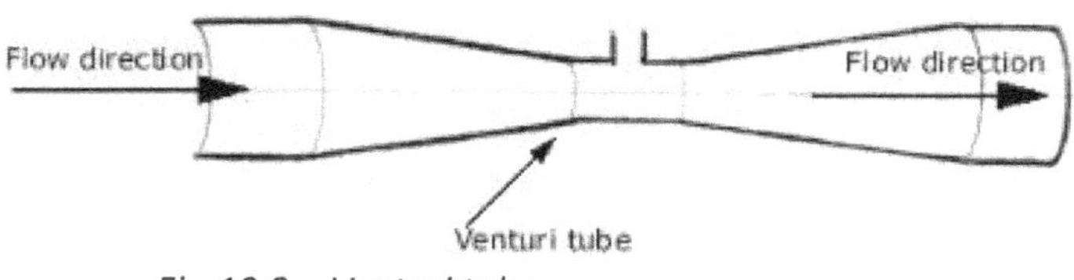

Fig 10.3 – Venturi tube

15. What are the differences between orifice plates and venturi tubes in terms of applications?

Ans: Differences Between Orifice Plates and Venturi Tubes :

Parameter	Orifice Plate	Venturi Tube
Measurement Principle	Creates a sharp pressure drop with a hole in the plate	Uses a smooth, tapered design for gradual pressure changes
Pressure Loss	High pressure loss due to sudden restriction	Low pressure loss due to gradual expansion
Accuracy	Moderate accuracy (~±2-4%)	High accuracy (~±1%)
Fluid Type	Best for clean fluids, gases, and steam	Suitable for dirty, viscous, and slurry fluids
Clogging Issues	More prone to clogging, especially in slurries	Less prone to clogging due to smooth design
Installation Space	Compact and easy to install	Large and requires more space

Cost	Low cost, widely used	Expensive due to complex design
Maintenance	Requires frequent maintenance due to wear	Low maintenance, longer lifespan
Application Suitability	Steam, compressed air, oil, and gas pipelines	Water treatment, slurry, and wastewater

16. What is a flow nozzles?

Ans: A flow nozzle is a device used in industrial systems to measure the flow rate of fluids like liquids, gases, or steam. It works on the principle of differential pressure. The nozzle has a smooth, tapered inlet and a narrow throat that causes the fluid to speed up as it passes through. This increase in velocity results in a drop in pressure, and by measuring the pressure difference between the wider section and the throat, the flow rate can be calculated using Bernoulli's principle.

Compared to orifice plates, flow nozzles offer better accuracy, usually around ±1% or better and cause less permanent pressure loss. Because of their durability and ability to handle high-speed and high-temperature flows, they are especially well-suited for steam and other demanding applications.

17. What is a dall tubes?

Ans: A Dall tube is a differential pressure (DP) flow measurement device similar to a Venturi tube, but with a shorter length and lower pressure loss. It consists of a converging inlet, a short throat, and a diverging outlet with an annular gap for improved pressure recovery. The annular gap in the diverging section helps recover pressure more efficiently than a Venturi tube.

It has lower pressure loss compared to Venturi tubes and orifice plates and shorter length than Venturi tubes, making installation easier. It is used in water supply and irrigation systems, Petrochemical and gas pipelines.

18. What is a pitot tube?

Ans: A Pitot tube is a simple device used to measure the velocity of a fluid (like air or water) flowing through a pipe or duct. It works on a basic principle: when a fluid hits a solid object, it slows down and comes to a stop at a point called the stagnation point.

As the moving fluid hits the front opening of the Pitot tube, its velocity drops to zero, and its kinetic energy is converted into pressure, this is known as stagnation pressure. Meanwhile, the side opening of the tube (placed at 90° to the flow) measures the static pressure of the fluid.

By comparing these two pressures, stagnation and static, we can calculate the fluid's velocity using Bernoulli's principle.

A typical Pitot tube has a small front-facing hole (usually 3 to 6 mm in diameter) to catch the fluid head-on, and a side hole to measure the static pressure. The difference in pressure between these two points is proportional to the square of the flow velocity.

Pitot tubes have minimum pressure loss and economical to install but have poor accuracy. The accuracy of a pitot tube may range from ±1/2 to ±5%.

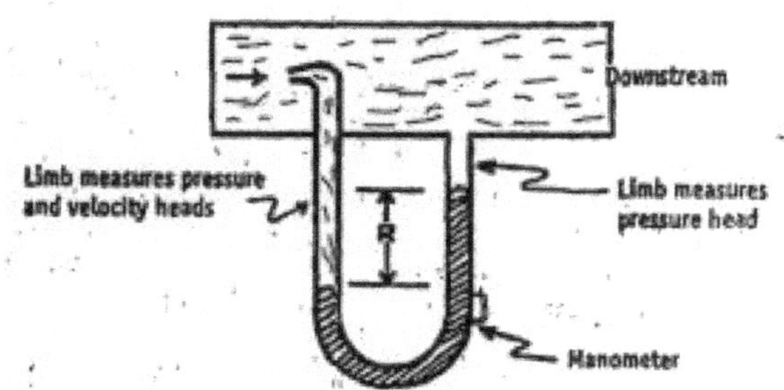

Fig 10.4 – Pitot tubes

19. What is an Annubar Tube?

Ans: An Annubar tube is a type of averaging Pitot tube used for differential pressure (DP) flow measurement. It consists of a hollow probe with multiple sensing ports positioned across the diameter of a pipe. These ports measure both static and total pressure, providing a more accurate average velocity compared to a single Pitot tube.

Fluid flows through the pipeline, and the Annubar tube is inserted across the flow direction. The upstream ports measure stagnation (total) pressure, while the downstream ports measure static pressure. The differential pressure (ΔP) is calculated using Bernoulli's equation.

It is more accurate than single Pitot tubes due to multiple sensing points. The accuracy of an annubar tube may range from ±1/2 to ±3/2%.

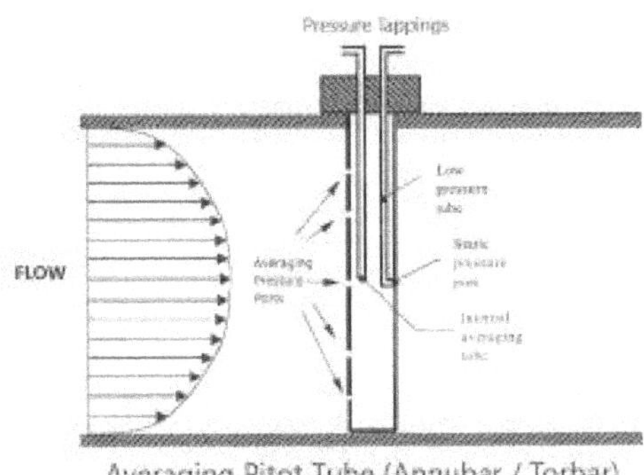

Fig 10.5 – Annubar tube

20. How is DP flow transmitter installed at pipe for gas and liquid flow measurement?

Ans: For gas and vapor flows, it is important that no stray liquid droplets collect in the impulse lines leading to the transmitter, this would generate an error-producing pressure.

For liquid flows, it is important that no gas bubbles collect in the impulse lines, or else those bubbles may displace liquid from the lines and thereby cause unequal vertical liquid columns, which would generate an error-producing differential pressure.

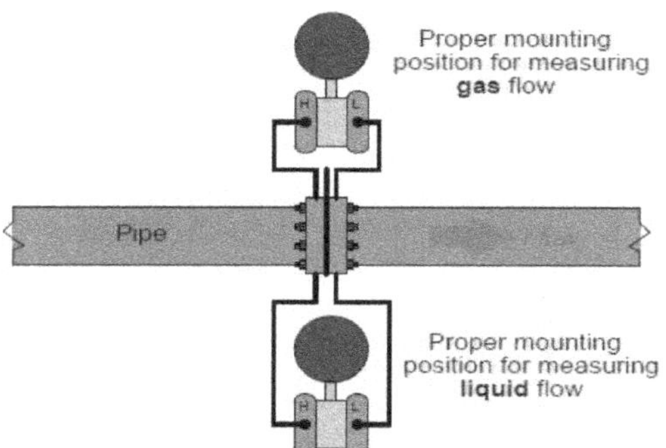

Fig 10.6 – DP transmitter

Hence, the transmitter is installed above the pipe for gas flow applications and below the pipe for liquid flow applications.

21. How is re ranging of DP flow transmitter done?

Ans: DP flow transmitter can be re range by the equation:

$$\frac{Existing\ flow}{Revised\ flow} = \frac{sqrt\ of\ existing\ DP}{sqrt\ of\ revised\ DP}$$

$$=> Revised\ flow = \frac{sqrt\ of\ revised\ DP}{sqrt\ of\ existing\ DP} \times Existing\ flow$$

Where,

Existing DP   = DP value as per orifice datasheet

Existing Flow = Flow value as per orifice datasheet

Revised DP   = Actual DP value in the field

Revised Flow = Calculated transmitter flow max range.

22. What is the working principle of a rotameter?

Ans: A rotameter is a variable area flowmeter used to measure the flow rate of liquids or gases. It operates on the principle of gravity and differential pressure. Rotameter consists of a vertical tapered tube with a float which is free to move up or down within the tube. The free area between float and inside wall of the tube forms an annular orifice. The tube is mounted vertically with the small end at the bottom.

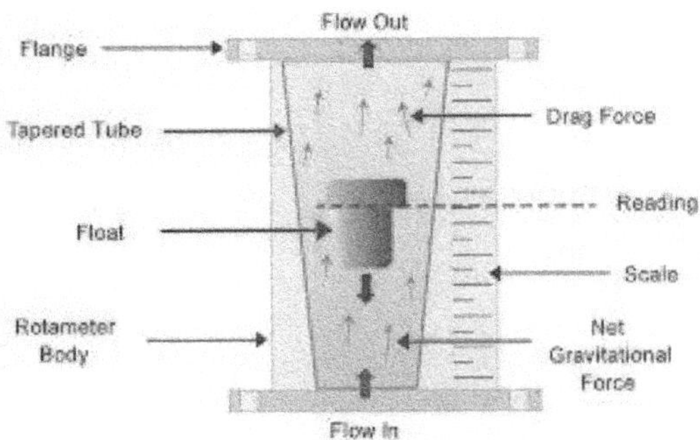

Fig 10.7 - Rotameter

The fluid to be measured enters the tube from the bottom and passes upward around the float, and exit at the top. When there is no flow through the rotameter, the float rests at the bottom of the metering tube. As fluid flows upward, it exerts a drag force on the float. The float moves up until the upward force (fluid flow) balances the downward force (gravity). The higher the flow rate, the higher the float rises in the tube. A calibration scale printed on the tube or near it, provides a direct indication of flow rate. The tube materials of rotameter may be of glass or metal.

23. What is the working principle of a magnetic flowmeters?

Ans: A magnetic flowmeter (or electromagnetic flowmeter) operates based on Faraday's Law of Electromagnetic Induction to measure the flow rate of conductive fluids. Faraday's law states that whenever a conductor moves through a magnetic field of given strength, a voltage is induced in the conductor which is proportional to the relative velocity between the conductor and the magnetic field. In case of magnetic flowmeter, electrically conductive flowing liquid work as the conductor.

The magnetic flowmeter consists of an electrically insulated or non-conducting pipe, with a pair of electrodes mounted opposite to each other and with magnetic coil mounted around the pipe. Magnetic coils generate a magnetic field perpendicular to the flow inside the non-metallic pipe. As the liquid passes through the pipe section, it also passes through the magnetic field set up by the magnetic coils, thus inducing the voltage in the liquid which is detected by the pair of electrodes mounted in the pipe wall. The amplitude of the induced voltage is proportional to the velocity of the flowing liquid. The induced voltage is given by the equation:

$$E = BVD,$$

Where,

E – Voltage induced

B - Magnetic field strength

V – Flow velocity

D – Pipe diameter

The flowmeter converts this velocity into a flow rate, considering the pipe's cross-sectional area.

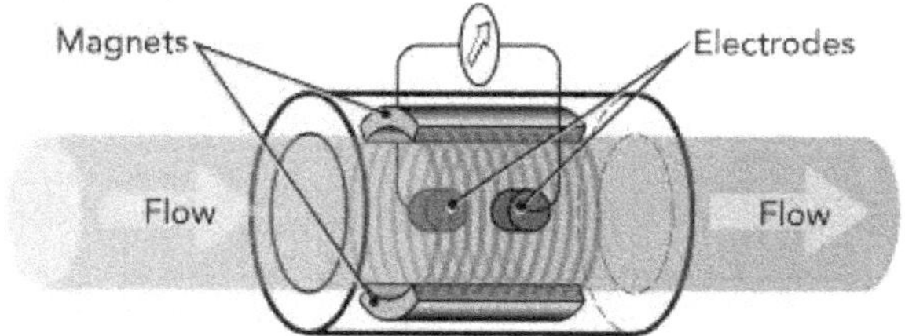

Fig 10.8 – magnetic Flowmeter

24. What are the advantages and disadvantages of magnetic flowmeter?

Ans: Following are the advantages:

- No Moving Parts → Low maintenance and long lifespan.
- Minimal Pressure Drop → No obstructions in the flow path.
- High Accuracy → Typically ±0.5% of flow rate.
- Measures Dirty & Corrosive Fluids → Works well with wastewater, slurries, and acids.
- Wide Range of Pipe Sizes → Can be used for small to large pipelines.
- Bidirectional Flow Measurement → Can measure flow in both directions.

    Following are the disadvantages:

- Only Works with Conductive Fluids → Cannot measure gases, oils, or pure water.
- Expensive → Higher initial cost compared to mechanical flowmeters.
- Requires Power Supply → Needs external power to operate.
- Sensitive to Pipe Lining & Electrode Coating → Scaling or coating can affect accuracy.
- Not Suitable for High-Temperature Applications → Limited use in extreme heat conditions.

25. What is the working principle of a turbine flowmeters?

Ans: A turbine flowmeter operates based on the principle of fluid velocity measurement using a rotating turbine inside the flow path.

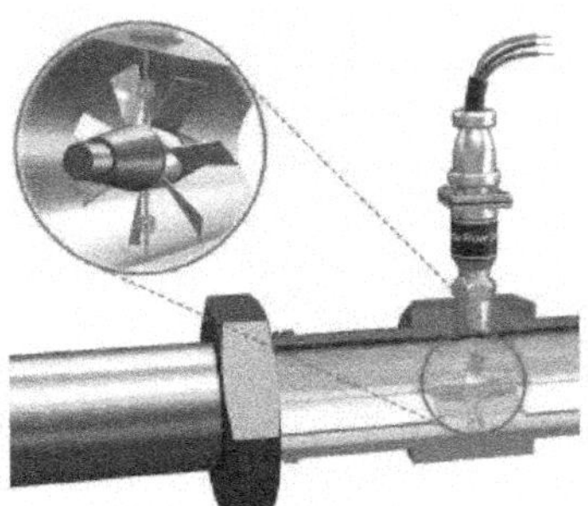

Fig 10.9 – Turbine flowmeter

It consists of a multi bladed turbine which is mounted at right angle to the axis of the flowing liquid. Fluid flows through the meter, striking the turbine blades, causing them to rotate. The rotational speed of the turbine is proportional to the flow velocity. A magnetic or optical sensor detects the number of turbine rotations. The sensor converts this into an electrical pulse signal, which is processed to determine flow rate. The final output is displayed as volumetric flow rate.

It has high accuracy in steady flow conditions and Suitable for clean liquids and gases. Its use is limited for slurry applications.

26. What is the working principle of a target flowmeters?

Ans: A target flowmeter measures flow rate based on the force exerted by a fluid on a target (disc or plate) placed in the flow path.

A target element is suspended in the flow path inside the pipe. As the fluid flows, it exerts a force on the target, causing it to deflect. This force is directly proportional to the flow rate. A strain gauge or force sensor measures this deflection as force which is proportional to the square of the flow and converts it into an electrical signal.

27. What is the working principle of a ultrasonic flowmeters?

Ans: An ultrasonic flowmeter measures fluid flow by using high-frequency sound waves. It is a non-invasive method suitable for liquids and gases. There are two main types of ultrasonic flowmeters: Transit-Time Ultrasonic Flowmeter and Doppler Ultrasonic Flowmeter.

Transit-Time Ultrasonic Flowmeter: It measures flow by measuring the time taken for ultrasonic wave to transverse a pipe section, both with and against the flow of liquid within the pipe. It consists of two transducers placed diagonally across the pipe. One transducer sends a sound wave to other and vice versa, both the transducer works as a transmitter and receiver. The detector measures the transit time from upstream to downstream transducers and vice versa. The difference in travel time between upstream and downstream waves is proportional to the flow velocity. The flow rate is then calculated based on this velocity. This type of flowmeter is used for clean fluids.

Doppler Ultrasonic Flowmeter: In doppler flowmeter, an ultrasonic wave is projected at an angle through the pipe wall into the liquid by a transmitting crystal in a transducer mounted outside the pipe. Part of the waves reflect off particles or bubbles in the flow. Since the reflectors (bubbles) are travelling at the fluid velocity, the frequency of the reflected wave is shifted according to the Doppler principle. The frequency shift (Doppler Effect) is measured to determine the flow velocity. This type of flowmeter is used for dirty or slurry fluids.

28. What are the advantages and limitations of ultrasonic flowmeter?

Ans*: Following are the advantages:*

- Non-Intrusive Measurement → No contact with the fluid, reducing contamination and maintenance.
- No Pressure Drop → Unlike mechanical flowmeters, it does not obstruct flow.
- Bi-Directional Flow Measurement → Measures flow in both directions.
- Its output relationship is linear.
- Works for Large Pipe Sizes → Suitable for industrial pipelines with large diameters.

Following are the limitations:

- Expensive → Higher initial cost compared to mechanical flowmeters.
- Requires Proper Sensor Alignment → Incorrect installation affects accuracy.

29. What is the volumetric flow and mass flow? What is the significance of mass flow rate?

Ans: Volumetric flow rate is he volume of fluid passing through a given point per unit time. It is measured in: Cubic meters per second (m³/s), liters per minute (L/min), gallons per minute (GPM). Example: A water pipeline delivering 100 L/min to a tank.

Mass flow rate is he mass of fluid passing through a given point per unit time. It is measured in: Kilograms per second (kg/s), pounds per hour (lb/h). Example: Steam flow in a boiler at 500 kg/h.

Volumetric flow rate can be converted to mass flow rate by multiplying the density of the fluid with the volumetric flow.

The volume of compressible fluid changes with changes in pressure and temperature. The mass remains constant irrespective of changes in the pressure and temperature of the fluid. It is therefore convenient to measure mass flow rate.

Applications for mass flow measurement include custody transfer (where a fluid product is bought or sold by its mass), chemical reaction processes (where the mass flow rates of reactants must be maintained in precise proportion in order for the desired chemical reactions to occur), and steam boiler control systems (where the out-flow of vaporous steam must be balanced by an equivalent in-flow of liquid water to the boiler – here, volumetric comparisons of steam and water flow would be useless because one cubic foot of steam is certainly not the same number of H_2O molecules as one cubic foot of water).

30. What is a Square Root Extractor in a DP Flowmeter?

Ans: In a differential pressure (DP) flowmeter, the relationship between flow rate and pressure is not linear. When the flow rate doubles, the differential pressure actually increases four times. This is because the pressure drop created by devices like venturi tubes, orifice plates, and pitot tubes is proportional to the square of the flow rate.

As a result, if a pressure transmitter is used to measure this differential pressure, the output it provides doesn't directly represent the actual flow rate—it represents the square of the flow rate. To get an accurate flow reading, the signal must go through a process called square root extraction.

Square root extraction converts the nonlinear pressure signal into a linear flow signal by mathematically taking the square root of the measured differential pressure. In the past, this was done using a separate device called a square root extractor, installed between the transmitter and the flow indicator. Today, this function is typically built into either the transmitter itself or the receiving instrument, such as a controller, recorder, or display. No matter where it's done, applying the square root function is essential for accurately measuring flow across the full operating range of the system.

31. How will you convert 4-20mA current loop output to a square root extraction and vice versa?

Ans: 4-20mA current loop output to a square root extraction conversion formula:

$$output\ sqrt\ = 4\ mA + \left(4 \times \sqrt{(output linear)} - 4mA\right)$$

Example : For 8 mA linear output, sqrt output will be:

$$= 4 + \left(4 \times \sqrt{8} - 4\right) = 4 + (4 \times 2.82 - 4) = 4 + 7.28 = 11.28\ mA$$

The reverse formula for converting a square root extraction output to a linear one is:

$$output\ linear = 4mA + \left(\frac{(output\ sqrt - 4mA)^{\wedge}2}{16}\right)$$

Example : For 10 mA sqrt output, linear output will be:

$$= 4 + \left(\frac{(10-4)^2}{16}\right) = 4 + \left(\frac{36}{16}\right) = 6.25\ mA$$

32. What is actual Volumetric flow rate and Standardized Volumetric Flow Rate?

Ans: When dealing with gases flow measurement, where pressure and temperature variations affect volume and hence volumetric flow rate. So, it is necessary to standardize the volumetric flow rate under standard pressure and temperature to nullify the effect of change in pressure and temperature.

The volume of fluid (gas or liquid) flowing through a pipe at the existing, real-time pressure and temperature conditions is the actual volumetric flow. Its unit is cubic meters per second (m^3/s), liters per minute (L/min). Example: A gas pipeline delivering 500 m^3/h at 8 bar and 50°C.

The volume flow rate corrected to a standard reference condition (e.g., 1 atm pressure and 0°C or 25°C), allowing for consistent comparisons across different systems. This corrected flowrate is the standardized volumetric flow rate. Its unit is Normal cubic meters per hour (Nm³/h), standard cubic feet per minute (SCFM). Example: The same gas at 500 m³/h (actual) at 8 bar, 50°C, when corrected to 1 atm, 0°C, may become 75 Nm³/h.

$$Q_{standard} = Q_{actual} \times (P_{actual}/P_{standard}) \times (T_{standard}/T_{actual})$$

Where,

$P_{standard}$ = Standard pressure (e.g., 1 atm or 101.325 kPa)

$T_{standard}$ = Standard temperature (e.g., 0°C = 273.15K or 25°C = 298.15K).

33. Why is pressure and temperature compensation required in flow measurement?

Ans: Pressure and temperature compensation are important in flow measurement because gases and steam change their volume quite a bit when pressure and temperature vary. Without compensating for these changes, the flow readings wouldn't be accurate or consistent. By adjusting the measured flow to standard reference conditions, like 1 atmosphere of pressure and a specific temperature such as 0°C or 25°C, we can compare flow rates fairly across different systems.

Usually, the pressure sensor is placed upstream of the flow measurement device, while the temperature sensor is positioned downstream. This setup helps ensure the velocity profile inside the flow element isn't disturbed, keeping the measurement reliable.

34. What is the working principle of vortex flowmeter?

Ans: A vortex flowmeter works on the principle of the Von Kármán Vortex Street. This means when a fluid flows past a bluff body, a blunt object placed in the flow, it creates a repeating pattern of swirling vortices behind it. These vortices shed alternately from each side, and the frequency at which they form is directly related to how fast the fluid is moving.

The bluff body, often called a shedder bar, sits right in the flow path. As the fluid moves around it, these vortices form one after another, creating pressure changes that can be detected as tiny fluctuations. Sensors like piezoelectric, capacitive, or ultrasonic ones pick up these fluctuations. By measuring how often the vortices occur, the flowmeter calculates the fluid's velocity. Then, using the cross-sectional area of the pipe, it converts that velocity into a volumetric flow rate.

35. What is the working principle of coriolis flowmeter?

Ans: A Coriolis flowmeter works by directly measuring the mass flow rate of a fluid using the Coriolis effect, an apparent force that acts on a mass moving in a rotating or vibrating system. In this case, the flowmeter uses vibrating tubes to create this effect.

Inside the meter, the fluid flows through one or two curved or straight tubes that are continuously vibrated at their natural frequency by an internal driver. As the fluid moves through these vibrating tubes, the inertia of the moving fluid interacts with the vibration and causes the tubes to twist slightly. This twisting effect creates a time delay, also called a phase shift, between the vibration at the inlet and the outlet of the tube.

Sensors placed at both ends of the tube detect this phase shift. The greater the flow of mass through the tube, the more pronounced the twisting becomes. Because this phase shift is directly proportional to the mass flow rate, the meter can calculate the actual amount of fluid passing through it, independent of its temperature, pressure, or density.

36. What is the working principle of Thermal flowmeter?

Ans: A thermal flowmeter measures mass flow rate based on the principle of heat transfer between a heated sensor and the flowing fluid. It relies on the relationship between mass flow rate and heat dissipation to determine the flow of gases.

The flowmeter has two temperature sensors: One heated sensor (actively heated by an electrical current) and One reference sensor (measures ambient temperature). The heated sensor is maintained at a fixed temperature difference (ΔT) above the reference sensor. When gas flows over the heated sensor, it carries away heat (forced convection). The amount of heat lost depends on the mass flow rate of the gas. The flowmeter compensates by increasing electrical power to maintain the temperature difference. The additional electrical power required to sustain $\Delta T\backslash Delta\ T\Delta T$ is proportional to the mass flow rate of the gas.

37. What is the working principle of a positive displacement flowmeter? What are its key features?

Ans: A Positive Displacement (PD) flowmeter measures fluid flow rate by trapping and transferring discrete volumes of fluid through a chamber. It directly measures volumetric flow rather than inferring it from velocity or pressure changes, making it one of the most accurate flow measurement techniques.

The fluid flows into a chamber with rotating or oscillating mechanical components. The internal mechanism (gears, pistons, or lobes) traps a known volume of fluid within compartments. As fluid moves through, the mechanism rotates or oscillates, pushing the trapped fluid forward. The number of rotations or oscillations is directly proportional to the fluid volume. A sensor or mechanical counter tracks the number of cycles. The flow rate is calculated using the known volume per cycle.

Following are the key features: -

- *Highly Accurate* → Direct volumetric measurement without needing compensation for temperature or pressure.
- *Works with High-Viscosity Fluids* → Ideal for measuring oils, syrups, fuels, and lubricants.

- **No Upstream or Downstream Straight Pipe Required** → Unlike other flowmeters, PD meters are unaffected by flow disturbances.

38. What is flowmeter turndown ratio? What is the importance of turndown ratio?

Ans: Turndown ratio (also called rangeability) of a flowmeter refers to the range over which a flowmeter can accurately measure flow, expressed as the ratio of the maximum to minimum measurable flow rate while maintaining accuracy.

If a flowmeter can measure flow from 10 LPM to 1000 LPM, then:

Turndown Ratio=1000/10=100:1

Following are the importance of turndown ratio:

- **Indicates Flexibility** → A higher turndown ratio means the meter can measure a wider range of flows.
- **Critical for Process Control** → Ensures accurate measurements at both high and low flow conditions.
- **Prevents Meter Overloading or Underutilization** → Ensures proper meter selection for varying flow rates.

39. What factors affect the stability of Flow Meter readings? What are the best solutions of those factors affecting the stability of Flow Meter readings?

Ans: Following are the factors that affect the Stability of Flow Meter Reading:

- **Fluid Characteristics:** Changes in fluid properties like viscosity or density can lead to unstable readings. Different flow meters are sensitive to different fluid characteristics.
- **Air Bubbles:** Air or gas entrained in the fluid can cause fluctuating readings.

- ***Pipe Vibration:*** Mechanical vibrations in the pipe can interfere with the meter's sensing elements, causing erratic readings.
- ***Pulsating Flow:*** In some pumping configurations, particularly with diaphragm or piston pumps, the flow can be pulsatile rather than smooth, affecting the reading stability.
- ***Improper Installation:*** Incorrect installation, such as too close to a bend, pump, or valve, can lead to turbulent flow and affect readings.
- ***Temperature Fluctuations***: Rapid changes in fluid temperature can cause transient changes in flow meter readings.
- ***Electrical Interference***: Electrical noise or interference from nearby equipment can corrupt the signal.
- ***Wear and Tear***: Mechanical wear over time can lead to degradation of the meter's internal components, affecting its accuracy and stability.
- ***Calibration:*** An improperly calibrated meter will provide unstable or inaccurate readings.
- ***Pressure Fluctuations:*** Variability in line pressure can also cause the readings to be unstable.
- ***Blockages:*** Partial blockages or fouling can cause unpredictable flow profiles, affecting meter readings.
- ***Software Glitches:*** If the flow meter is software-driven, firmware or software issues could lead to unstable readings.
- ***Scaling and Fouling:*** The accumulation of material on the meter's internals can lead to unstable readings over time.
- ***Manual Interference:*** Sometimes the tampering of settings or manual adjustments can cause unstable readings.
- ***Instrumentation Issues:*** Finally, signal processing issues, faulty wiring, or problems in the control system itself can contribute to instability.

The best solutions of these factors are:

Factors	Flow Meter Solutions to Solve Stability Issues
Fluid Properties	Adopt flow meters with built-in compensation for variations in density or viscosity. Calibrate regularly based on fluid properties.
Air Bubbles	Incorporate air eliminators or air traps in the system to remove entrained air before the fluid reaches the meter.
Pipe Vibration	Employ vibration isolation techniques or materials. Alternatively, reposition the meter away from sources of vibration.
Pulsating Flow	Introduce a flow smoother or flow conditioner upstream to equalize the flow before it reaches the meter.
Installation Errors	Adhere to manufacturer guidelines on proper installation. Make sure to have sufficient straight pipe lengths upstream and downstream.
Temperature Fluctuations	Utilize flow meters with temperature compensation features or stabilize the temperature around the flow meter.
Electrical Interference	Install shielded cabling and ensure proper grounding to minimize electrical noise. Isolate power supplies if possible.
Wear and Tear	Schedule regular maintenance and inspections to identify and replace worn components.
Calibration Issues	Follow a strict calibration schedule as per manufacturer guidelines or industry norms to ensure accurate measurements.
Pressure Changes	Employ pressure-compensating flow meters or stabilize the line pressure through control valves or other means.

40. What is a 'zero check' and 'static zero check' on a DP flow transmitter?

Ans: *Zero Check*: A procedure for checking the transmitter output is equal to 4.00 mA when its HP & LP chambers are equalized and are at atmospheric pressure.

Static Zero Check: A procedure for checking the transmitter output is equal to 4.00 mA when its HP & LP chambers are equalized and are at the operating pressure.

41. What is MSCMD?

Ans: MSCMD stands for Million Standard Cubic Meters per Day and is a unit of gas flow rate measurement. It represents the volume of gas flowing per day under standard conditions. This unit is used in natural gas production, pipeline transport, and distribution systems and it ensures accurate volume comparison regardless of pressure fluctuations.

42. Why Generally a Flow Transmitter Installed Upstream of a Flow Control Valve?

Ans: A flow transmitter is always installed on the upstream of the flow control valve in order to maintain the operating pressure across the flow transmitter sensors.

Downstream of the control valve the pressure changes as the control valve open or closes.

43. Why is RTD installed after the Orifice Flow element?

Ans: The location of RTD (thermowell), is positioned downstream of the orifice plate so the turbulence it generates will not create additional turbulence at the orifice plate.

44. Can an Electromagnetic Flow meter be used for the measurement of the flow of liquids like Petrol, Diesel,

Kerosene, Various types of oil, Edible oil, or other organic solvents?

Ans: The electrical conductivity of liquid under measurement should have a minimum of 5 micro-Siemens per cm. conductivity. However, some transmitter, can measure the flow rate of liquids having conductivity as low as 1 micro-Siemens per cm.

The conductivity of the liquids like Petrol, Diesel, Kerosene, Various types of oil, Edible oil, or other organic solvents is nearing almost zero. Hence, Electromagnetic Flow meter be used for the measurement of the flow.

45. What do we need to know about the system when ordering a new flow meter?

Ans: The following parameters needed to know:

- Type of fluid
- Expected flow rate
- Max. fluid temp and system pressure
- % suspended particles by volume
- Pipe size (ID) material and wall thickness.

46. How are flowmeters selected based on different applications?

Ans: Based on various applications flowmeters can be selected as:

Applications	*Recommended Flowmeter*
Mass Flow	Coriolis, Thermal flowmeter
Steam Flow Measurement	DP (Orifice, Venturi), Vortex
High Accuracy Liquid Flow	Coriolis, Magnetic, Positive displacement
Corrosive Fluids	Magnetic, Ultrasonic
Gases & Airflow	Thermal, Vortex, DP, Ultrasonic

Chapter: 11

Vibration Measurements

1. What do you mean by vibration in a mechanical equipment?

Ans: Vibration is static and dynamic imbalance of equipment. Vibration is the oscillation, or moving back and forth of an object.

2. What is a bearing?

Ans: A bearing is a mechanical component that supports and guides moving parts, reducing friction between surfaces in relative motion. Bearings allow controlled movement and increase the efficiency and lifespan of machines.

3. What is thrust bearing and journal bearing?

Ans: A thrust bearing is designed to support axial loads, meaning forces that act along the axis of a shaft. It keeps the shaft from moving back and forth. It is commonly used in vertical pumps, turbines.

A journal bearing supports radial loads, meaning forces that act perpendicular to the shaft. The shaft (journal) rotates inside the bearing surface with a thin film of lubrication separating them. Journal bearings are widely used in motors, turbines, and compressors.

4. Why vibration measurement is important?

Ans: Vibration analysis is often used as a diagnostic tool to monitor the health of machinery. Changes in vibration patterns can indicate issues such as imbalance, misalignment, looseness, or bearing failures. By monitoring these patterns, maintenance can be performed proactively, reducing the risk of unexpected breakdowns.

Excessive vibration can negatively impact the performance of mechanical equipment. It can lead to increased wear and tear, reduced efficiency, and even catastrophic failure if not addressed.

High levels of vibration can pose safety risks to both the equipment and the operators. It can cause components to loosen or fail, which might result in accidents or injuries.

5. What Causes vibration?

Ans: Unbalance of shaft, Bearing problem, Cracking of the rings, Fluid coupling problem, Shaft misalignment, and other dynamic instabilities.

6. What is a vibration spectrum?

Ans: A vibration spectrum is a graphical representation of vibration amplitude versus frequency. It shows how the energy of a vibration signal is distributed across various frequencies and is a fundamental tool in machinery condition monitoring and diagnostics.

7. What are the principal characteristics of the vibration signal that we measure in mechanical equipment?

Ans: The principal characteristics of the vibration signal are:

- Ampliude
- Frequency
- Phase

8. Explain Amplitude measurement of vibration signals.

Ans: In vibration measurement, amplitude refers to the maximum extent of a vibration or oscillation, measured from the position of equilibrium. Essentially, it indicates the strength or intensity of the vibration.

9. What are the different ways to quantify Amplitude?

Ans: There are different ways to quantify amplitude, including peak-to-peak, Zero to peak, and root mean square (RMS) values:

- ***Peak to Peak:*** This measures the total displacement between the maximum positive and maximum negative peaks of the vibration signal. It provides a complete range of the vibration motion

- ***Zero to peak:*** This is the maximum displacement from the position of equilibrium to the peak of the vibration wave. It's useful for identifying the maximum instantaneous force exerted by the vibration.

- ***Root mean square (RMS):*** RMS amplitude provides a statistical measure of the magnitude of the varying quantity. It is calculated by taking the square root of the average of the squares of the instantaneous values over a period. RMS is particularly useful because it provides a consistent measure of the vibration energy, making it a good indicator of the vibration's overall effect on the equipment.

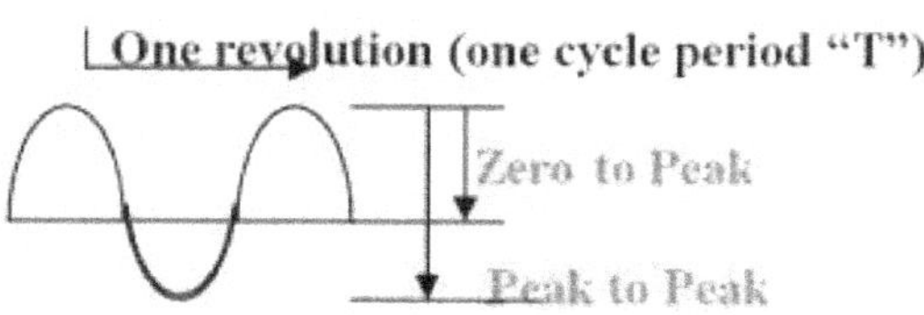

Fig 11.1 – Vibration amplitude

10. What are the different units used for measuring vibration displacement, velocity, and acceleration?

Ans: Vibration displacement is measured in mils or micrometres and expressed as peak-to-peak. Vibration velocity is measured in inches per second or millimetres per second and is expressed as zero-to-peak or RMS. Vibration acceleration is measured in meters per second squared and is also expressed as zero-to-peak or RMS.

11. Explain Frequency measurement of vibration signals.

Ans: Frequency measurement of vibration signals involves determining the number of oscillations or cycles that a vibrating system undergoes per unit of time. The unit of frequency is Hertz (Hz). Frequency is a measure of how fast a body is vibrating and is used to identify the source of vibration. Normally Frequency is expressed in shaft rotative speed. If a vibration is at the same frequency as the shaft speed, this will be 1X or 1 time shaft speed. If it is twice, it is 2X. This 2X harmonics indicates misalignment in the rotating equipment.

12. What are the types of sensors for vibration monitoring?

Ans: The three principal vibration sensor types are displacement, velocity, and accelerometer.

13. Explain the working principle of displacement type or proximity sensor for vibration measurement.

Ans: A displacement-type or proximity sensor works based on the principle of electromagnetic induction. It is commonly used to measure the vibration of rotating equipment by detecting the small movements (displacement) of a conductive target, like a shaft.

The sensor system mainly includes a probe and a proximeter. The probe contains a coil that generates an alternating electromagnetic field when energized by an AC signal. This signal is provided by the proximeter, which also processes the returning signals from the probe.

When a conductive target, such as a metal shaft, comes near the probe tip, it enters the electromagnetic field. This causes eddy currents to be induced on the surface of the target. These eddy currents generate their own electromagnetic field, which interferes with the field from the probe. The nature of this interference depends on how close the target is to the probe. As the distance between the probe and the target changes, due to vibration, the interaction between the two fields changes. This affects the impedance of the coil inside the probe. The proximeter detects these impedance changes and converts them into a voltage signal.

The output voltage is directly proportional to the gap (distance) between the probe and the target.

So, as the target vibrates and moves closer or farther from the probe, the sensor outputs a changing voltage signal. This varying voltage corresponds to the vibration displacement, allowing us to measure the vibration of the equipment accurately.

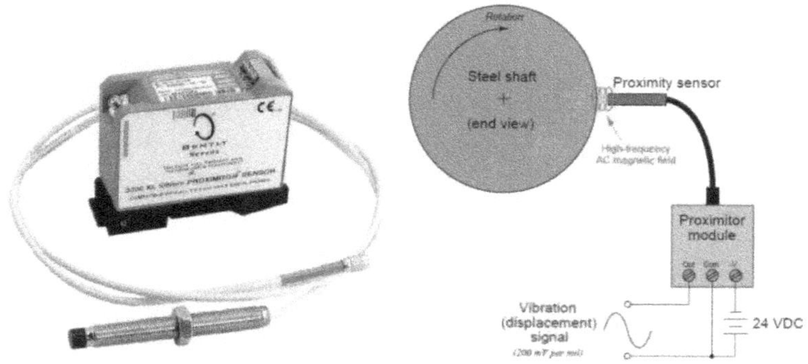

Fig 11.2 Proximeter

14. What is a Proximeter?

Ans: The Proximeter powers the probe and processes the raw signal from the probe. It converts the changes in the electromagnetic field into a voltage signal proportional to the distance between the probe and the target.

15. What are the three wires used on a Proximeter?

Ans: The three wires terminated on the Proximeter are: -24V DC (power supply), common and output signal.

16. What is gap voltage for proximity probe?

Ans: The gap voltage for a proximity probe refers to the DC voltage that is measured when the probe is positioned at a specific distance (or gap) from the conductive target surface. Gap voltage is the output voltage of the proximity probe when it is measuring the distance to the target. It indicates the distance between the probe tip and the target surface.

Gap voltage of Bently Nevada vibration probe is usually set at -10V. Reason for setting at -10 volt is that as proximitor allows probe to work from -2 volt to -18 volt. So voltage difference of 2 to 10 and 10 to 18 is 8 volt. When setting at -10 volt, probe can equally measures vibration at both sides i.e. when shaft is going away from probe or towards probe).

17. What are the reasons for a vibration 'spike signal'?

Ans: The following may cause a 'spike signal' in the vibration measurement.

- Loss of signal cable insulation.
- Signal cable passing next to high voltage lines.
- Improper earthing facility.
- Grounding of the wires.
- Loose mounting of the instrument field components.

18. What is the typical output signal of an eddy current vibration probe?

Ans: DC voltage proportional to displacement.

19. What is the main advantage of using a non-contact vibration probe?

Ans: No wear and tear on the probe or the machine.

20. How gap voltage is adjusted during installation of the probe?

Ans: Generally, the GAP voltage of the Bently Nevada Vibration Probe is set to -10V DC. Because the proximity permits the vibration probe to operate in its region of linearity from -2VDC to -18VDC. Following steps are followed during installation of proximity sensor:

- Install the probe in the mounting bracket and insert the vibration probe fully till it touches the shaft or the body whose vibration is to be measured.
- Connect the probe to the proximeter and measure the gap

voltage using a voltmeter on the output from the proximeter.

- If the gap voltage is less than -10VDC (say -8VDC), probe too close, move the probe slightly away from the target.
- If the gap voltage is more than -10VDC (say -12VDC) probe too far, move the probe slightly closer to the target.
- Recheck the gap voltage after each adjustment until it falls within the specified range.
- Once the correct gap voltage is achieved, securely lock the probe in place to maintain the proper distance during operation.

21. What is a TK-3 Calibrator?

Ans: A TK-3 Calibrator is a portable instrument used to test, calibrate, and verify the performance of eddy current (proximity) vibration sensor. It is manufactured by Bently Nevada.

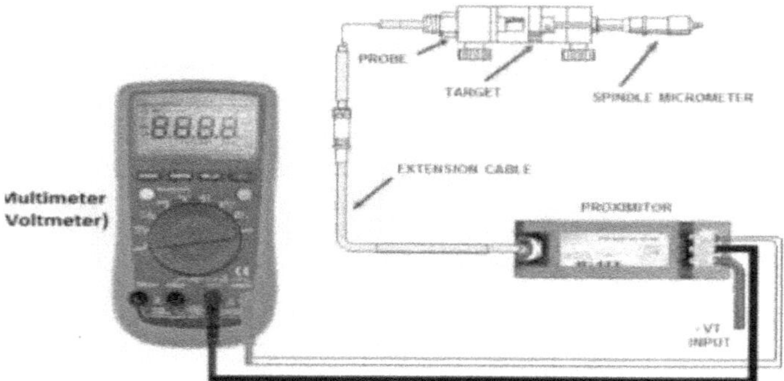

Fig 11.3- TK-3 calibrator

The calibrator includes two main components: a wobulator and a spindle micrometer. The spindle micrometer helps verify the voltage-to-distance relationship of proximity probes and their associated electronics (proximitors). The wobulator, on the other hand, is used to simulate controlled vibration. It creates precise mechanical motion that mimics actual machine vibration. This motion is regulated by a manual swing arm and monitored using a dial indicator included in the kit.

The speed of the wobulator can be adjusted using a control knob, allowing users to fine-tune the test conditions. By applying a known mechanical input using the calibrator and observing the output on a monitor or meter, technicians can evaluate the full vibration monitoring system for accuracy and proper function.

22. What is the Bently Nevada Vibration Monitoring System?

Ans: The Bently Nevada Vibration Monitoring System is a comprehensive suite of hardware and software solutions designed for continuous monitoring, protection, and diagnostics of rotating machinery. It is one of the most trusted and widely used systems in industries.

23. What are the components of Bently Nevada Vibration Monitoring System?

Ans: Following are the components of Bently Nevada Vibration Monitoring System:

- *Power supply Module*: The power supply module installed on the leftmost side of the rack and installed one above the other creating a redundant system.
- *Transient data interface Module*: The TDI module is always placed in the rack beside the power supply module. This module continuously collects data from all modules and sends them to other systems connected to this module through Ethernet
- *4 Channel proximitor Module*: The Proximitor Monitor is a four-channel monitor which accepts input from Bently Nevada vibration monitoring system/proximity transducers and converts the data to vibration.
- *16 Channel temperature Module*: This module provides 16 channels of temperature monitoring and accepts both resistance temperature detector (RTD) and isolated tip thermocouple (TC) temperature inputs.

- **_4 Channel Relay Module_**: The 4-Channel Relay Module is a full-height module that provides four relay outputs which is user settable i.e. NO or NC contact from the back of the module.
- **_4 Channel Keyphasor Module_**: The Keyphasor Module is a half-height, two-channel module used to provide Keyphasor signals to the monitor modules in the rack.
- **_Communication Module:_** The Communication Gateway module allows communication with other systems using both Ethernet TCP/IP and serial (RS232/RS422/RS485) communications capabilities.

24. At what angle a pair of proximity sensor installed for vibration measurement in rotating shaft?

Ans: A pair of sensors are installed 45 degrees from the identified centre line of the rotor shaft. This will constitute the left and right sectional vibration measurements.

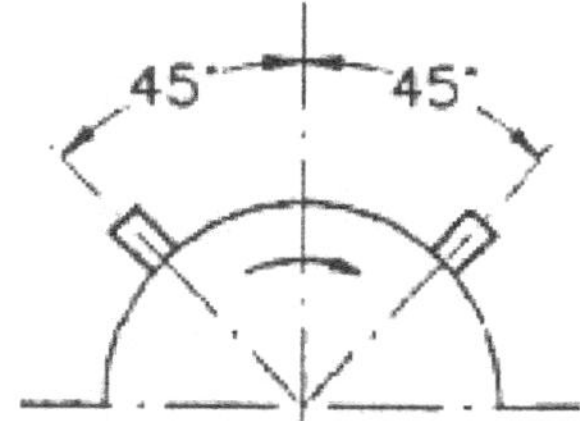

Fig 11.4 – Proximity sensor installation

25. Explain the working procedure of velocity sensor or seismic sensor for vibration measurement.

Ans: A velocity sensor converts the velocity of a vibrating object into an electrical signal that can be measured and work based on Faraday's Law of Electromagnetic Induction.

It consists of a wire coil suspended within a magnetic field created by a permanent magnet. The coil and magnet assembly housed in a casing that protect it from damage.

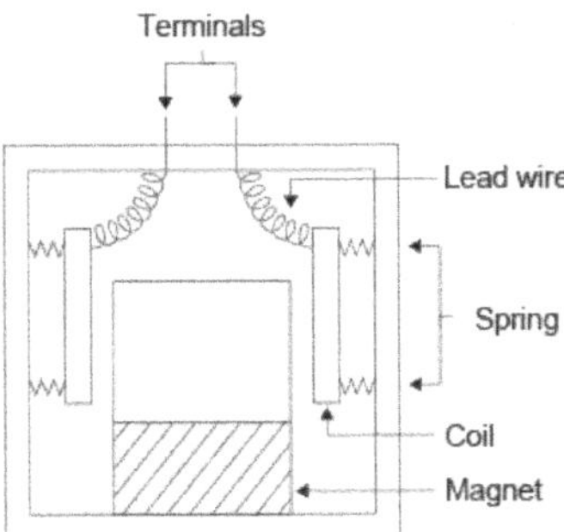

Fig 11.5 – Sesimic sensor

As the vibrating object (to which the sensor is attached) moves, it causes relative motion between the coil and the magnet. this relative motion induces a voltage in the coil. The voltage induced is proportional to the velocity of the motion. The induced voltage is the sensor's output signal, which represents the velocity of the vibration.

26. Explain the working procedure of Piezoelectric accelerometers for vibration measurement.

Ans: It consists of a crystal or ceramic material that generates an electrical charge when subjected to mechanical stress and a mass attached to the piezoelectric element. The piezoelectric element generates a charge proportional to the acceleration of the vibrating object. The acceleration signal is then passed through an electronic integrator circuit and the integrator circuit outputs a voltage signal that represents the acceleration of the vibration.

27. How to check the healthiness of Proximity probe and seismic probe?

Ans: The health of a proximity probe can be assessed by measuring its coil resistance. A resistance value between 5 Ω and 9 Ω is considered acceptable. For seismic probes, the coil resistance should be within the range of 110 Ω to 115 Ω to be deemed healthy.

28. What are the differences between a seismic probe and a proximity probe?

Ans: Following are the differences between seismic probe and a proximity probe.

Feature	Seismic Probe	Proximity probe
Working Principle	Piezoelectric or moving coil (measures acceleration or velocity)	Eddy current (electromagnetic field)
Measures	Absolute motion of machine casing or structure	Relative motion of shaft to bearing
Vibration Type	Casing vibration	Shaft vibration
Units	Velocity (mm/s) or Acceleration (g)	Displacement (μm, mils)
Signal Type	AC voltage proportional to velocity or acceleration	Negative DC voltage + AC vibration
Mounting	Mounted on machine casing or structure	Close to the rotating shaft
Installation complexity	Low (surface mount with bolts or adhesives)	High (requires exact gap, alignment, calibration)
Best for	Medium/low-speed machines	High-speed machines

29. What is a key phasor?

Ans: A key phasor is a reference signal used in rotating machinery to mark a specific point on the shaft during each revolution. It's typically generated by a proximity sensor that detects a unique feature on the shaft, such as a keyway, notch, or pin. This setup produces one distinct electrical pulse for every full rotation of the shaft.

The key phasor signal plays a crucial role in vibration analysis. It provides a timing reference that helps correlate other dynamic signals with the shaft's position. This makes it possible to analyze conditions like unbalance, misalignment, and other mechanical issues. It provides a reference point in the machine's rotation to correlate other vibration signals against.

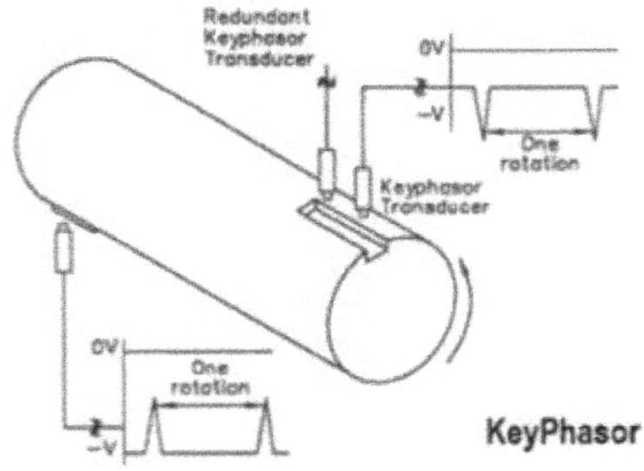

Fig 11.6 – key Phasor

30. What is eccentricity?

Ans: Eccentricity in rotating machinery refers to a condition where the center of rotation doesn't align with the physical center of the shaft or rotor. In simple terms, the rotating part isn't spinning evenly around its own center, it's slightly off-center. In electric motors, this often shows up as an uneven air gap between the rotor and the stator. One side of the rotor might be closer to the stator than the other, which creates an imbalance during rotation.

This misalignment can cause vibrations and uneven forces, leading to faster wear on components like bearings and seals. Eccentricity is typically detected using proximity sensors and vibration analysis, which help identify these subtle shifts in shaft position during operation.

31. What is axial displacement of a turbine and how is it measured?

Ans: Axial displacement in a turbine refers to the movement of the rotor along the direction of the shaft, essentially, forward or backward along its length. This can happen due to thermal expansion, uneven pressure, or thrust forces that develop while the turbine is running.

If the rotor moves too much in this direction, it can come into contact with stationary parts like thrust bearings or seals. That kind of contact can damage the bearings, cause rubbing, or even lead to serious mechanical failure.

To keep an eye on this, a proximity probe is installed at the end of the turbine shaft. It measures how much the shaft moves in the axial direction, helping operators monitor and protect the machine from excessive movement.

32. What is differential expansion of a turbine and how is it measured?

Ans: Differential expansion in a turbine refers to the difference in thermal expansion between the rotor (shaft) and the stator (casing) as the turbine heats up during startup, shutdown, or load changes. Since the rotor and casing are made of different masses and materials, and are heated or cooled at different rates, they expand at different rates, which can lead to mechanical interference or misalignment if not properly monitored. Excessive differential expansion can cause rotor-to-stator rubbing, leading to damage.

Differential expansion is measured using a proximity probe system mounted on the turbine casing. The probe is aimed at a collar or target on the rotor near the thrust end. The measured value represents how much more (or less) the rotor has expanded compared to the casing.

33. Explain the working principle of vibration switch.

Ans: A vibration switch works by detecting excessive vibration in a machine and triggering a response, like shutting down the equipment or sounding an alarm. Inside the switch, there's a tension spring and a pivoting plate mounted on a special kind of balance point called an over-center fulcrum. There's also a micro-switch connected to the system to provide an electrical signal when needed.

Under normal conditions, the spring holds the plate in a steady position, and nothing happens—the circuit stays open, so no alarm or trip signal is sent. But if the machine starts vibrating too much, the force causes the plate to snap over the fulcrum and shift to the tripped position. When this happens, it activates the micro-switch, which changes the electrical circuit's state, usually to stop the machine or alert the operator.

To get things back to normal, the switch needs to be manually reset by pressing a button or plunger on the outside of the device.

34. How mounting in different orientation affects the operation of the vibration switch?

Ans: Orientation affects how gravity interacts with the mechanism:

- ***Horizontal Mounting***: Best orientation; gravity has negligible effect.
- ***Vertical Up***: Gravity resists tripping; requires more vibration (more than 1 g).
- ***Vertical Down***: Gravity assists tripping; requires less vibration (1–2 g less).

On the basis of orientation switch can be set accordingly.

Chapter:12

Discrete process Measurements (switches)

1. What do you mean by normal status of a switch?

Ans: The normal status of a switch refers to the position of its electrical contacts when the switch is at rest, that is, when there is no physical force or external action applied to it. In other words, it's the default condition of the switch under normal, inactive circumstances.

Electrical switches are always drawn in schematic diagrams in their "normal" statuses, regardless of their application.

2. What are normally open (NO) and normally close switch (NC)?

Ans: A normally open (NO) switch is an electrical contact that remains open in its normal state and changes to a closed state upon the application of external simulation.

A normally closed (NC) switch is an electrical contact that remains closed in its normal state and changes to an open state upon the application of external stimulation.

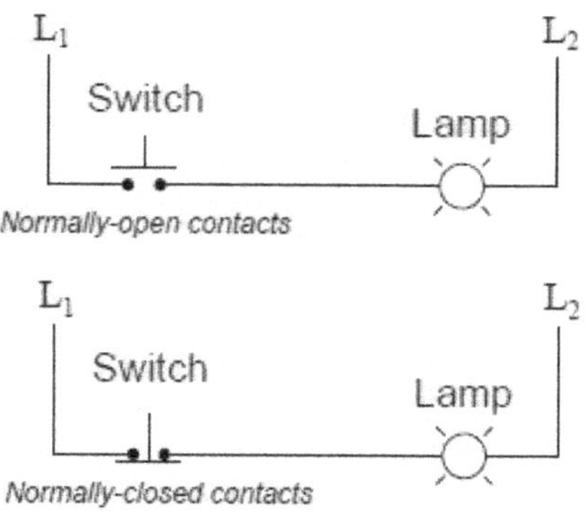

Fig 12.1 – NO & NC switches

3. What is a limit switch?

Ans: A limit switch detects the physical motion of an object by direct contact with that object.

An example of a limit switch is the switch detecting the open position of a refrigerator door, automatically glowing the refrigerator's light when the door opens.

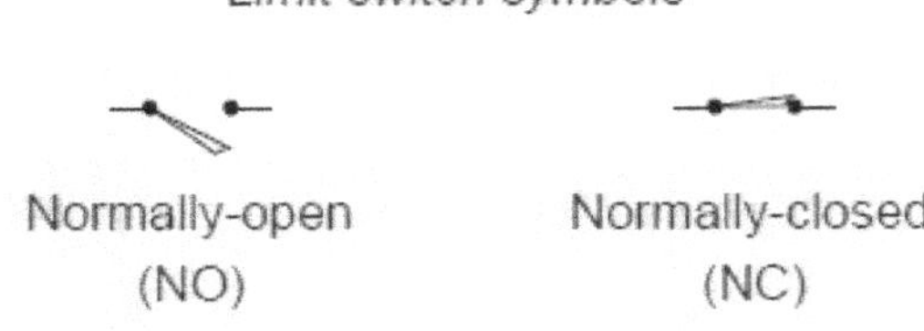

Fig 12.2 – Limit Switches

4. Mention some of the industrial application of limit switch.

Ans: In industry, limit switches are used for the indication of opening and closing positions of the valve. A lever, plunger, or roller on the limit switch is actuated by moving part attached to the valve stem or actuator. When the valve reaches its fully open or closed position, the corresponding mechanical action makes or breaks contact of the limit switch. The limit switch sends an electrical signal when triggered, indicating whether the valve is fully open, fully closed.

Moreover, a limit switch also used for indication of status of electrical breaker positions.

Fig 12.3 – Limit switches

5. What is proximity switch?

Ans: A proximity switch is a type of sensor that detects the presence or absence of an object without requiring physical contact. It operates by sensing changes in a specific field or signal caused by an object's presence, such as electromagnetic, capacitive, or magnetic fields.

Being non-contact in nature, proximity switches are often used in industrial applications to sense metal parts, machinery, or tools.

6.   What is Dry Contact and Wet Contact?

Ans: A dry contact is a mechanical switch that is electrically isolated from any internal voltage. It does not supply any voltage or current by itself. The user must provide an external power source to use the contact in a circuit. It is also known as potential free contact.

Example: Pressure switch, which requires external power source to use in a circuit.

A wet contact is a contact that already has a voltage present supplied from within the device or system. When the contact is closed, it sends a powered signal (voltage) to the receiving circuit. It is used when a signal needs to be directly transmitted to another device. It is also called as Powered contact.

Example: A PLC module with wet outputs sends a 24V signal directly to an actuator or another control system when the contact closes.

7.   What is electromechanical relay?

Ans: An electromechanical relay is an electrically operated switch that uses an electromagnetic coil to mechanically open or close one or more sets of contacts. It is commonly used to control circuits and devices, allowing a low-power signal to control a higher-power circuit.

8.   How electromechanical relay works?

Ans: The relay has an electromagnetic coil that generates a magnetic field when current flows through it. This magnetic field pulls or pushes a mechanical armature. The movement of the armature opens or closes the relay's contacts, switching the connected circuit on or off. The contacts can be normally open (NO), normally closed (NC), or a combination of both. When the current to the coil is removed, a spring returns the armature to its original position, reversing the state of the contacts.

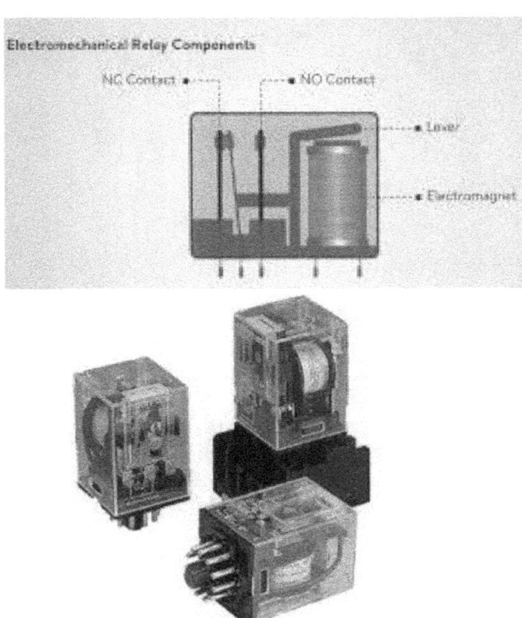

Fig 12.4 – Electromechanical relay

9. What is Single pole single throw (SPST), single pole double throw (SPDT) and Double pole double throw (DPDT) relay?

Ans: Single pole single throw (SPST) has one pole and one contact only (either NO or NC). It acts as a simple on/off switch.

SPDT relay has one pole and two contacts (both NO & NC). It allows to connect a single input to one of two outputs or both the outputs.

DPDT relay has two pole and four contacts (either NC or NO or both). Both poles operate simultaneously, allowing control of two independent circuits.

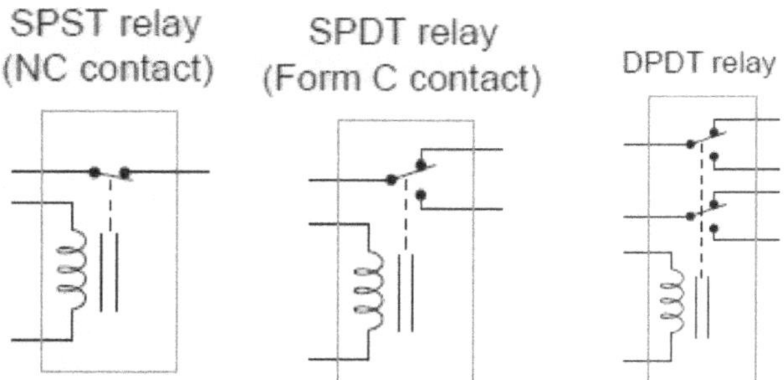

Fig 12.5 – SPST, SPDT, DPDT relay

10. What is latching relay?

Ans: A latching relay (also known as a bistable relay) is a type of relay that maintains its last switching state (ON or OFF) even after the control signal is removed. Unlike standard relays, it does not require continuous power to the coil to hold its state, which makes it energy-efficient.

It typically has two coils: Set Coil that energized to switch the relay to the ON position and reset Coil that energized to switch the relay back to the OFF position. Once the relay is latched, it stays in that state until an opposing pulse (from the reset coil) is applied.

11. What is time delay relay?

Ans: A time delay relay is a relay equipped with a timer that delays the opening or closing of its contacts after the relay coil is energized or de-energized.

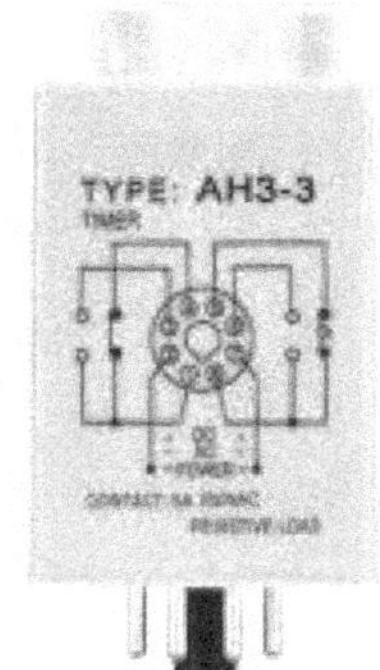

Fig 12.6 – Time delay relay

When the coil of relay gets energized, the timer starts and relay change the contacts after the completion of set time.

12. What are the different types of time delay relay?

Ans: Following are the different types of time delay relay:

- **On Delay Relay**: When power is applied to the relay coil, the timer starts counting. After the preset delay time has passed, the contacts change their state (e.g., from open to closed). This type is commonly used to turn a load on after a delay, such as in motor start sequences.

- **Off Delay Relay:** In this type, the contacts change state immediately when power is applied. However, when the power is removed, the timer begins counting. After the preset time has elapsed, the contacts return to their original state. This is useful when you want a device to keep running for a short time after power is turned off, such as an exhaust fan that runs briefly after a machine stops.

- **Interval time relay or Time pulse**: When the relay is energized, the contacts remain in the actuated state for a fixed period. After the preset time, they return to their normal state, regardless of whether the power is still applied. These are typically used when a device needs to be activated for a set time, such as a warning light or buzzer that stays on for a few seconds.

13. What is a level switch?

Ans: A level switch is one detecting the level of liquid or solid (granules or powder) in a vessel. Level switches often use floats as the level-sensing element, the motion of which actuates one or more switch contacts.

14. How is a float type level switch function?

Ans: A float type level switch is a device used to detect the level of liquid within a tank or vessel. It works based on the buoyancy principle, using a float that rises and falls with the liquid level.

It consists of a hollow float (usually made of stainless steel, plastic, or other buoyant material) is attached to a lever or rod. As the liquid level rises or falls, the float moves accordingly. When the float reaches a certain point, it triggers a switch to either open or close an electrical circuit, sending a signal for level control or alarm purposes.

15. What is a temperature switch?

Ans: A temperature switch is a device used to detect temperature and control a circuit based on that temperature. It activates or deactivates electrical contacts when a certain temperature level (called the set point) is reached.

One common type uses a bimetallic strip, which bends when the temperature changes. This bending motion is used to open or close the switch contacts. Another design uses a sealed metal bulb filled with a fluid. As the temperature rises, the fluid expands, increasing pressure. This pressure acts on a diaphragm or bellows, triggering the switch mechanism.

When the temperature reaches the set point, a physical or electrical change occurs in the sensing element. This causes the switch to either open or close the circuit, depending on how it's configured. Temperature switches are widely used in heating, cooling, and safety systems to control equipment based on temperature changes.

16. What is a flow switch?

Ans: A flow switch is one detecting the flow of some fluid through a pipe. Flow switches often use "paddles" as the flow-sensing element, the motion of which actuates one or more switch contacts.

Chapter: 13

Instrumentation Documents

1. What is process flow diagram (PFD)?

Ans: A Process Flow Diagram (PFD) is a visual representation that illustrates the relationships between major components within an industrial process. It includes process piping, major equipment, process stream names and operational data (pressure, temperature etc).

For e.g, water is being evaporated from a process solution under partial vacuum (provided by the compressor). The compressor then transports the vapours to a "knockout drum" where they condense into liquid form. As a typical PFD, this diagram shows the major interconnections of process vessels and equipment, but omits details such as instrument signal lines and auxiliary instruments.

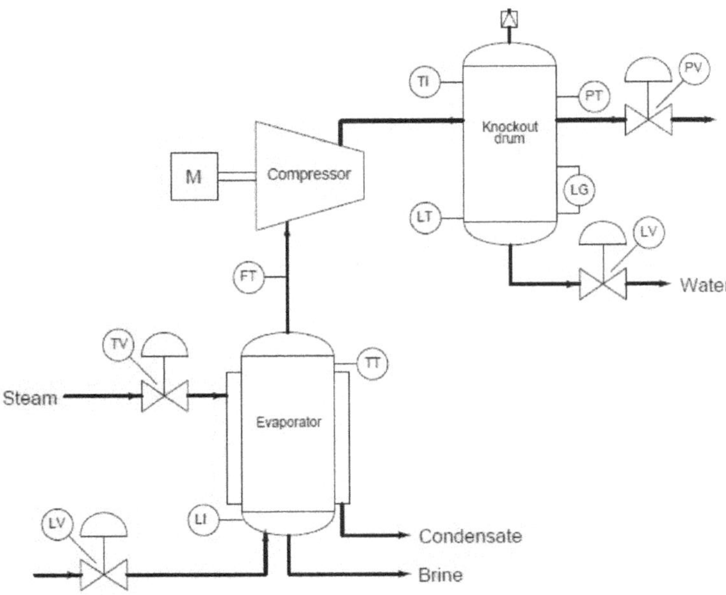

Fig 13.1 – Process Flow Diagram

2. What is process and Instrumentation drawing (P&ID)?

Ans: P&ID shows the layout of all relevant process vessels, pipes, and machinery, but with instruments superimposed on the diagram showing what gets measured and what gets controlled. Here, one can view the flow of the process as well as the "flow" of information between instruments measuring and controlling the process.

Below fig shows an example of P&ID

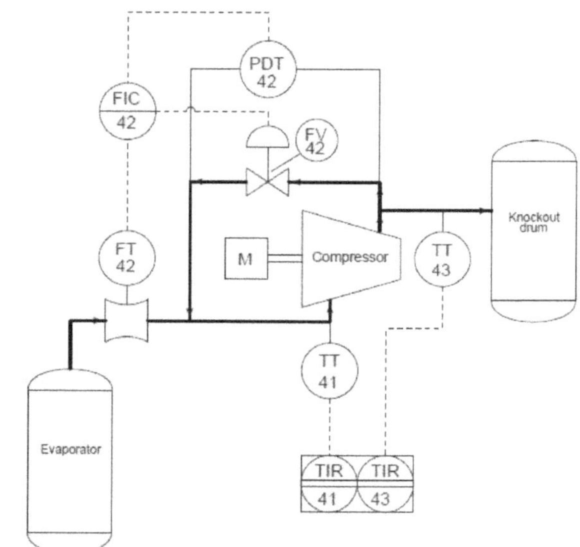

Fig 13.2 – P &ID

3. What is loop diagram?

Ans: Loop diagram is the proper form of fine details which includes all the wire numbers, terminal numbers, cable types, instrument calibration ranges, etc. Here, the process vessels and piping are sparsely represented, because the focus of the diagram is the instruments themselves.

In Loop diagrams field instruments are always placed on the left-hand side, while control-panel or control-room instruments must be located on the right-hand side. Text describing instrument tags, ranges, and notes are always placed on the bottom.

Below fig shows an example of Loop diagram:

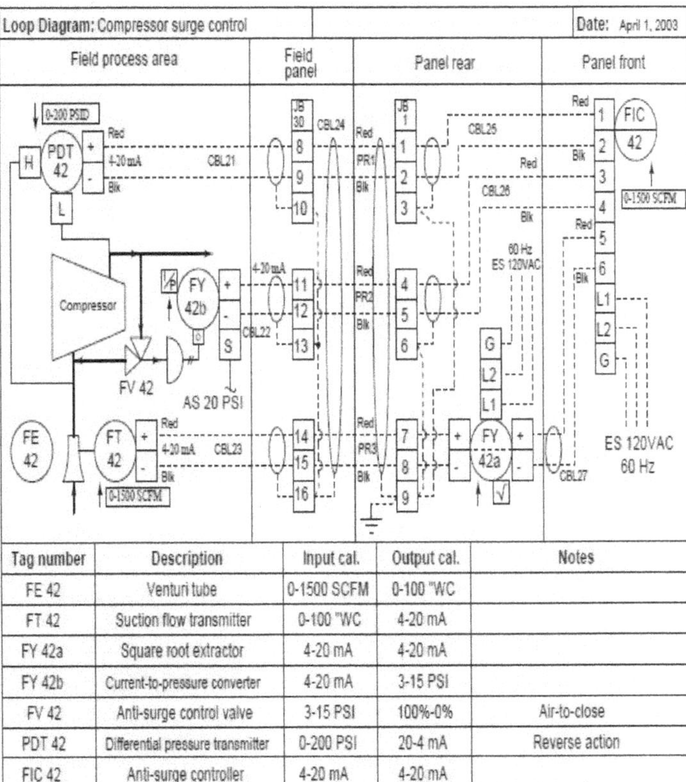

Fig 13.3 -Loop Diagram

Tag number	Description	Input cal.	Output cal.	Notes
FE 42	Venturi tube	0-1500 SCFM	0-100 "WC	
FT 42	Suction flow transmitter	0-100 "WC	4-20 mA	
FY 42a	Square root extractor	4-20 mA	4-20 mA	
FY 42b	Current-to-pressure converter	4-20 mA	3-15 PSI	
FV 42	Anti-surge control valve	3-15 PSI	100%-0%	Air-to-close
PDT 42	Differential pressure transmitter	0-200 PSI	20-4 mA	Reverse action
FIC 42	Anti-surge controller	4-20 mA	4-20 mA	

4. What is Functional diagram (FD)?

Ans: Functional diagrams are used to document the strategy of a control system. Functional diagrams focus on the flow of information within a control system rather than on the process piping or instrument interconnections (wires, tubes, etc.). The general flow of a functional diagram is top-to bottom, with the process sensing instrument (transmitter) located at the top and the final control element (valve or variable-speed motor) located at the bottom.

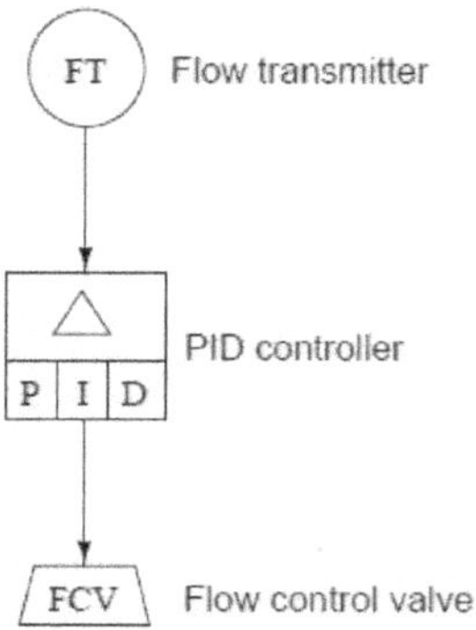

Fig 13.4 – Functional diagram

Above fig shows a functional diagram appears here, showing a flow transmitter (FT) sending a process variable signal to a PID controller, which then sends a manipulated variable signal to a flow control valve (FCV):

5. How different line types are represented in P&ID?

Ans: Below figure shows the different line representation:

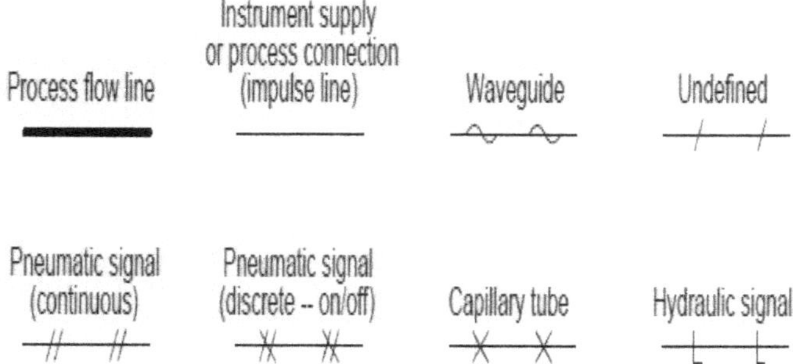

Fig 13.5 – Line representation for P&ID

6. How different process valves are represented in P&ID?

Ans: Below fig shows the representation of Process valve:

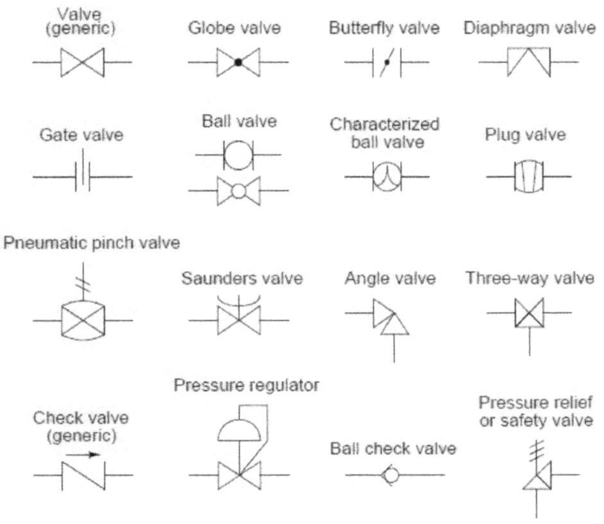

Fig 13.6 – Process valves

7. How different valve actuators represented in P&ID?

Ans: Below figure shows representation of different actuators:

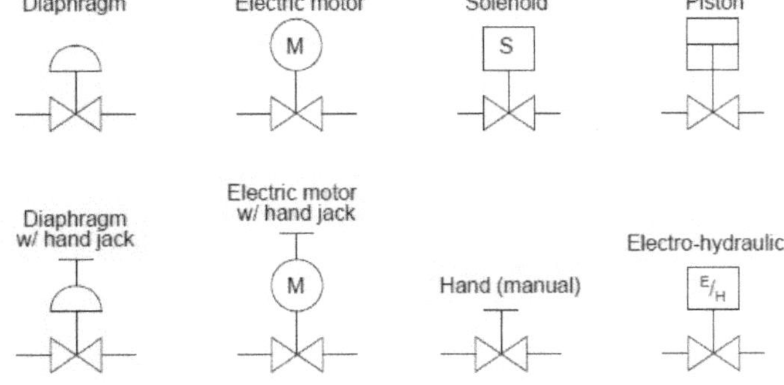

Fig 13.7 – Valve actuators

8. What is instrumentation hook up drawing?

Ans: It is a detailed drawing showing typical installation of an instrument in a correct manner so that the instrument operates properly and prevent issues which could potentially affect the measurement such as liquid trap in gas impulse.

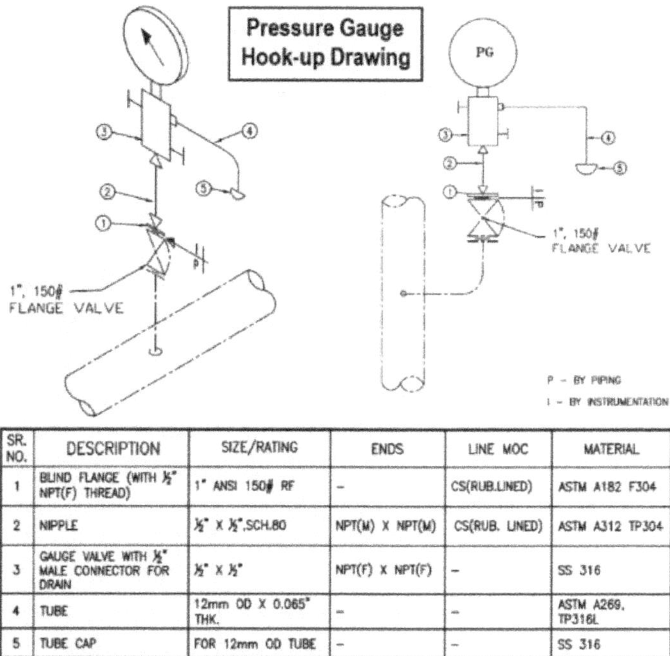

SR. NO.	DESCRIPTION	SIZE/RATING	ENDS	LINE MOC	MATERIAL
1	BLIND FLANGE (WITH ½" NPT(F) THREAD)	1" ANSI 150# RF	–	CS(RUB.LINED)	ASTM A182 F304
2	NIPPLE	½" X ½",SCH.80	NPT(M) X NPT(M)	CS(RUB. LINED)	ASTM A312 TP304
3	GAUGE VALVE WITH ½" MALE CONNECTOR FOR DRAIN	½" X ½"	NPT(F) X NPT(F)	–	SS 316
4	TUBE	12mm OD X 0.065" THK.	–	–	ASTM A269, TP316L
5	TUBE CAP	FOR 12mm OD TUBE	–	–	SS 316

Fig 13.8 -Hook up drawings

Hook-up drawing indicates tubing slopes, position of instrument in reference to process tapping point, scope break between instrument vs piping. Hook-up drawing also gives information the requirement of bulk material for each installation. It also details its specification (size, type and material) and the quantity.

During project construction phase, this drawing is also referred as a guidance of how to install the instrument properly.

The below diagram shows the required components and tubing for installation of a pressure gauge.

9. What is the difference between instrumentation hook up drawing and P&ID drawing?

Ans: P&ID drawing shows where to install an instrument in process line and Hook up drawing shows how to install an instrument correctly in a process line.

10. How do you verify that installed instrumentation meets the project requirements?

Ans: Verification involves reviewing approved data sheets, installation drawings, and manufacturer certificates to confirm correct model numbers, materials, and calibration ranges.

Inspections also cover physical installation details such as mounting orientation, accessibility, and weatherproofing. Functional testing and calibration checks confirm that each device's performance matches project specifications.

11. Why is loop checking important in instrumentation?

Ans: Loop checking ensures that the entire signal path from the field instrument, through wiring and marshalling, to the control system is correct and functioning as intended.

It identifies wiring mistakes, calibration errors, or defective components before the system is commissioned, preventing costly downtime or safety incidents later on.

12. How do you ensure proper grounding of electrical and instrumentation equipment?

Ans: Proper grounding involves confirming grounding conductors are correctly sized and installed, all metal parts are bonded together, and the grounding network meets project specifications and electrical code requirements. Inspections check continuity from equipment to earth, measure earth resistance with a ground resistance tester, and ensure corrosion-resistant connections.

13. What does a 'continuity test' involve, and when would you conduct it?

Ans: A continuity test verifies that an electrical path is complete, ensuring there are no breaks or loose connections in wiring or grounding. It's conducted before energizing cables, during loop checks, and when troubleshooting suspected open circuits.

A multimeter or dedicated continuity tester is typically used for this purpose.

14. What is a cable schedule? What is its significance?

Ans: A cable schedule lists all the cables used in a project, including cable type, length, routing, source, and destination terminals.

It is significant because it helps Instrumentation Engineers confirm correct cable installation, alignment with design drawings, labelling accuracy, and compliance with voltage or signal requirements.

15. What is the purpose of colour coding in instrument wiring?

Ans: Colour coding helps identify wire functions (e.g., power, return, signal, ground) or system usage (e.g., thermocouple leads). It reduces the likelihood of cross-connections or incorrect terminations.

16. What is the difference between a 'soft tag' and 'hard tag' for instruments?

Ans: A 'soft tag' is the logical identification used within control software or a database, while a 'hard tag' is the physical label attached to the instrument or cable. Example: For a pressure transmitter hard tag in field can be PT-1101 and in DCS soft tag can be 0PT1101

Chapter: 14

Pneumatic Instrumentation

1.   What is the range of pressure signal use in Pneumatic system?

Ans:- 3- 15 PSI and 0.1 to 1 kgf. A 3 PSI pressure value represents 0% of scale, a 15 PSI pressure value represents 100% of scale, and any pressure value in between 3 and 15 PSI represents a commensurate percentage in between 0% and 100%.

2.   What is a flapper nozzle mechanism?

Ans: A flapper nozzle mechanism is a key component in many pneumatic control systems. It is used to convert mechanical motion (usually from a force or displacement) into a pneumatic signal.

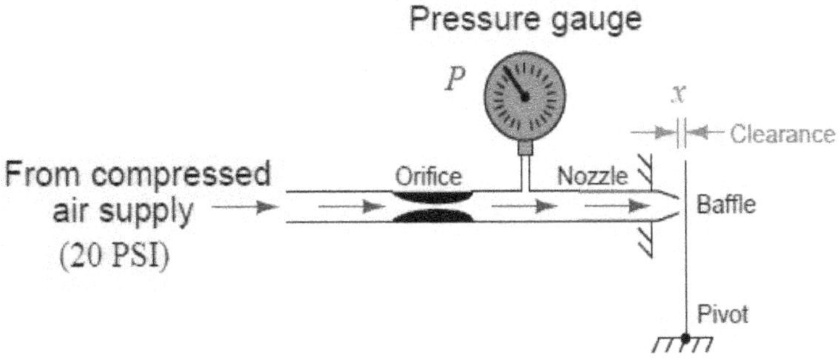

Fig 14.1 – Flapper nozzle mechanism

The system consists of two main parts: Flapper (a movable mechanical element) and a Nozzle (a small orifice through which air escapes). The flapper is pivoted at one end. When compressed air is supplied to the system, it tries to escape through the nozzle. The flapper is positioned close to the nozzle, and its distance from the nozzle controls how much air can escape.

When the flapper is far from the nozzle, more air escapes, resulting in low back pressure. When the flapper moves closer to the nozzle, it restricts air flow, causing increased back pressure in the nozzle chamber. This back pressure can then be used to operate pneumatic relays, valves, or other control elements.

3. What is a pneumatic relay?

Ans: A pneumatic relay is a device used in pneumatic control systems to amplify, reverse, or switch pneumatic signals. It functions similarly to an electronic relay but works using air pressure instead of electricity. A pneumatic relay takes a small, low-power air signal and uses it to control a larger flow of compressed air, thereby amplifying the signal or redirecting it.

4. What are the different types of pneumatic relay?

Ans: Following are the different types of pneumatic relay:

- *Volume Booster Relay*: It amplifies flow rate of air and used when a fast response is required from actuators.
- *Reverse-Acting Relay*: Outputs pressure that decreases when input pressure increases, and vice versa.
- *Positive Bias Relay*: It adds a constant pressure offset to the input signal.
- *Negative Bias Relay*: It subtracts a constant pressure offset from the input signal.
- *Differential Relay*: It compares two pressures and outputs based on their difference.

5. What is the working principle of pneumatic relay?

Ans: A pneumatic relay consists of a closed chamber, a pilot mechanism, a diaphragm for pressure sensing, and a continuous supply of compressed air. It is used to amplify or control pneumatic signals in response to small input pressure changes. The pilot mechanism is positioned in such a way that it controls the passage of air through the inlet and vent ports.

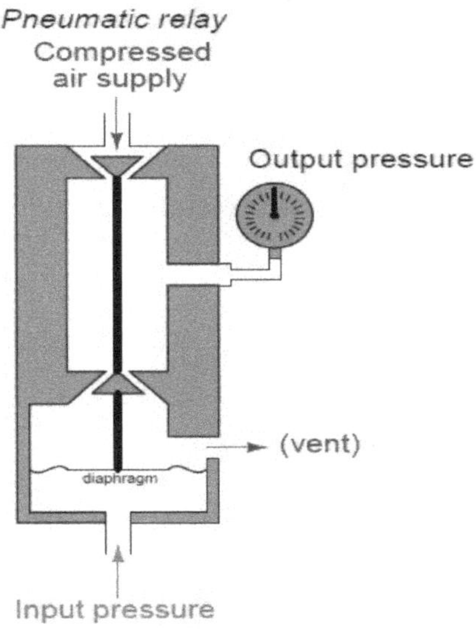

Fig 14.2 – Pneumatic relay

When input pressure is applied to the diaphragm, it causes the piston mechanism to move slightly upward. This movement allows more compressed air to enter the chamber through the inlet, and restricts the air flow through the vent port. As a result, the pressure inside the chamber increases, which leads to a corresponding increase in output pressure. With a further increase in input pressure, the piston mechanism moves further upward, allowing even more compressed air to enter and further increasing the output pressure.

6. What is the self-balancing concept in pneumatic instruments?
Ans: The self-balancing concept in pneumatic instruments is a design principle where the system automatically maintains a steady output by adjusting itself based on the input. This is done through negative feedback, meaning the system reacts to changes by correcting them to bring everything back to balance.

The self-balancing concept can be understood by comparing it to a mass balance beam, where the weight in one pan is counterbalanced by an equal weight in the other pan. In pneumatic instruments, this balance is achieved using a combination of mechanical parts and pneumatic components. The system typically consists of a mass balance beam, bellows, a pneumatic relay, a nozzle-flapper mechanism, and a compressed air supply.

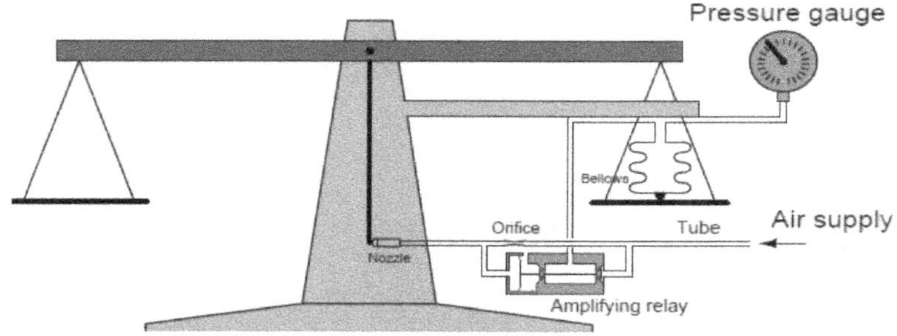

Fig 14.3 – Self balancing in pneumatic instruments

One side of the beam (pan) contains the flapper-nozzle arrangement connected to a bellows. The other side of the beam is used for placing a weight, which represents the input signal (e.g., a process variable or setpoint). When a weight is placed or increased on the input pan, the beam tips, causing the flapper to move closer to the nozzle. This reduces the nozzle gap, generating back pressure. The back pressure acts as the input signal for the pneumatic relay. The pneumatic relay responds by generating an amplified output pressure, which is supplied to the bellows. The bellows expand, adding force to their side of the beam and restoring balance. The degree of expansion (and therefore the pressure) in the bellows corresponds to the weight placed on the input pan. This pressure can be measured using a pressure gauge, allowing for a calibrated readout of the input signal.

The pneumatic relay ensures fast response and amplification of the weak back pressure signal, making the system more sensitive and responsive. This mechanism achieves self-balancing, as the system continuously adjusts itself to maintain equilibrium between the input weight and the feedback force from the bellows.

7. What is the function of I/P Converter? How it works?

Ans: An I/P converter (current-to-pressure converter) is a device used to convert an electrical current signal (typically 4-20 mA) into a proportional pneumatic output pressure signal (usually in the range of 3-15 psi or 0.2-1 bar). I/P converters are commonly where electronic control signals need to be translated into pneumatic signals to operate control valves, dampers, or other pneumatic devices.

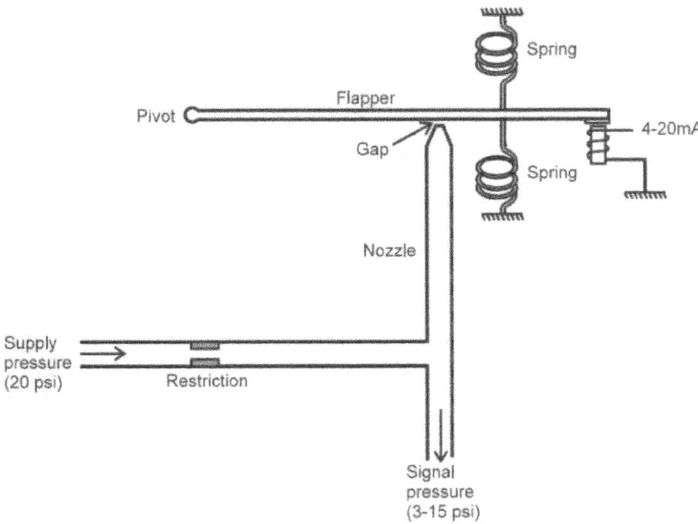

Fig 14.4 – I/P converter

It works on Flapper-Nozzle method. It consists of a Flapper, nozzle and electromagnet. The Flapper of the Flapper-Nozzle instrument is connected to Pivot so that it can move up and down and a magnetic material was attached to other end of flapper and it is kept near the electromagnet. A regulated supply of pressure, usually 20 psi, provides a source of air through the restriction. The nozzle is open at the end where the gap exists between the nozzle and flapper, and air escapes in this region. As the magnet gets activated, due to increase in current signal, the flapper moves towards the electromagnet and the nozzle gets closed to some extent. So, some part of 20 P.S.I supplied will escape through nozzle and remaining pressure will come as output. With the increase in current signal, the power of the magnet will increase, then flapper will move closer to the nozzle, so less pressure will escape through nozzle and output pressure increases. The force generated by the magnetic coil modulates the flapper nozzle mechanism, allowing a specific amount of compressed air to pass through. In this way the output pressure will be proportional to the input current.

8.   How flapper nozzle mechanism can be used as P/I Converter?

Ans: For P/I converter in flapper nozzle mechanism, LVDT can be used in place of electromagnet. A P/I converter (pressure-to-current converter) works on the opposite principle of an I/P converter, converting a pneumatic pressure signal (typically 3-15 psi) into an equivalent electrical current signal (usually 4-20 mA).

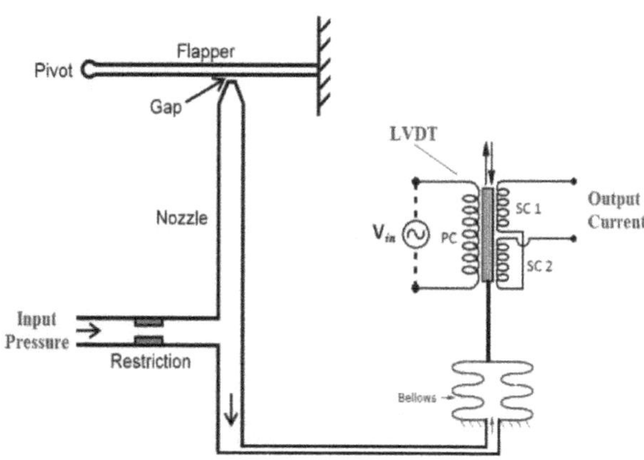

Fig 14.5 – P/I converter

Input pressure is supplied to the Flapper- Nozzle arrangement. Then it will supply through a pipe and that pressure is given as input to the bellows. These bellows are connected to the Core of LVDT. When pressure is applied to bellows, they will expand thus core displaces and the voltage is induced on the secondary coils of LVDT. As voltage is induced, current will flow through the coil. That current is proportional to the input pressure applied. Thus, Pressure is converted into equivalent current.

9.   Explain the working principle of Pneumatic transmitter.

Ans: When the pressure applied on the "High pressure" input port, the large diaphragm capsule is forced to the right.

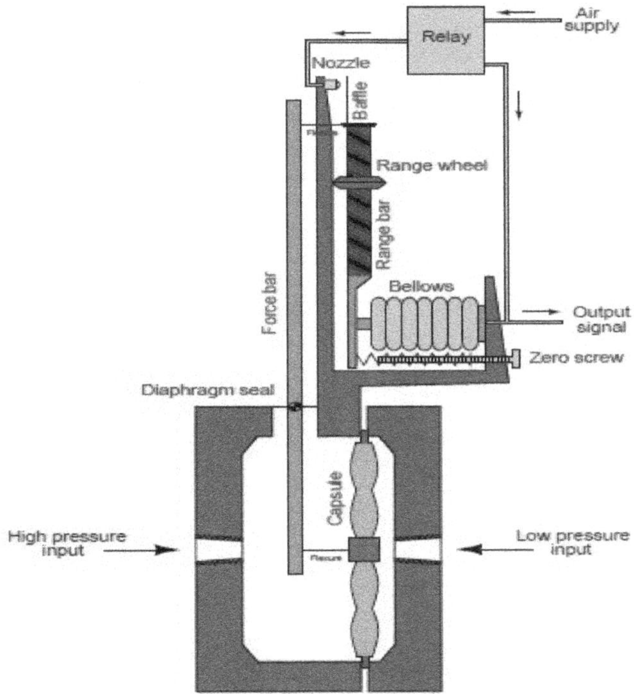

Fig 14.6 – Pneumatic instruments

The same effect would occur if the pressure on the "Low pressure" input port were to decrease. This resultant motion of the capsule tugs on the thin flexure connecting it to the force bar. The force bar pivots at the fulcrum (where the small diaphragm seal is located) in a counter-clockwise rotation, tugging the flexure at the top of the force bar. This motion causes the range bar to also pivot at its fulcrum (the sharp-edged "range wheel"), moving the flapper closer to the nozzle.

As the flapper approaches the nozzle, air flow through the nozzle becomes more restricted, accumulating backpressure in the nozzle. This backpressure increase is greatly amplified in the relay, sending an increasing air pressure signal both to the output line and to the bellows at the bottom of the range bar. Increasing pneumatic pressure in the bellows causes it to push harder on the bottom of the range bar, negating the initial motion and returning the range bar (and force bar) to their near-original position

10. What is air filter regulator?

Ans: An air filter regulator is a pneumatic device used to condition compressed air before it enters sensitive control instruments or actuators. It combines two essential functions:

- Air filtration – to remove dust, oil, moisture, and other contaminants
- Pressure regulation – to maintain a steady and precise output pressure regardless of fluctuations in supply pressure.

11. What are the precautions to be taken for the pneumatic system?

Ans: Following precautions to be taken for ensuring reliable and long-lasting operation of pneumatic systems:

- Always use filtered and dried compressed air, with automatic air dryers in the system. As contaminants like dirt, rust, oil, and especially moisture can clog tiny orifices and nozzles inside pneumatic instruments.

- Always use local pressure regulators to ensure each instrument gets air at the correct pressure, regardless of line fluctuations.
- Install instruments in vibration-isolated or well-supported locations, away from heavy machinery or unstable mounting points. As Pneumatic instruments are precision mechanical devices, sensitive to movement. Vibration can shift calibration or even break components.

12. What are the advantages and disadvantages of pneumatic system?

Ans: Following are the advantages of pneumatic system-

- Pneumatic instruments do not use electricity, so they cannot produce sparks, making them ideal for explosive or flammable environments.
- Constant bleeding of compressed air creates a positive internal pressure, keeping dust, moisture, and vapors out, and keeping the inside of the instrument clean even in dirty environments.
- Pneumatic instruments are naturally resistant to heat and radiation, unlike electronic instruments which may require special hardening.

Following are the disadvantages of pneumatic system-

- Pneumatic instruments are more sensitive to vibration, temperature changes, and mounting position, which can cause inaccuracies in calibration.
- Compressed air is more expensive than electricity per unit energy, and installation requires special tubing (stainless steel, copper, or plastic) which increases overall cost.
- Long air tube runs act like low-pass filters, slowing response time, and pneumatic instruments cannot be made "smart" (no diagnostics or digital communication).

13. What is a Pneumatic Cylinder?

Ans: Pneumatic Cylinder is a mechanical device that uses compressed air to produce linear motion (movement in a straight line). When air enters the cylinder, it pushes against a piston inside, causing the piston rod to extend or retract, depending on which side the air pressure is applied. Pneumatic cylinders are widely used in industries for automation tasks like lifting, pressing, clamping, and moving parts because they are simple, fast, reliable, and safe to operate.

14. What is the importance of an air dryer in a Pneumatic System?

Ans: In pneumatic systems, compressed air often contains moisture. If this moisture is not removed, it travels through pipes and enters sensitive instruments like pneumatic positioners and control valves. Over time, accumulated water can cause corrosion, sticking, freezing, and malfunctioning of these devices. An air dryer removes moisture from compressed air, ensuring reliable and long-term performance of pneumatic equipment, preventing failures, and reducing maintenance costs.

Chapter:15

Valves and Actuators

1. Mention the different types of valves used in process application.

Ans: Ball valve, Gate Valve, Plug Valve, Butterfly Valve, Globe Valve, Pinch Valve, Disc Check valve.

2. What is ball valve? Mention its features.

Ans: A ball valve is a type of valve that uses a rotating ball with a hole through its centre to control fluid flow. It's a quarter-turn valve, meaning it only requires a 90-degree turn to open or close. When the valve is open, the ball's hole aligns with the valve body's ports, allowing fluid to flow. When the valve is closed, the ball rotates, blocking the flow path and sealing the valve.

Fig 15.1 – Ball valve

Advantages:
- Low maintenance
- Quick operation.
- Bi-directional flow control.

Disadvantages
- Limited throttling capabilities.

Applications:

Ball valves are mostly used in shutoff applications. Ball valves are commonly used in steam, water, oil, gas, air, corrosive fluids. They can handle slurries and dusty dry fluids. Ball valves are not used with abrasive and fibrous materials as it poses risk of damage to the seat and plug surface.

3. What is gate valve? Mention its features.

Ans: A gate valve is a type of valve that controls fluid flow by lifting a gate (or disc) out of the fluid's path. It's a linear motion valve, typically operated by a handwheel or electric actuator.

Gate valve should ideally be used as on-off valve. It is not advisable to use them as throttling valves because in partly open conditions, erosion of gate might take place. In partially open conditions, due to vibrations, valve is exposed to quick wear and tear. Also, during closing and opening, there is considerable amount of friction and hence, opening and closing these vales quickly and frequently is not possible.

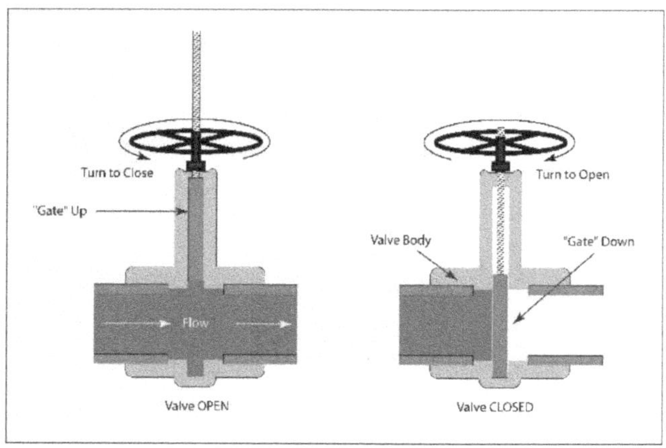

Fig 15.2 – Gate valve

4. What is Plug valve? Mention its features.

Ans: This valve consists of a plug which can be either cylindrical or conical in shape. The plug has a through slit which remains in-line with the flow in the open condition. When the plug is turned by 90

Deg., this slit becomes perpendicular to flow and the valve gets closed.

Plug valves are primarily used for on-off applications. When used for throttling purpose, the pressure drop through the valve is higher because of misalignment between flow direction and the direction of the opening (slit).

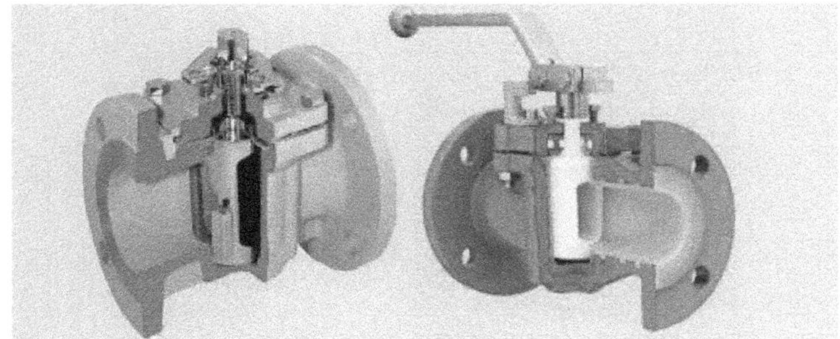

Fig 15.3 – Plug valve

5. What is butterfly valve? Mention its features.

Ans: A butterfly valve is quarter turn operated valves commonly used in industrial applications to regulate or isolate fluid flow.

Fig 15.4- Butterfly valve

It consists of a circular disc (the "butterfly") that is mounted on a rotating shaft. When the valve is fully closed, the disc blocks the flow entirely, and when it's open, the disc is turned so that fluid can pass through the valve. It can be opened or closed quickly by rotating the disc 90 degrees. Compared to other types of valves, butterfly valves are generally smaller and lighter.

In the open condition there is minimum obstruction to the fluid flow through the valve as the flow passes around the disc aerodynamically. This results in very less pressure drop through the valve.

6. What is globe valve? Mention its features.

Ans: A globe valve is a type of valve used for regulating the flow of a fluid (liquid or gas) in a pipeline. It gets its name from its spherical body shape and is designed to offer good throttling capabilities, making it effective for controlling flow. It consists of a movable plug or disc that fits against a stationary ring seat inside the valve body. The flow enters below the seat and exits through an opening above it.

Due to its design, globe valves tend to create more pressure drop in the system compared to valves with a straight flow path. Commonly used in systems where flow needs to be regulated, such as cooling systems, fuel oil systems, and high-pressure steam lines.

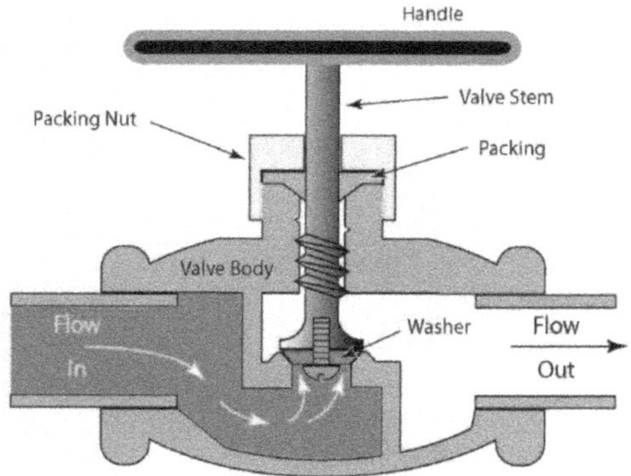

Fig 15.5 – Globe valve

7. What is needle valve? Mention its features.

Ans: A needle valve is a type of valve used to precisely control the flow of fluid in small systems. It is similar in function to a globe valve but is designed for finer adjustments in flow. The valve body typically has a small port and a threaded, slender plunger that fits into this port to open and close the valve. As the valve stem is turned, the needle either moves further into or out of the seat, adjusting the flow path.

Needle valves are suited for controlling low flow rates of fluids or gases because of the small passageways inside the valve. These valves are typically used for applications requiring accurate, low flow rates and are common in instrumentation, calibration, and flow metering systems.

Fig 15.6 – Needle valve

8. What is disc check valve?
Ans: Disc check valves, also called as non-return valves allow the flow to pass through them in only one direction and stop the flow in reverse direction.

9. What are the Industrial Applications of Gate Valve, Globe Valve, Ball Valve, Plug Valve, Diaphragm Valve, Buterfly Valves, Check Valves and Safety/Relief valve, thermal relief valve?
Ans*: **Gate valves** are generally used in systems where low flow resistance for a fully open valve is desired and there is no need to throttle the flow.

Globe valves are used in systems where good throttling characteristics and low seat leakage are desired and a relatively high head loss in an open valve is acceptable.

Ball valves allow quick, quarter turn on-off operation and have poor throttling characteristics.

Plug valves are often used to direct flow between several different ports through use of a single valve.

Diaphragm valves and pinch valves are used in systems where it is desirable for the entire operating mechanism to be completely isolated from the fluid.

Butterfly valves provide significant advantages over other valve designs in weight, space, and cost for large valve applications.

Check valves automatically open to allow flow in one direction and seat to prevent flow in the reverse direction.

Safety/relief valve are used to provide automatic over pressurization protection for a system.

Thermal relief Valve is typically used to relieve over pressure due to thermal expansion of liquid in pipelines.

10. Which are the multi turn Valve?

Ans: Gate, Globe, Pinch, Needle, Diaphragm.

11. Which are the quarter turn valve?

Ans: Ball, Butterfly, Plug

12. Which is the self-actuated valve?

Ans: Check and Relief valve

13. What is a Control Valve?

Ans: A control valve is a power-operated used to regulate or manipulate the flow of fluids, such as gas, oil, water, and steam. It is a critical part of a control loop and is an example of a final control element.

14. Mention the different parts of control valve.

Ans: Following are the parts of control valves:

Actuator: This part of the valve is for controlling purposes. An actuator may be a manually operated hand wheel, manual lever, motor operator, solenoid operator, pneumatic operator, or hydraulic.

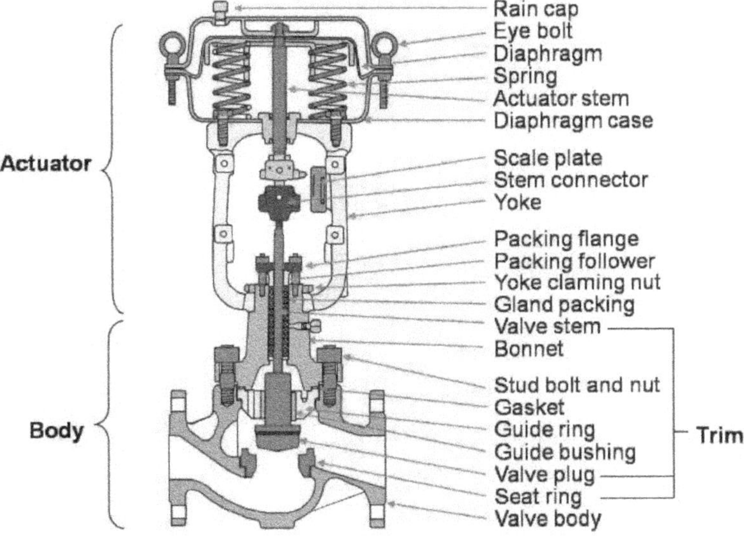

Fig 15.7 – Control valve parts

- ***Rain Cap***: The purpose of a rain cap in a valve actuator is to protect the actuator from rain, dust, and debris, preventing moisture and contaminants from entering and potentially damaging the internal components.
- ***Eye Bolt***: It is used as hook for moving the valve.
- ***Diaphragm***: It is a flexible membrane, usually made of rubber or a synthetic material. It receives air pressure (in pneumatic actuators) or hydraulic pressure (in hydraulic actuators) and flexes accordingly. This movement is transmitted to the valve stem, which opens or closes the valve.
- ***Spring***: The spring provides a restoring force that opposes the diaphragm movement. It ensures the valve returns to a fail-safe position when control air pressure is lost.
- ***Diaphragm Case***: These are the parts that are used for packing

Diaphragm plate.

- **Scale Plate:** It is used for indication of the position of the valve between 0-100%.
- **Stem Connector:** It is the link between them for Actuator Stem and Plug Stem.
- **Yoke:** It is a component that is used for connecting sections of the Actuator and Valve Body.

Body Part: Part of Body Valve is included in the Bonnet valve with which this segment is exposed to the fluid (fluid) directly.

- **Packing Flange:** It is used for compression of the stud bolt to make the most of all the Gland Packing tight and fluid cannot leak out of the neck Bonnet.
- **Packing Follower:** It is the strength of Packing Flange. A metal sleeve that compresses the packing.
- **Yoke Claim Nut:** It secures the yoke in a valve actuator, ensuring proper alignment and stability of the actuator to the valve.
- **Gland Packing:** It is a sealing material around the valve stem, inside the bonnet. It prevents fluid leakage along the stem while still allowing it to move. It is made up of PTFE (Teflon), graphite, asbestos, or modern composite materials.
- **Valve Stem:** The valve stem is a rod that connects the actuator to the valve plug. It transfers motion from the actuator to open, close, or throttle the valve. It is made up of stainless steel.
- **Bonnet:** The bonnet is the top cover of the valve body. It provides a pressure-tight enclosure and guides/supports the valve stem. It Houses the gland packing and allows stem motion.
- **Stud Bolt and Nut:** These are used to join two components securely. The stud bolt is a threaded rod, and nuts are tightened on each end to hold the parts together, commonly used in flanged connections.
- **Gasket:** A gasket is a seal placed between two stationary surfaces , typically between the valve body and bonnet. Its job is to prevent leakage of process fluid. It is made from

compressed fiber, graphite, PTFE and must withstand temperature, pressure, and chemical exposure of the process.

- **_Guide Ring_**: A guide ring keeps the valve stem or valve plug aligned properly inside the valve. It prevents sideways movement, ensuring smooth linear travel and reducing wear. Often located inside the bonnet or within the valve body.

- **_Guide Bushing_**: It is used for supporting Guide Ring.

- **_Valve Plug_**: The valve plug is the part that modulates flow inside the valve. It's attached to the valve stem and moves in relation to the seat ring to control flow. It determines the flow properties as Linear, Equal Percentage or Quick Opening.

- **_Seat Ring or valve seat_**: The seat ring is the sealing surface against which the plug rests to stop flow completely.

- **_Valve body_**: It is the primary pressure boundary of a valve. It serves as the principal element of a valve assembly because it is the framework that holds everything together. The body, the first pressure boundary of a valve, resists fluid pressure loads from connecting piping. It receives inlet and outlet piping through threaded, bolted, or welded joints.

15. What is a Single-Seated and Double-Seated Control Valve?

Ans: A single-seated control valve has one plug and one seat. The plug moves up and down to control the flow, creating a tight seal when closed. These valves provide better shutoff capability because there's only one sealing surface, which allows for minimal leakage.

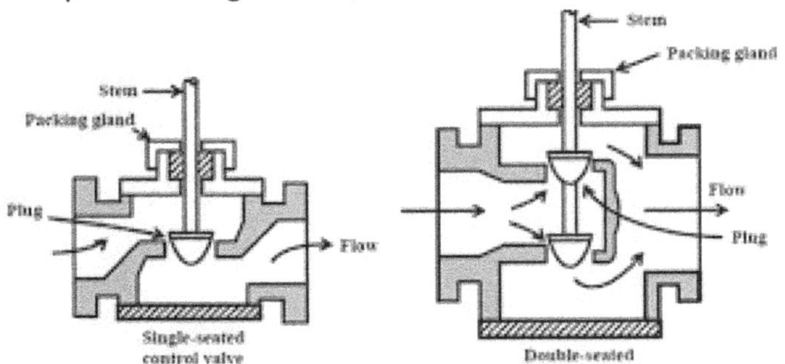

Fig 15.8 – Single seated and double seated control valves

A double-seated control valve has two plugs and two seats arranged in opposite directions. This design helps balance the hydraulic forces acting on the plugs, making it easier to open and close under high-pressure conditions.

Single-seated valves are preferred when tight shutoff is required and Double-seated valves are used when handling high-pressure differentials and larger flows, but with less critical shutoff requirements.

16. Which is the material used in valve gland packing? What are its important properties?

Ans: The two most common packing materials in use today are Teflon (PTFE) and graphite. Teflon is the better of the two with regard to fluid sealing, stem friction, and stem wear5. Teflon is also quite resistant to attack from a wide variety of chemical substances. Unfortunately, it has a limited temperature range and cannot withstand intense nuclear radiation (making it unsuitable for use near reactors in nuclear power plants).

Graphite is another self-lubricating packing material, and it has a far greater temperature range than Teflon6 as well as the ability to withstand harsh nuclear radiation, but creates much more stem friction than Teflon. Graphite packing also has the unfortunate property of permitting galvanic corrosion between the stem and bonnet metals due to its electrical conductivity.

17. What is valve seat leakage classification?

Ans: Valve seat leakage classification defines how much a control valve is allowed to leak when it is supposed to be fully closed. Each class specifies a maximum allowable leakage rate, based on the valve size, seat design, and test pressure.

Class	Description	Leak Rate (typical for 1" valve)	Notes
I	No test required		Basic commercial quality
II	Minimal leakage	0.5% of full capacity	Often achievable without lapping
III	Tight shutoff	0.1% of full capacity	Requires better machining
IV	Metal-to-metal seat (standard)	~0.01% of full capacity	Common for control valves
V	Tight metal seat	5×10^{-3} ml/min per psi per inch of dia.	Higher tightness than IV
VI	Soft seat / bubble-tight	≤ 0.15 ml/min of air (per size limits)	For air/gas service, soft seats used

Class IV: Sufficient for most standard process control with metal seats.

Class VI: Required where leakage could be dangerous, or zero leakage is specified.

18. What is the bubble test used for Class VI seat leakage?

Ans: The "bubble test" used for Class VI seat leakage is based on the leakage rate of air or nitrogen gas past the closed valve seat as measured by counting the rate of gas bubbles escaping a bubble tube submerged under water. For a 6-inch valve, this maximum bubble rate is 27 bubbles per minute. Class VI shut-off is often achievable only through the use of "soft" seat materials such as Teflon rather than hard metal-to-metal contact between the valve plug and seat.

19. What is the valve flow coefficient (Cv) of a control valve?

Ans: The valve flow coefficient (Cv) is a numerical value that measures a control valve's ability to allow a liquid or gas to flow through it.

It is defined as the volume of water (in Gallon) at 60°F that will flow through a fully open valve with a pressure differential of 1 psi across the valve. Its unit is Gallon per meter (GPM).

If a valve has a Cv of 10, it means 10 GPM of water will flow through it with a 1 psi pressure drop.

20. What is the significance of valve flow coefficient (Cv)?

Ans: It is a crucial factor in valve sizing, as it helps determine the appropriate valve size for optimal performance.

21. Which factor should be considered while selecting a control valve for a process?

Ans: The type of fluid, the pressure drops across the valve, and the desired flow rate should be taken into account when selecting a control valve.

22. Why is control valve sizing so important?

Ans: An undersized valve has restricted flow capacity and could potentially cause a higher pressure drop across the valve, leading to poor performance and potential harm to the system.

An oversized valve is very sensitive to process operating conditions. Even the smallest changes in valve position will cause significant changes in inflow. This makes it difficult or even impossible for the valve to the exact tune of the required flow.

23. What is a valve actuator?

Ans: A valve actuator is a device that operates a valve, controlling the flow of fluids (liquids, gases, or steam) in a system.

24. What are the different types of actuators?

Ans: Pneumatic actuators, Hydraulic Actuators, Electric Actuators, Mechanical actuators and Smart actuators.

- Pneumatic actuators: Use compressed air or gas to operate the valve.
- Electric Actuators: Use electric motors to operate the valve.
- Hydraulic Actuators: Use liquid fluid pressure to operate the valve.
- Mechanical Actuators: Use levers, gears, or linkages to operate the valve.
- Smart Actuators: Intelligent, microprocessor-controlled actuators.

25. Explain the working of pneumatic actuators.

Ans: A pneumatic actuator works by using the combined action of air pressure and spring force to position a control valve. Inside the actuator, a flexible rubber diaphragm divides the housing into two chambers. The upper chamber receives compressed air through an inlet at the top, while the lower chamber holds a spring that pushes upward against the diaphragm.

Attached to the diaphragm is a stem that transmits the diaphragm's motion directly to the valve, allowing it to open or close. A local position indicator is also connected to the stem to show the current position of the valve. The movement of the valve is controlled by adjusting the supply air pressure to the upper chamber. When there is no air pressure, the spring pushes the diaphragm upward, which in turn moves the valve to the fully open position, resting against the upper mechanical stops.

As air pressure is gradually applied, the force from the compressed air starts to overcome the spring force. This pushes the diaphragm downward, causing the valve to close. The more air pressure applied, the more the diaphragm moves down, and the more the valve closes. When the supply pressure is reduced, the spring pushes the diaphragm back upward, allowing the valve to open again.

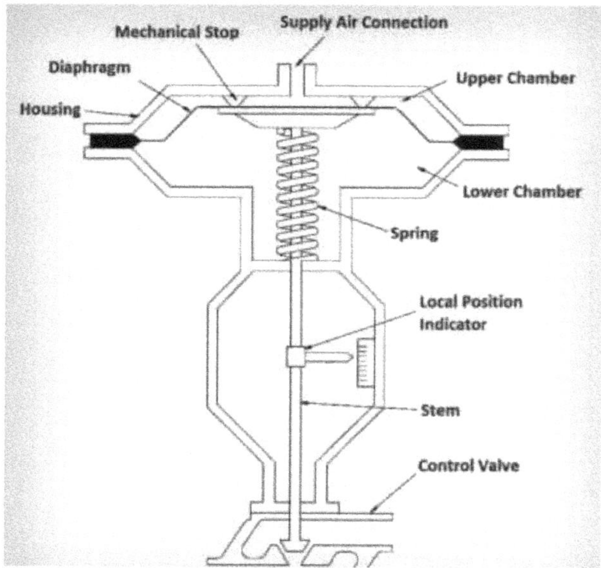

Fig 15.9 – Pneumatic actuators

By adjusting the air pressure somewhere between zero and the maximum, the diaphragm can settle at an intermediate position, allowing the valve to be partially open or closed. This enables precise control of flow, making pneumatic actuators ideal for throttling applications.

26. Explain the working principle of Hydraulic Actuator.

Ans: A hydraulic actuator uses hydraulic pressure and spring force to operate a control valve. The actuator typically consists of a cylinder, piston, spring, hydraulic supply and return line, and a stem that connects to the valve.

Inside the cylinder, the piston moves vertically and divides it into two chambers. The upper chamber houses the spring, while the lower chamber is filled with hydraulic oil. Hydraulic fluid enters and exits this lower chamber through the connected supply and return lines.

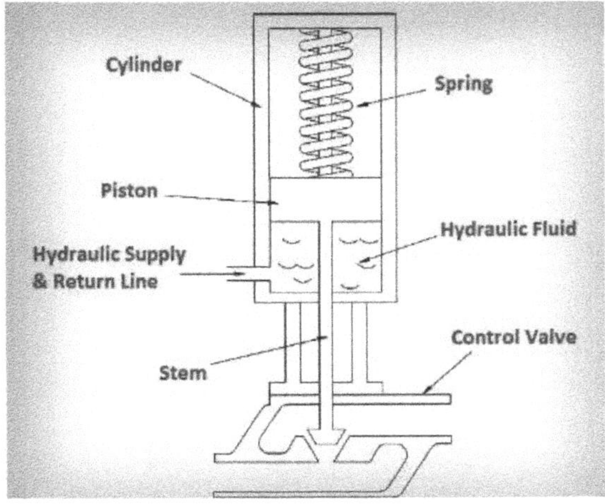

Fig 15.10 – Hydraulic actuators

The stem, attached to the piston, transfers its motion to the valve. When there is no hydraulic pressure, the spring in the upper chamber pushes the piston downward, keeping the valve in the closed position. As hydraulic fluid flows into the lower chamber, the pressure begins to rise, creating an upward force on the bottom of the piston. When this hydraulic force exceeds the spring force, the piston starts to move upward, compressing the spring and causing the valve to open.

The more the hydraulic pressure increases, the further the valve opens. If the fluid is gradually drained from the lower chamber, the hydraulic pressure decreases. Once it becomes less than the spring force, the spring pushes the piston back down, and the valve closes. By carefully controlling the amount of hydraulic fluid supplied or drained, the actuator can position the valve anywhere between fully open and fully closed, allowing for precise flow control.

27. What is the difference between Hydraulic actuator and Pneumatic actuator in application.

Ans: When a large amount of force is required to operate a valve (for example, the main steam system valves), hydraulic actuators are normally used.

Pneumatic actuators are normally used to control processes requiring quick and accurate response, as they do not require a large amount of motive force.

28. Explain the working principle of Electric Motor actuator.

Ans: It consists of an electric motor, clutch and gear box assembly, manual handwheel, and stem connected to a valve. The motor moves the stem through the gear assembly. The motor reverses its rotation to either open or close the valve. The clutch and clutch lever disconnects the electric motor from the gear assembly and allows the valve to be operated manually with the handwheel.

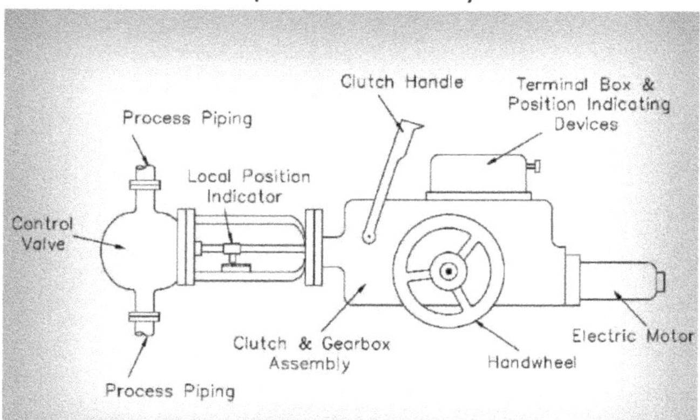

Fig 15.11 – Electric motor actuators

29. What is the function of Limit Switches and Torque limiters in Motor operated actuators?

Ans: Limit switches de-energize the electric motor when the valve has reached a specific position.

Torque limiters de-energize the electric motor when the amount of turning force has reached a specified value. The turning force normally is greatest when the valve reaches the fully open or fully closed position. This feature can also prevent damage to the actuator or valve if the valve binds in an intermediate position.

30. Explain the working principle of self operated control valve?

Ans: Self-operated valves are a type of control valve that regulate pressure, or flow without the need for external power or control signals (like electricity, compressed air, or control systems). Instead, they operate using the process fluid that may be directly tubed to the actuating element (diaphragm or piston).

An externally-loaded pressure regulator, using a source of external gas pressure from upstream tries to force the plug off the seat, while "feedback" gas pressure from the downstream side of the valve acts against a flexible diaphragm to move the plug toward the seat.

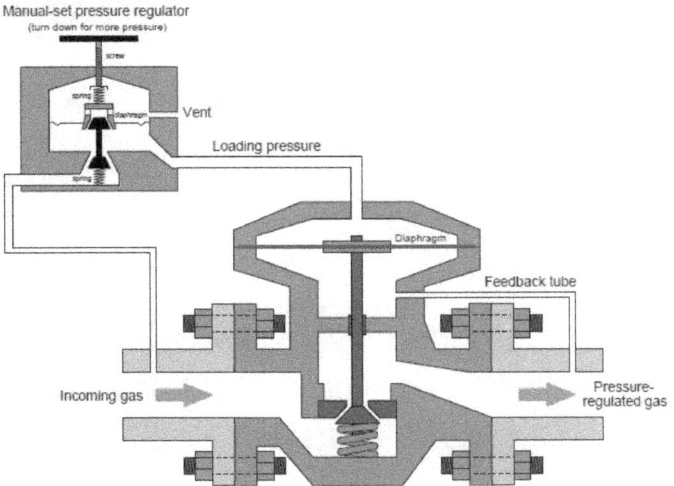

Fig 15.12 – Self operated control valves

The less downstream pressure, the more the trim opens up; the more downstream pressure, the more the trim shuts off. This loading pressure is easily adjusted by turning the knob on the manual-set pressure regulator, the main regulator now becomes adjustable as well. The pilot mechanism controls the main gas throttling mechanism.

31. What is double acting and single acting actuator?

Ans: The single acting actuator is actuated by air on one side while on the other side it moves with help of a spring or membrane. Therefore, only one side of the actuator needs to be pressurized.

The double-acting actuator only uses one piston as an element to operate the valve, therefore, the actuator must be pressurized alternately from both sides to operate the valve.

32. Under what conditions Single acting actuator is used?

Ans: In most of application, that require the valve to become in close position or in open position when the signal or the supply is lost, then the Single acting actuator is used.

33. Under What conditions Double acting actuator is used?

Ans: In some applications that require the valve to become in last position when the signal or the supply is lost, then the Double acting actuator is used.

34. What is fail safe action in Control Valve?

Ans: A fail safety system is how the valve should operate when there is a loss of power or signal. The valve's fail position is a safety precaution that protects the process in emergency situations.

Fail Open or Air to Close: Fail open means a valve would open at a loss of signal or power. These types of valves require air pressure to stay closed. Once the required air pressure is gone, the valve will naturally open, under the action of spring mechanism. In this type of valve, spring is under the piston which forces the piston up and forces the valve open and air supply is provided above piston. These types of valves are called air to close or normally open valve or direct acting valve.

Fail Close or Air to Open: Fail close means a valve would close at a loss of signal or power. These types of valves require air pressure to stay opened. Once the required air pressure is gone, the valve will naturally close. In this type of valve, spring is over the piston which forces the piston down and forces the valve close and air supply is provided below piston. These types of valves are called air to open or normally close valve or reverse acting valve.

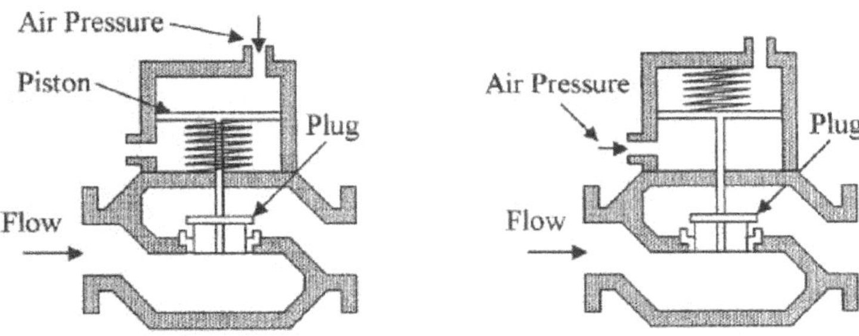

Fig 15.13 – Fail open & fail close valve

35. What are the flow characteristics of a control valve?

Ans: Control valve has inherent flow characteristic, which describes the relationship between the flow rate and valve travel. As a valve opens, the flow characteristic, which is inherent to the design of the selected valve, allows a certain amount of flow through the valve at a particular percentage of the stroke. There are three most common types of flow characteristics: **a. *Linear, b. Equal Percentage, c. Quick opening.***

36. Explain the flow characteristics: Linear, Equal percentage and Quick opening.

Ans: ***Linear valve characteristics***: This characteristic provides a linear relationship between the valve position and the flowrate. The flow through a linear valve varies directly with the position of the valve stem. This flow- travel relationship, if plotted on rectilinear coordinates, approximates a straight line. For example, at 40% valve lift, 40% of the full flow to pass.

Equal percentage characteristics: in these valves, equal increments of valve lift produce an equal percentage in flow change. The relationship between valve lift and orifice size (and therefore flowrate) is not linear but logarithmic. For example, for a valve of rangeability 100, for every 10% change in valve lift, flow rate will change by 58%.

Quick Opening characteristics: A quick opening valve plug produces a large increase in flow for a small initial change in stem travel. For example, a valve lift of 50% may result in an flowrate up to 90% of its maximum potential. Unlike linear and equal percentage characteristics, the exact shape of the fast-opening curve is not defined in standards.

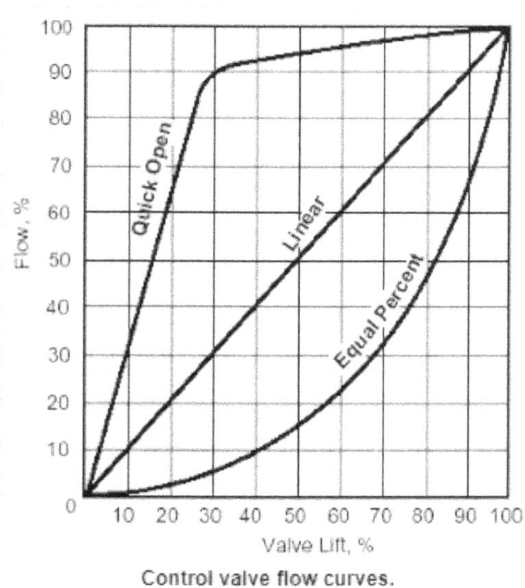

Control valve flow curves.

Fig 15.14- Control valve characteristics curve

37. What determines the control valve flow characteristics?

Ans: The physical shape of the plug and seat arrangement, which also called the valve 'trim', causes the difference in valve flow characteristics.

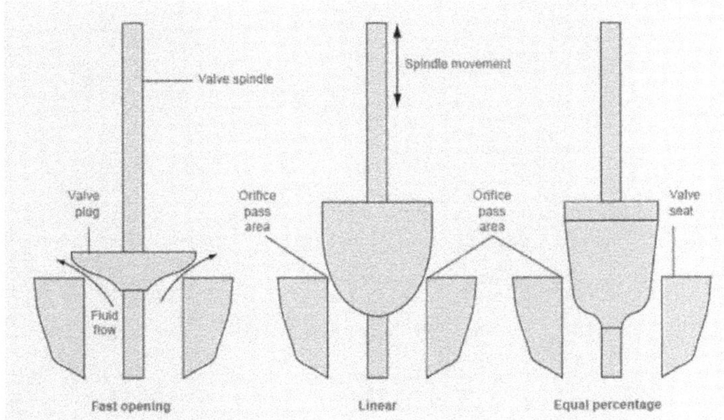

Fig 15.15 – Control valve trim

38. What are the typical applications of the quick opening, linear and equal percentage valves?

Ans: *Quick Opening Characteristics*:
- Used for frequent on-off service.
- Used for processes where "instantly" large flow is needed

Linear Characteristics:
- Used in liquid level or flow control loops.
- Used in systems where the pressure drop across the valve is expected to remain fairly constant.
- Used when the pressure drop across the valve is a large proportion of the total pressure drop.

Equal Percentage Characteristics:
- Used in processes where large changes in pressure drop are expected.
- Temperature and pressure control loops.

39. How will you select the control valve characteristics for flow, pressure, temperature and liquid level control?

Ans: Control valve characteristics chosen as:

- **Flow control:** normally Equal percentage valve is used.
- **Pressure Control:** Normally linear valve is used to maintain a constant pressure drop.
- **Temp. Control:** Normally equal percentage valve is used.
- **Liquid Level Control:** Normally linear valve is used.

40. What is the inherent and installed flow characteristics of the control valve?

Ans: An inherent flow characteristic is the relation between valve opening and flow under constant pressure conditions. The inherent characteristic of a valve is the characteristic published by the manufacturer.

When valves are installed with pumps, piping and fittings, and other process equipment, the pressure drop, caused by frictional losses in the piping, across the valve will vary as the valve travel changes. When the actual flow in a system is plotted against valve opening, the curve is called the installed flow characteristic and it will differ from the inherent valve characteristic.

41. What are the control valve accessories?

Ans: Positioners, I/P Transducers, Volume Boosters, Position Transmitters, Limit Switches, Solenoid Valves, Air Lock relay, Handwheel.

42. What are the different types of Positioners?

Ans: Different types of Positioners: Pneumatic Positioner, Electro-Pneumatic Positioner, Electronic positioner Digital/Smart positioner.

43. What are a pneumatic Positioners? How it works?

Ans: A pneumatic positioner is a device used to ensure that a control valve moves to the correct position based on a signal from a controller. It adjusts the air pressure sent to the valve actuator so that the valve opens or closes precisely as needed. These devices are especially useful in systems that require accurate and stable control of fluid flow.

The positioner receives a pneumatic control signal, typically in the range of 3–15 psi (or 0.2 to 1.0 kgf/cm^2), from a process controller. It is mechanically connected to the valve stem, allowing it to detect the valve's current position in real-time.

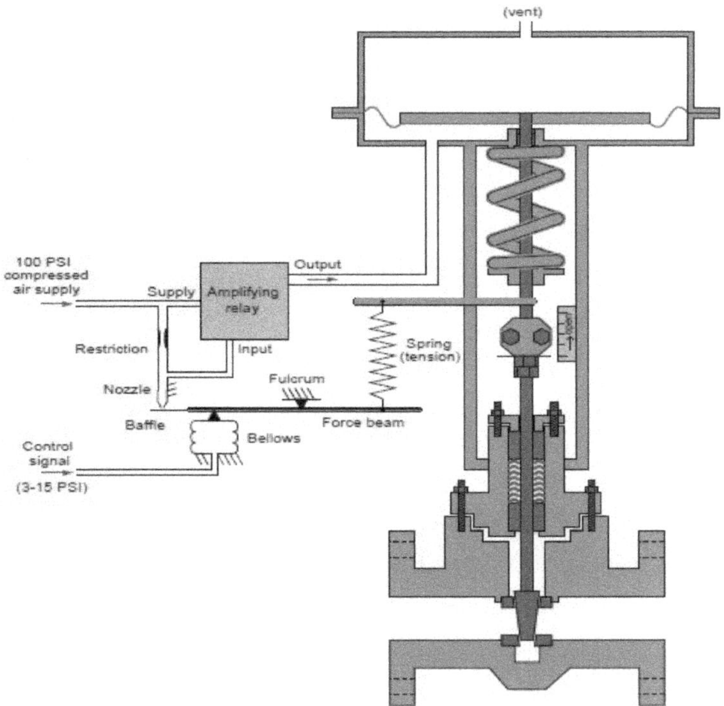

Fig 15.16 – Pneumatic Positioners

Inside the positioner is a flapper-nozzle mechanism. When the control signal is applied, it creates a force that moves a beam, causing the flapper to move closer to the nozzle. As the flapper approaches the nozzle, the backpressure in the nozzle increases.

This increase in pressure activates a pneumatic relay, which then boosts the air pressure sent to the actuator.

As the actuator receives more air pressure, it moves the valve stem, opening the valve. As the stem moves, it also stretches a spring connected to the beam, creating a balancing force. Once this force balances the pressure force from the control signal, the system reaches a steady position.

The positioner keeps adjusting in real-time, making fine corrections to maintain the valve at the correct position—even if there are changes in pressure or load. This ensures consistent and precise control of the process.

44. What is single acting and double acting positioner?

Ans: *Single-Acting Positioner*: Used with single-acting actuators, where the positioner only controls air in one direction, and a spring provides the force to move the valve in the opposite direction.

Double-Acting Positioner: Used with double-acting actuators, which require air pressure to both open and close the valve. The positioner controls airflow in both directions.

45. What is Electro Pneumatic Positioner and Electronic Positioner?

Ans: Electro Pneumatic Positioner performs the same function as the pneumatic type, but uses electrical current usually 4-20mA instead of air as the input signal which and uses I/P converter.

Electronic Positioner replaces the I/P convertor with a microprocessor inside the positioner itself to perform the same function as the Electro-Pneumatic Positioner.

46. What is Smart Positioner?

Ans: A smart positioner is an advanced type of valve positioner that uses microprocessor technology to provide highly accurate, automated control of valve positioning. Unlike traditional pneumatic positioners, which rely solely on mechanical and pneumatic feedback systems, smart positioners combine electronic components, sensors, and digital communication protocols to enhance precision, diagnostics, and control capabilities. Smart positioners can communicate with a Distributed Control System (DCS) or a Programmable Logic Controller (PLC).

The smart positioner receives a digital or analog input signal that indicates the desired valve position. It converts this input into a command for the actuator. Integrated sensors continuously monitor the valve position, comparing it with the target position to check for discrepancies. The microprocessor in the positioner uses this feedback to make precise adjustments to the actuator pressure, achieving the desired position quickly and accurately.

47. What are the advantages of smart positioner over Pneumatic positioners?

Ans: Following are the advantages of the smart positioner over Pneumatic positioners:

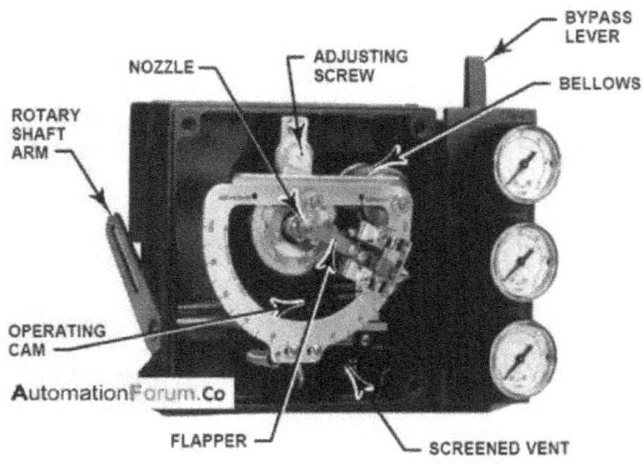

Fig 15.17 - Pneumatic positioner

- Smart positioners can communicate with a Distributed Control System (DCS) or a Programmable Logic Controller (PLC).
- They can automatically calibrate themselves and diagnose

issues, providing feedback on valve health and performance, which helps in predictive maintenance.

- Using microprocessor control, smart positioners offer highly precise valve positioning and can correct small deviations without mechanical feedback.

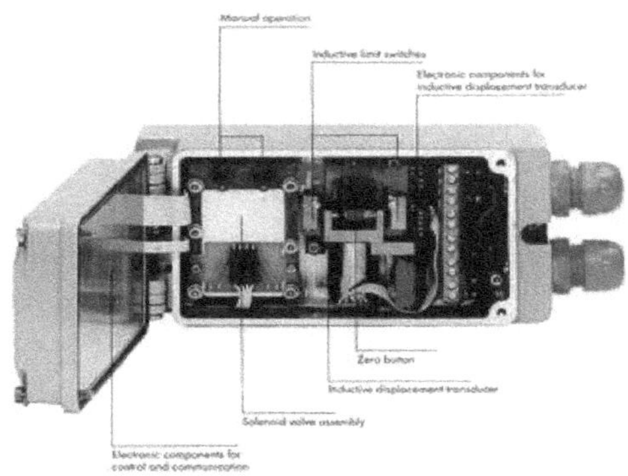

Fig 15.18 - Smart Positioner

48. What is the function of I/P Converter? How it works?

Ans: An I/P converter (current-to-pressure converter) is a device used to convert an electrical current signal (typically 4-20 mA) into a proportional pneumatic output pressure signal (usually in the range of 3-15 psi or 0.2-1 bar). I/P converters are commonly where electronic control signals need to be translated into pneumatic signals to operate control valves, dampers, or other pneumatic devices.

It works on Flapper-Nozzle method. It consists of a Flapper, nozzle and electromagnet. The Flapper of the Flapper-Nozzle instrument is connected to Pivot so that it can move up and down and a magnetic material was attached to other end of flapper and it is kept near the electromagnet. A regulated supply of pressure, usually 20 psi, provides a source of air through the restriction.

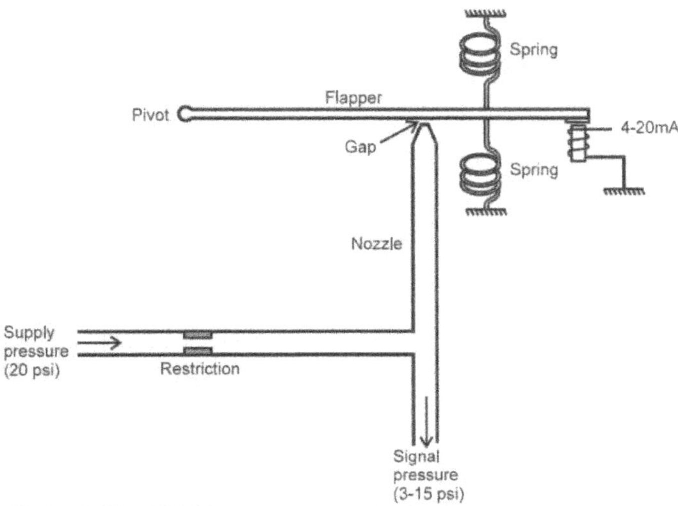

Fig 15.19 – I/P converter

The nozzle is open at the end where the gap exists between the nozzle and flapper, and air escapes in this region. As the magnet gets activated, due to increase in current signal, the flapper moves towards the electromagnet and the nozzle gets closed to some extent. So, some part of 20 P.S.I supplied will escape through nozzle and remaining pressure will come as output. With the increase in current signal, the power of the magnet will increase, then flapper will move closer to the nozzle, so less pressure will escape through nozzle and output pressure increases. The force generated by the magnetic coil modulates the flapper nozzle mechanism, allowing a specific amount of compressed air to pass through. In this way the output pressure will be proportional to the input current.

49. How flapper nozzle mechanism can be used as P/I Converter?

Ans: For P/I converter in flapper nozzle mechanism, LVDT can be used in place of electromagnet. A P/I converter (pressure-to-current converter) works on the opposite principle of an I/P converter, converting a pneumatic pressure signal (typically 3-15 psi) into an equivalent electrical current signal (usually 4-20 mA).

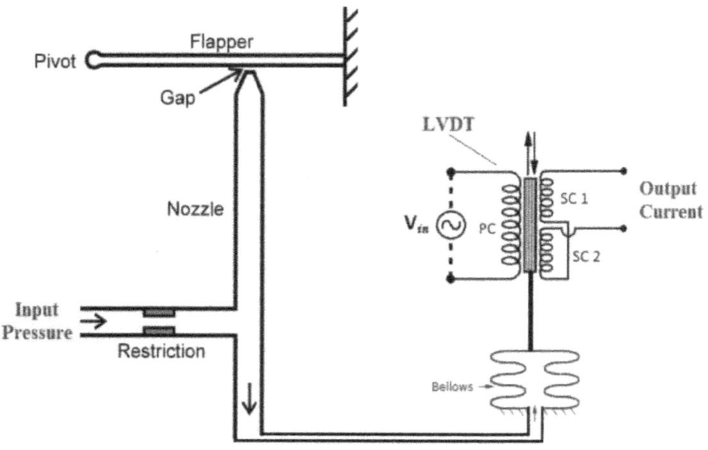

Fig 15.20 – P/I converter

Input pressure is supplied to the Flapper- Nozzle arrangement. Then it will supply through a pipe and that pressure is given as input to the bellows. These bellows are connected to the Core of LVDT. When pressure is applied to bellows, they will expand thus core displaces and the voltage is induced on the secondary coils of LVDT. As voltage is induced, current will flow through the coil. That current is proportional to the input pressure applied. Thus, Pressure is converted into equivalent current.

50. What is a volume booster?

Ans: A volume booster is a pneumatic device used to speed up the response of control valves and actuators. It works by increasing the amount of air that flows to the actuator when a control signal is received. This helps the actuator move faster and respond more quickly to changes in the control signal. In simple terms, it acts like an amplifier for airflow.

Volume boosters are commonly used in systems where quick valve movements are important, such as in fast control loops or emergency shutdown systems. By improving the speed and responsiveness of actuators, volume boosters help ensure better control performance and system reliability.

51. How volume booster functions?

Ans: The volume booster receives a low-flow pneumatic control signal from a positioner or controller, typically at the standard 3-15 psi range.

The booster connects to a larger air supply source and uses this high-volume supply to amplify the air going to the actuator. When the input signal changes, the booster rapidly adjusts the air volume supplied to the actuator.

The booster's internal mechanism (usually a diaphragm or piston) adjusts the output airflow to match the input signal's pressure. If the input signal is at 9 psi, for instance, the booster ensures the output to the actuator is also at 9 psi, but at a much higher airflow rate than the controller alone could supply.

52. In what type of control valve volume booster is used?

Ans: Used in applications with large valves that require high air volume for quick and efficient operation and suitable for systems where rapid control actions are necessary, such as emergency shutdown systems or safety relief valves.

53. What are the uses of limit switch and position transmitter in control valve?

Ans: Limit Switch is used for the indication of open and close status of the control valve.

Position transmitter is used to provide valve position feedback to the control system. Position feedback of the control valve often becomes necessary as it is used for process monitoring, troubleshooting, or startup/shutdown verification from the control room by an operator.

54. Why in some control applications solenoid valves used with control valves?

Ans: The use of solenoid valve is to trap air in the actuator to lock the valve in its current position.

55. What is the function of air lock relay in the control valve?

Ans: An air lock relay is a pneumatic device used in control valve systems to maintain the last position of a control valve in case of a failure in the instrument air supply. Its primary purpose is to "lock" the control valve in its current position to prevent uncontrolled movement that could disrupt the process or cause unsafe conditions.

56. How air lock relay works?

Ans: An air lock relay is used in pneumatic control systems to hold a valve in its last position if the air supply pressure drops unexpectedly. Under normal conditions, it simply lets the air signal from the controller or positioner pass through to the actuator, which adjusts the valve as needed.

However, if the air supply pressure falls below a set level, the relay automatically cuts off the supply and locks in the pressure that's already in the actuator. This prevents the valve from moving and keeps it in its current position, which helps avoid unwanted process changes during a loss of supply pressure.

When the air pressure comes back to a normal level, the relay unlocks and resumes regular operation, letting the control signal once again reach the actuator.

57. Why does the air pressure tubing between valve actuator and the air supply pipe bent into a loop?

Ans: The air pressure tubing between the valve actuator and the air supply pipe, bent into a loop to minimize strain on the metal tubing from vibration that may occur. This is called a vibration loop.

58. What is split ranging in control valve? What are the different types of split ranging?

Ans: There are many process control applications in industry where it is desirable to have multiple control valves respond to the output of a common controller. Control valves configured to follow the command of the same controller are said to be split-ranged or valve sequencing.

The different types of split ranging are: complementary, exclusive, and progressive.

59. Explain the functions of complementary, exclusive, and progressive valve sequencing.

Ans: *In complementary valve sequencing*, each valve operates in coordination with the other's position. When one valve reaches the fully open position, the other valve reaches the fully closed position. Both valves are actuated by the same 3–15 PSI pneumatic signal from the I/P transducer (AY). However, one valve is configured as Air-to-Open and the other as Air-to-Close. As the control air pressure increases from 3 PSI, one valve begins to open while the other begins to close. This arrangement allows continuous flow through one path while gradually closing the other, which helps switch flow smoothly from one line to another without interruptions.

In exclusive valve sequencing, both valves (A and B) are fully closed at a 50% controller output signal. At 0% controller output (i.e., 3 PSI), Valve A is fully open while Valve B is fully closed. As the controller output increases from 0% to 50%, Valve A begins to close and reaches the fully closed position at 50%, while Valve B remains fully closed. As the controller output increases beyond 50% up to 100%, Valve B begins to open and reaches the fully open position at 100%, while Valve A remains fully closed. It ensures that only one valve operates at a time, providing precise flow switching between two control elements.

In progressive valve sequencing, one small valve and one large valve are controlled by a single controller output signal. This configuration provides more precise flow control across the entire operating range than a single control valve could achieve alone. At 0% controller output, both valves are fully closed. As the controller output increases from 5% to 50%, the small valve begins to open and reaches the fully open position at 50%, while the large valve remains fully closed. As the controller output continues to increase from 50% to 100%, the large valve starts to open and becomes fully open at 100%, while the small valve remains open. It provides fine control at low flow rates (via the small valve) and full-capacity flow at higher ranges (via the large valve), improving control accuracy across the full range.

60. What are the common control valves problem?

Ans: The common control valves problem: Mechanical friction, Flashing, Cavitation, choked flow, Valve noise, Erosion, chemical attack.

61. What are the causes of mechanical friction in control valve and what are its remedies?

Ans: Following are the causes of mechanical in control valve:

- The contact between the valve stem and the packing material. It gets worse by over-tightening of packing nuts.
- In designs like cage-guided globe valves or rotary ball valves, internal components slide or rotate against each other.
- Dry or hardened packing leads to high friction during stem movement.
- Worn or misaligned internal parts increase resistance to motion.

Following are the remedies from mechanical friction:

- ***Proper Packing Maintenance***: Avoid over-tightening the packing nuts. And use correct torque values recommended by manufacturers.
- ***Lubrication***: Apply packing lubricants using a lubricator device threaded into the valve bonnet.
- ***Component Inspection and Replacement***: Rebuild or replace damaged trim, worn packing, or misaligned parts to restore smooth operation.

62. What are the effects of mechanical friction in a control valve?

Ans: Following are the effects of mechanical friction in a control valve:

- Friction increases the force needed by the actuator to move the valve stem.
- Static friction must be overcome to start valve movement, often leading to "jerky" or non-linear motion. After motion begins, the reduced dynamic friction causes the valve stem to accelerate unpredictably, then stop again, resulting in slip-stick behaviour.
- Changing the direction of stem movement introduces another challenge. The actuator has to again overcome static friction in the opposite direction, requiring a noticeable pressure change before the valve responds. This leads to what's called deadband, where small adjustments to the control signal don't cause any movement at all. It also causes hysteresis, where the valve doesn't return to the same position for the same signal after a reversal.
- The valve's stem position may not reflect the input signal accurately. This results in degraded loop control performance.

63. What is flashing in a control valve? What are its effects in control valve?

Ans: Flashing occurs when a liquid flowing through a control valve starts to boil due to a drop in pressure. As the liquid moves through the narrow parts of the valve (especially around the trim), its velocity increases. According to the principle of energy conservation, as the velocity goes up, pressure goes down. If the pressure drops below the liquid's vapor pressure at that point, the liquid begins to vaporize, this is call flashing.

This change from liquid to vapor doesn't reverse once the fluid leaves the narrow passage. Instead, the vapor continues downstream. Because of this, the flow can become restricted or "choked," reducing the valve's ability to pass fluid effectively. The valve's capacity (Cv) decreases as a result.

Flashing is also quite damaging to the valve itself. When the liquid turns into vapor, small, high-speed droplets form and hit the valve trim, especially the plug and seat, causing erosion over time. This kind of wear can shorten the valve's life and lead to performance issues if not addressed.

64. How Can Flashing Be avoided or minimized?

Ans: Following methods can be adopted to minimise flashing:

- Select a control valve type having less pressure recovery.
- Increase both upstream and downstream pressures by relocating the valve to a higher-pressure location in the process.
- Use multiple control valves in series to reduce the lowest pressure at either one.
- Use multi-stage trim to reduce pressure gradually and keep it above the vapor pressure throughout the valve.

65. How valve trim design affects flashing?

Ans: The globe valve does a better job of evenly distributing pressure losses throughout the path of flow. By contrast, the butterfly valve can only drop pressure at the points of constriction between the disk and the valve body, because the rest of the valve body is a straight-through path for fluid offering little restriction at all. As a consequence, the butterfly valve experiences a much lower vena contracta than the globe valve for any given amount of permanent pressure loss, making the butterfly valve more prone to flashing than the globe valve with all other factors being equal.

66. What is cavitation in control valve? What are the impacts of cavitation in control valve?

Ans: Cavitation happens in control valves when a liquid starts to boil due to a drop in pressure inside the valve, just like in flashing. However, unlike flashing, the pressure then rises again after the fluid passes through the narrow sections of the valve. If this recovered pressure goes above the liquid's vapor pressure, the vapor bubbles that formed earlier collapse back into liquid. This collapse is what defines cavitation.

The sudden collapse of these vapor bubbles creates intense, localized shock waves inside the valve. These micro-explosions can damage internal parts, especially the valve trim and body, leading to pitting, erosion, and eventually leakage or failure. Cavitation is typically more destructive than flashing.

Aside from physical damage, cavitation also creates loud noise, often a rattling or crackling sound, and can cause significant vibration.

67. How Can Cavitation Be Avoided or Reduced?

Ans: Following methods can be adopted to minimise cavitation:

- Prevent flashing in the first place by selecting proper trim of control valve.
- A nonreacting gas may be injected into the liquid stream to provide some "cushioning" within the cavitating region. The presence of non-condensable gas bubbles in the liquid stream disturbs the gas bubble pathways, helping to

dissipate their energy before striking the valve body walls.

- If pressure falling below the vapor pressure of the liquid cannot be avoided as the flow stream moves through the valve, there is an option of ensuring the downstream liquid pressure never rises above the liquid's vapor pressure, at least until the fluid clears past the valuable control valve and into an area of the system where cavitation damage will not be so expensive. This avoids cavitation at the cost of guaranteed flashing within the control valve, which is generally not as destructive as cavitation.

68. Is flow through a Control Valve – Turbulent or Laminar?

Ans: Flow through control valves is almost always turbulent.

69. What is a control valve stroke test?

Ans: A stroke test checks how a control valve responds to input signals, measures travel distance or rotation, and confirms the valve's ability to reach its fully open and closed positions. It identifies mechanical binding, actuator issues, or calibration errors in the positioner. Performing stroke tests ensures the control loop will effectively regulate the process when operational.

70. How would you troubleshoot a control valve that is stuck and not functioning?

Ans: Following steps can be taken in troubleshooting:

- First of all, get the control valve out of operation by closing the isolation valve before it.
- Disconnect the actuator stem from valve stem.
- Stroke the actuator and see whether the actuator operates or not. It not then the diaphragm may be punctured.
- If the actuator operates connect it back to the plug stem stroke the control valve. If it does not operate loosen the

gland nuts a bit and see if it operates. If it does not then the control valve has to be removed from the line to w/shop.

71. What is a spool valve?

Ans: A spool valve is a type of valve commonly used in hydraulic and pneumatic systems to control the direction, flow, and pressure of fluid (liquid or gas) by shifting a cylindrical spool inside a machined valve body. The spool is a cylindrical piece with grooves or lands and is positioned inside the valve body. As the spool slides back and forth (either manually, electrically, or hydraulically), it opens or blocks various internal flow paths. This controls which port the fluid enters and exits from.

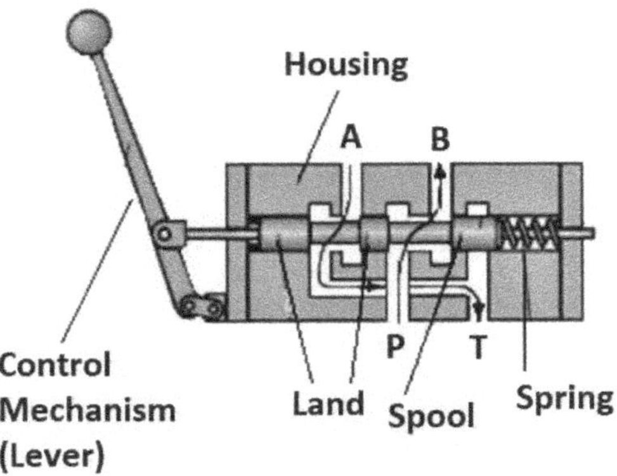

Fig 15.21 – Spool valve

72. What is normally closed valve and normally open valve?

Ans: Normally Closed Valves stays closed in de-energized state; opens when energized. Normally Open Valves stays open in de-energized state; closes when energized.

73. How does solenoid valve operates?

Ans: Solenoid valve is an electromechanically operated valve. It consists of a coil of wire designed to produce magnetic field and a ferrous plunger (centre part of solenoid). When solenoid is powered up, the coil gets energised and acts as a magnet. The energized solenoid coil acts as magnet and lifts the core or plunger of the solenoid. As the core or plunger of solenoid moves towards upsides, this movement creates a open flow for the fluid. When the power supply is disconnected, then solenoid coil de-energizes and magnetic field also stopped. Then the plunger will be pushed back to its original position with the help of a spring, this movement stops the flow for the fluid.

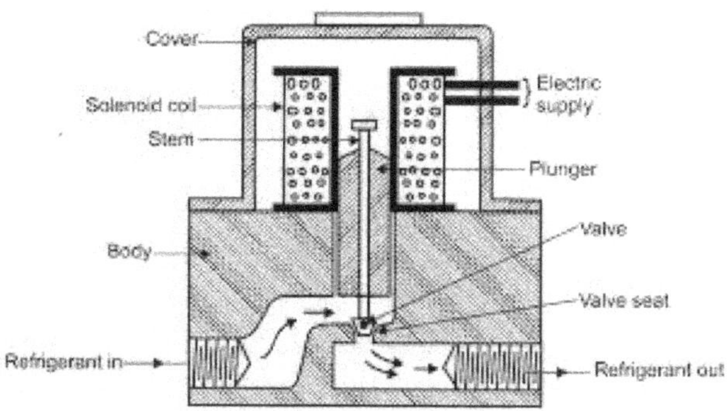

Fig 15.22 – Solenoid valve

74. How does a 2 way solenoid valve functions?

Ans: 2-way solenoid valves operate in a manner analogous to single-pole single-throw (SPST) electrical switches i.e. with only one path for flow. It has two ports—an inlet and an outlet, used to start or stop the flow of a fluid (liquid or gas) through a pipeline. The fluid enters the valve through inlet port and exit the valve through outlet port.

In NC (normally close) 2 way solenoid valve, fluid passes when solenoid energised, lifting the plunger and allowing flow from the inlet to the outlet. And in de-energised state, valve is closed, no flow occurs because the internal plunger blocks the outlet.

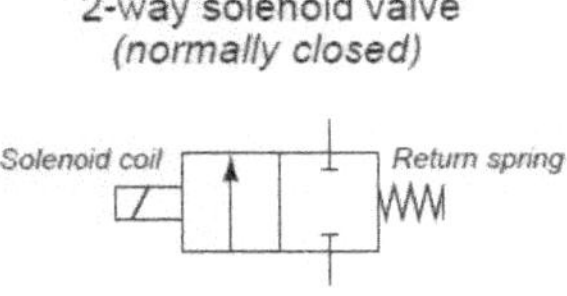

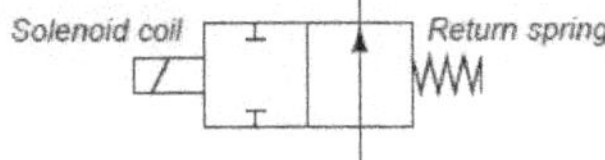

Fig 15.23 – 2 way solenoid valve

In **NO** (normally open) 2 way solenoid valve, fluid passes when solenoid de-energised. And when energised valve close and stop the flow.

75. How does a 3 way solenoid valve functions?

Ans: 3-way solenoid valves operate in a manner analogous to single-pole double-throw (SPDT) electrical switches i.e. with two paths for flow sharing and one common terminal. It has three ports: P (for supply), C (for outlet) and E (for exhaust or vent).

For NC (normally close) 3 way solenoid valve:
- In de-energised state, no fluid flows from the supply, as Port C (outlet)is connected to Port E (exhaust).
- In energised state, Port P (supply) is connected to Port C (outlet) and fluid passes from inlet to outlet.

For NO (normally open) 3 way solenoid valve:
- In energised state, Port C is connected to Port E (exhaust) and thus no fluid flows through the valve.
- In de-energised state, Port P is connected to Port C and fluid passes through the valve.

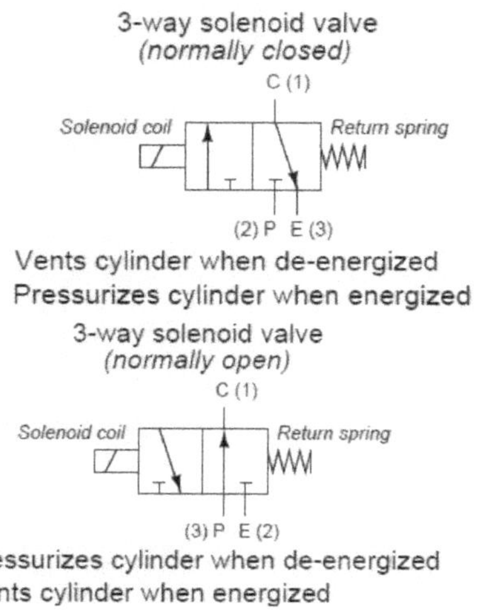

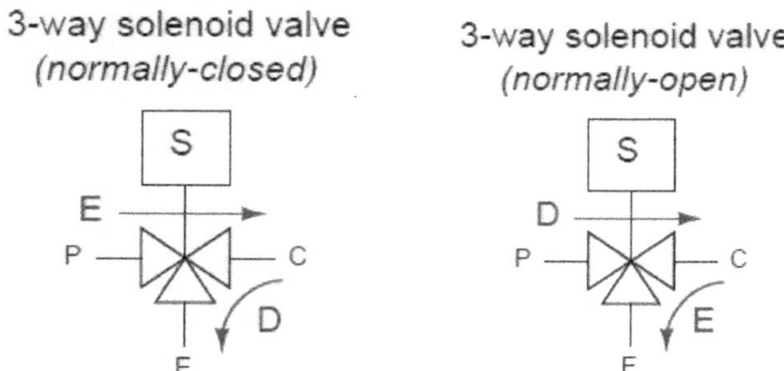

Fig 15.24- 3 way solenoid valve

76. How does a 4 way solenoid valve functions?

Ans: A 4-way solenoid valve is an electrically operated valve with four ports, commonly used to control double-acting cylinders in pneumatic or hydraulic systems. It has four ports: P (supply), E (exhaust), A& B (output). Port A and B connected to the two sides of a double-acting actuator or cylinder.

When the solenoid is de-energised, air is directed to the port A i.e. top of the piston and the air in bottom of the piston vented to atmosphere through E port, causing the piston-actuated valve stem to move down. When the solenoid is energised, air is directed to the bottom of the piston and the air in top of the piston vented to atmosphere through E port, causing the piston-actuated valve stem to move up.

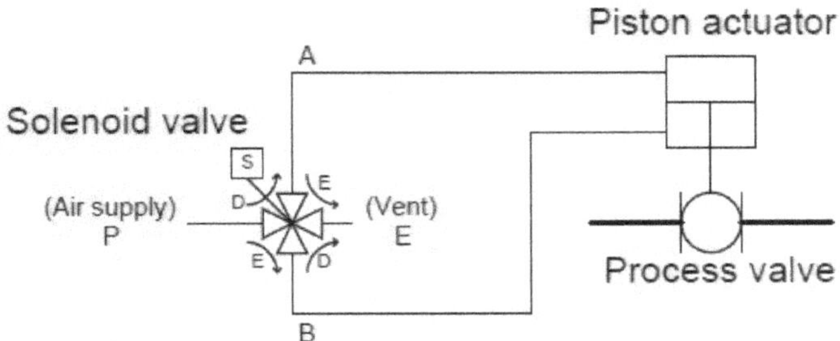

Fig 15.25 – 4 way solenoid valve

77. What is solenoid manual reset and solenoid manual override?
Ans: A solenoid with manual reset is a type of solenoid valve that requires human intervention to return to its operating position after it has been tripped due to a fault or intentional shutdown. After power failure, pressure loss, or emergency stop, the valve does not automatically reset. An operator must press or turn a mechanical reset button or lever to return the valve to service. It is commonly used in safety-critical applications, such as gas shutoff systems, where automatic re-energization could be dangerous.

A solenoid with manual override allows an operator to manually operate the valve regardless of its electrical control signal. It allows valve actuation without energizing the coil. It is typically provided with a lever, push button, or screw mechanism on the valve body. It is used for testing, maintenance, or emergency operation.

78. What is the function of the Bleed-Orifice or Bleed Hole in a solenoid valve?
Ans: To allow a small flow to control a larger flow.

79. What is the function of the Core Spring in a solenoid valve?
Ans: To close the valve when power is removed.

80. What is a servo valve?

Ans: A servo valve is a high-precision control valve used in hydraulic or pneumatic systems to accurately regulate the flow rate and direction of fluid based on an electrical input signal.

Inside a servo valve, there's a small torque motor connected to a flapper that sits between two nozzles. When an electrical signal is applied, the motor causes the flapper to shift slightly. This creates an imbalance in pressure between the two nozzles, which then pushes on a spool (a sliding part inside the valve). The spool's movement controls how much and in which direction the fluid flows.

A feedback spring is connected between the spool and the flapper. As the spool moves, it stretches the spring, which pushes back against the motor. This feedback mechanism helps the valve maintain accurate, smooth, and proportional control of flow based on the input signal. Because of this precise control, servo valves are commonly used in systems where fast and accurate fluid movement is essential, such as in aerospace, robotics, and industrial automation.

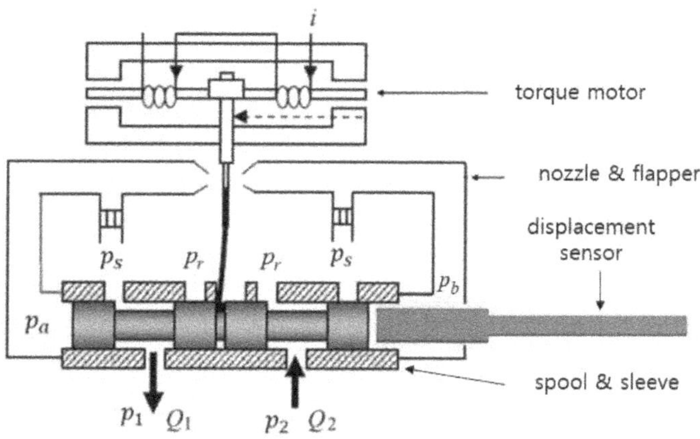

Fig 15.26 – Servo valve

Chapter: 16

Process Control

1. What is open loop control system?

Ans: An open-loop control system is a type of control system in which the output has no effect on the control action or input. For e.g. Traffic signal: operates on timer only, not concerned of traffic volume, Washing Machine: Operates based on a timer, irrespective of whether clothes are clean or not.

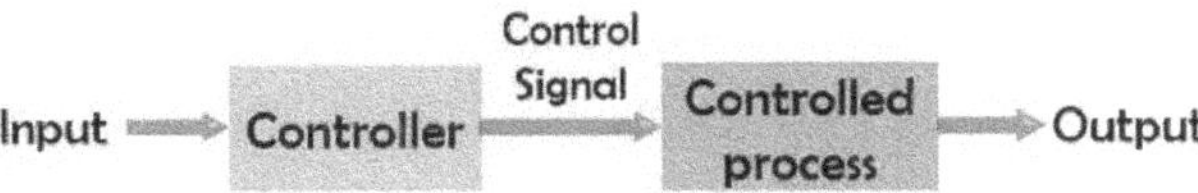

Fig 16.1 – Open loop control system

2. What is closed loop control system?

Ans: A closed-loop control system is a type of control system that continuously monitors its output and uses feedback to adjust its control actions to achieve the desired output.

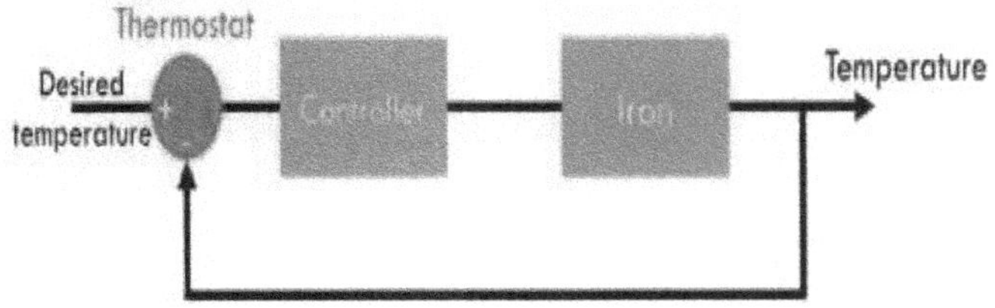

Fig 16.2 – Closed loop control system

The system compares the actual output with the desired setpoint and makes corrections based on the difference (called the error). This feedback mechanism allows the system to automatically compensate for disturbances and maintain desired performance. For e.g. Thermostat-Controlled Heater: Turns the heater on or off based on the actual room temperature relative to the set temperature.

3. What are the basic elements of closed loop control system?
Ans:

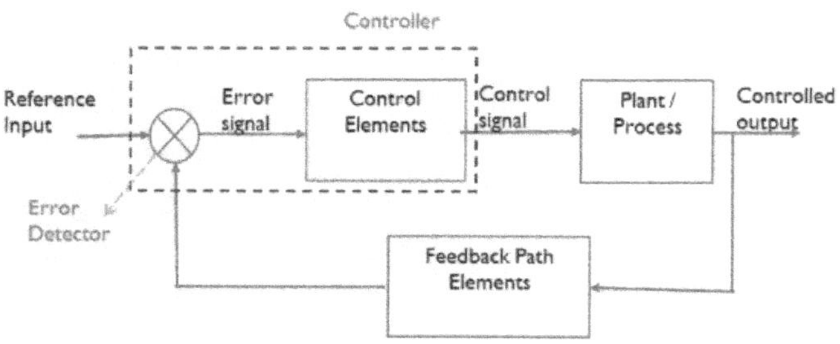

Fig 16.3 – Basic element of control loop

4. What are first order and second order control system?
Ans: In control systems, first-order and second-order systems are classifications based on the dynamics of the system. A first-order system is characterized by a first-order linear differential equation. The system's output depends on the current input and a single time constant that determines how quickly the system responds to changes. E.g. Simplified control systems, such as thermostats or level controllers.

A second-order system is characterized by a second-order linear differential equation. The system's output depends on the current input, the system's natural frequency, and its damping behavior. E.g. Precision control applications, such as robotics, automation, and servo systems.

5. What is transfer function?
Ans: A transfer function represents the relationship between the input and output of a system in the Laplace domain. It is used to analyze the system's dynamics, stability, and performance.

6. **Define the term time constant, settling time, steady state error, damping ratio, undamped system, overdamped sysytem, critically damped system.**

Ans: *Time constant*: The time constant is a measure of how quickly a system responds to a change in input. For a first-order system, it represents the time required for the output to reach 63.2% of the total change from its initial value to its final steady-state value. Smaller time constants mean faster system responses; larger time constants indicate slower responses.

Settling Time: The time it takes for a system's output to settle and remain within a s   pecified percentage (commonly 2% or 5%) of its final steady-state value. It indicates how quickly the system stabilizes after a disturbance or input change.

Steady-State Error (SSE): The difference between the desired output (setpoint) and the actual output as time approaches infinity. SSE measures how accurately the system tracks or reaches the desired output.

Damping Ratio: A dimensionless parameter that determines the nature of oscillatory behavior in a second-order system's response.

Undamped System: A system with no damping ($\zeta=0$), meaning it oscillates indefinitely at its natural frequency without losing energy. The output is a sinusoidal waveform with constant amplitude.

Overdamped System: A system with a damping ratio ($\zeta>1$), meaning the system does not oscillate but returns to steady state very slowly. The output exponential decay without oscillations. The system with excessively damped, leading to sluggish performance.

Critically Damped System: A system with a damping ratio ($\zeta=1$), representing the fastest possible response without oscillations. The system quickly reaches steady state without overshooting. It is ideal for systems that require fast, non-oscillatory behavior (e.g., control of a robotic arm).

7. What do you mean by the term control system gain?

Ans: In control systems, gain refers to the amplification factor applied to an input signal to produce an output signal. When we say "gain = 10", it means that the output is 10 times the input.

For e.g. a hydraulic system with a gain of 10. For 1 mm of displacement of the valve actuator there will be 10 mm of displacement in the piston.

8. What do you mean by set point and error signal?

Ans: The setpoint is the desired or target value of a system's output that want the control system to maintain. It acts as a reference for the system to achieve.

The error signal is the difference between the setpoint (desired value) and the actual output (measured value) of the system. It quantifies how far the system's current state is from the desired state.

For e.g. In a thermostat-controlled heating system, the setpoint is the temperature we set (e.g., 22°C). Consider, measured value is 20°C, error signal = 22°C -20°C =2°C. The controller uses this error signal to adjust the control actions to minimize the error and drive the system output closer to the setpoint.

9. What is feedforward control?

Ans: Feedforward control is a control strategy that tries to stay one step ahead of disturbances. Instead of waiting for a problem to show up and then correcting it (like feedback control does), feedforward control works proactively, it predicts what kind of changes might affect the system and makes adjustments before those changes have an impact.

For example, if a process is about to receive a sudden increase in input flow, a feedforward controller will detect this in advance and adjust the control valve early, so the system remains stable. In real-world applications, feedforward is usually combined with feedback control. Feedforward helps prevent problems, while feedback fine-tunes the response if anything unexpected still happens. Together, they create a more reliable and responsive control system.

10. Explain the difference of feedback and feedforward system with example.

Ans: Suppose a water tank that needs to maintain a specific water level, say set point of 50%. If outflow rate is 20L/min, feedforward system anticipates the effect of the outflow and increases the inflow to 20 liters per minute to maintain the water level. If the outflow suddenly increases to 30 liters per minute, the system detects this change and increases the inflow to 30 liters per minute without waiting for the water level to drop.

In feedback control system, the controller responds and modulate the inflow when there is a tank level set point (50% in this case). When tank level drops below 50%, the system increase inflow and when tank level rises above 50%, the system decrease inflow.

Feedback control system is reactive (responds after disturbance occurs) type and feedforward control system is proactive (anticipates disturbances) type system.

11. Explain cascade control system with example.

Ans: A cascade control system is an advanced control method where two (or more) controllers are used in a sequence, one acting as the primary controller and the other as a secondary controller. The primary controller manages the main process variable, while the secondary controller handles a related variable that influences the primary one. This setup allows the system to respond faster and more accurately to changes or disturbances.

Example: Boiler drum level control. Here, primary loop or controller maintains drum water level at desired set point. It measures the actual water level in the drum and calculates the desired feedwater flow rate as setpoint for inner loop. The inner loop or controller adjusts the feedwater control valve to maintain the required flow rate as set by primary loop. Once the flow rate stabilizes, the drum level controller ensures that the water level returns to the setpoint.

12. When cascade control should be used?

Ans: Cascade control should always be used in a process with relatively slow dynamics (like level, temperature, composition, humidity) and a liquid or gas flow, or some other relatively-fast process, has to be manipulated to control the slow process.

13. When Should Cascade Control Not be Used?

Ans: Cascade control is beneficial only if the dynamics of the inner loop are fast compared to those of the outer loop. Cascade control should generally not be used if the inner loop is not at least three times faster than the outer loop, because the improved performance may not justify the added complexity and there is also a risk of interaction between the two loops that could result in instability.

14. Explain ratio control system with example.

Ans: A ratio control system is a type of control strategy used to maintain a fixed ratio between two or more variables in a process. This is especially useful in processes where maintaining a specific proportion between variables is critical for proper operation or product quality.

In a combustion process (e.g., a gas-fired boiler), the air-to-fuel ratio must be maintained within a specific range for efficient combustion and to prevent issues like soot formation or incomplete combustion. A ratio controller ensures the air flow is always proportional to the fuel flow. For example, if the desired air-to-fuel ratio is 10:1 and the fuel flow increase to 5 units, the air flow is adjusted to 50 units.

15. What is Batch Process and Continuous Process?

Ans: A batch process involves producing a finite quantity of material in a series of steps. The production occurs in distinct batches, where each batch goes through the same sequence of operations. Production happens in cycles or "batches." The equipment is cleaned and prepared for the next batch after one cycle is completed. E.g. baking of bread or manufacturing of drugs.

A continuous process involves producing materials continuously without interruptions. It operates 24/7, with raw materials fed into the system and products extracted simultaneously. E.g. Refining crude oil into gasoline and other fuels.

16. What are the different types of control action?

Ans: ON-OFF control, Proportional Control (P), Reset or Integral action (I), Proportional plus Reset action (P+I), Rate or Derivative action (D), Proportional plus Derivative (P+D), Proportional plus Integral plus Derivative (P+I+D).

17. What is ON-OFF control action?

Ans: ON-OFF control is the simplest form of control system used to regulate a process variable. In this control action, the output is either fully ON or fully OFF, with no intermediate states. The controller switches the actuator between these two states based on whether the process variable is above or below a desired setpoint. E.g. Electric Heaters

18. What do you mean by hysteresis or deadband in ON-OFF control?

Ans: To reduce the frequent switching of the equipment a small range around the setpoint is introduced where no action is taken. This range is called hysteresis or deadband. For example: In a thermostat set to 22°C, the heater may turn ON if the temperature falls below 21.5°C and turn OFF if the temperature rises above

22.5°C. The range from 21.5°C to 22.5°C is hysteresis.

This reduces wear and tear and improves system stability.

19. What is proportional control action?

Ans: Proportional control action is a type of control mechanism in which the control output is proportional to the error between the process variable (measured value) and the setpoint (desired value). This means the controller adjusts the actuator's output in direct proportion to the size of the error.

Mathematical Representation:

The control output (u) is given by:

$u(t) = Kp \cdot e(t)$

Where:

u(t) Controller output

Kp: Proportional gain (a tuning parameter)

e(t)=Setpoint−Process Variable (error signal)

When the process variable deviates from the setpoint, the controller generates an output proportional to the error. The larger the error, the larger the corrective action. As the error decreases, the output also decreases, reducing the actuator's influence as the process approaches the setpoint.

20. What do you mean by the term gain in proportional control action?

Ans: In proportional control, the term gain refers to the proportional gain constant (Kp), which determines how strongly the controller reacts to the error between the setpoint and the process variable.

It is defined as the ratio of the controller's output change to the change in error. It defines the sensitivity of the control action to the error.

21. How proportional gain impact control action?

Ans: Excessively high Kp can cause overshoot and oscillations, while excessively low Kp makes the system unresponsive. Proper selection of Kp ensures the system is responsive, stable, and performs optimally for the specific application.

22. Which type of system require higher K_p?

Ans: Systems with fast dynamics (e.g., flow control) can tolerate higher Kp , while slow processes (e.g., temperature control) require lower Kp to avoid instability.

23.   What is proportional band?

Ans: Proportional Band (PB) is a term used in proportional control systems to define the range of the process variable over which the controller output changes proportionally.

24. What is the relationship between proportional band and Proportional gain?

Ans: Proportional band is inversely related to the proportional gain.

For high gain, proportional band is narrow and Controller reacts more aggressively to small errors. For low gain, proportional band is wide and Controller reacts less aggressively.

25. How controller responds within and outside the proportional band?

Ans: When the process variable moves outside the proportional band, the controller output saturates (either 0% or 100%).

For e.g. a temperature controller having input range 0°C to 400°C, Set point 200°C and proportional band 200±40°C (i.e. 160°C to 240°C),

At 160°C, controller output is 100%

At 240°C, controller output is 0%

Below 160°C, controller remains at 100%(saturation)

Above 240°C, Controller remains at 0%.

26. What is reset or integral control action?

Ans: Reset control action, also known as integral control action, is a type of control strategy where the controller output is proportional to the integral of the error over time. This action accumulates the error over time and adjusts the control output to eliminate the steady-state error (offset) present in proportional-only control.

The integral action sums up the error over time. As long as there is a non-zero error, the integral action continuously adjusts the controller output. Once the error becomes zero, the integral action stops accumulating, and the controller output stabilizes.

For e.g. consider a tank level control operating in following conditions:

Setpoint: Desired water level = 50%.

Process Variable: Measured water level (e.g., 45%).

Error: $e(t)$=Setpoint−Process Variable=50%−45%=5%$e(t)$

In a proportional-only system, a steady-state error may remain, causing the level to stabilize below 50%. Adding integral action:
The controller calculates the accumulated error over time (e.g., 5% continuously over several seconds). The integral action increases the pump output to compensate for the steady-state error. Eventually, the water level reaches the setpoint (50%).

27. What is reset time or integral time?

Ans: The speed of integral action is often expressed in terms of reset time, which is the time it takes for the integral action to produce the same change in controller output as the proportional action does for a given error.

For Short Reset Time, faster integral action, but can lead to instability or overshoot. And for Long Reset Time, Slower integral action, providing more stability.

28. What is integral windup? Explain with examples.

Ans: Integral windup is a condition in control systems where the integral term in a controller accumulates excessively large values due to a prolonged error. This typically occurs when the controller output saturates (reaches its maximum or minimum limit) and the integral action continues to integrate the error, even though no corrective action is possible.

As a result, the controller output can overshoot or take a long time to recover when the error is eventually corrected, causing instability or sluggish response.

Consider the example of Tank Level Control:

Setpoint: Water level = 50%.

Process Variable: Water level = 30%.

Controller Output: Controls a pump to fill the tank.

If the pump operates at maximum capacity but cannot quickly bring the level to the setpoint (e.g., due to system constraints), the integral action continues to accumulate the error (20% difference). Even when the process variable eventually reaches the setpoint, the controller output remains excessive due to the accumulated integral term, causing the tank to overshoot the desired level.

29. What are the causes of integral windup?

Ans: Following are the causes of integral windup:

- ***Actuator Saturation***: When the controller output reaches a physical limit (e.g., valve fully open/closed or pump at maximum capacity), the integral term keeps accumulating the error.
- ***Large Setpoint Changes:*** Sudden, large changes in the setpoint can create a significant error that persists long enough to cause windup.
- ***Disturbances:*** Persistent disturbances in the system that exceed the actuator's ability to correct them.

30. How proportional plus integral control action works?

Ans: A Proportional-Integral (P+I) Controller combines the actions of

Proportional Control and Integral Control to improve the performance of a control system.

The proportional term provides immediate correction for large errors, ensuring quick response. The integral term compensates for smaller, persistent errors over time, eliminating steady-state error.

For e.g. Tank Level Control: Setpoint: Water level = 50%, Process Variable: Measured water level, Controller Output: Controls the pump to maintain the desired water level.

- ***Proportional Action***: If the water level is 40% (error = 10%), the proportional term increases the pump output proportional to this error to bring the level closer to 50%. However, it may stabilize slightly below the setpoint (e.g., at 49%).
- ***Integral Action***: The integral term accumulates the 1% error (50% - 49%) and gradually adjusts the pump output to bring the level to exactly 50%.

31. What is rate or derivative control action?

Ans: A derivative controller produces a control action proportional to the rate at which the process variable's error is changing. It does not act on the error directly but rather on how quickly the error is increasing or decreasing.

By reacting to the rate of error change, the derivative action anticipates future error trends and adjusts the controller output accordingly. The derivative component does not respond to a constant error (steady-state error) because the rate of change (de(t)dt) is zero in such cases.

32. What are the key effects of derivative control?

Ans: Following are the key features of derivative control: -

- ***Damping Oscillations***: It reduces overshoot and oscillations caused by proportional or integral action.
- ***Improved Stability***: It slows down the system response to rapid changes, helping the process settle smoothly at

the setpoint.

- ***Faster Response to Disturbances***: Enhances the system's ability to respond to sudden disturbances or changes in setpoint.

33. How proportional plus derivative controller works?

Ans: A P + D (Proportional + Derivative) controller combines the proportional (P) and derivative (D) actions to control a process. The proportional action (P) adjusts the control output based on the current error (the difference between the setpoint and the process variable). The derivative action (D) predicts future behavior by reacting to the rate of change of the error (de(t)/dt). It dampens rapid changes and stabilizes the response.

34. How PID controller works?

Ans: A PID controller, is a widely used control algorithm in industrial automation. It combines three control actions — Proportional (P), Integral (I), and Derivative (D) — to provide accurate and stable control of a process.

The control output (u(t)) is calculated as the sum of the Proportional, Integral, and Derivative actions:

$$u(t) = K_p e(t) + K_i \int_0^t e(t)\,dt + K_d \frac{de(t)}{dt}$$

Where:

u(t): Controller output (control signal)

K_p: Proportional gain (amplifies the error)

K_i: Integral gain (eliminates steady-state error)

K_d: Derivative gain (stabilizes the system)

e(t): Error (setpoint - process variable)

$\int_0^t e(t)\,dt$: Accumulated error over time (integral action)

$\frac{de(t)}{dt}$: Rate of change of error (derivative action)

PID controller compliments the limitation of each P or I or D controller and forms a stable system. The P action handles the current error to provide an immediate response. The I action corrects cumulative errors and ensures long-term accuracy by eliminating offset. The D action anticipates future changes in the error and stabilizes the system, preventing overshoot or oscillations.

35. Explain PID controller with example.

Ans: Consider a process where to maintain the furnace temperature at 750°C for an industrial process, such as metal forging or heat treatment. The furnace is equipped with a heating element, a temperature sensor (thermocouple), and a PID controller.

The PID controller compares the setpoint (750°C) with the measured temperature and calculates an output to the heating element to adjust the furnace's heat. The heating element increases or decreases the heat based on the PID controller's output signal. If the furnace temperature is below 750°C (e.g., 720°C), the proportional action generates a control signal proportional to the temperature difference (error = 750 - 720 = 30°C). The P controller quickly responds to large errors by increasing heating power.

If the furnace consistently lags behind the setpoint (e.g., stabilizes at 745°C), the integral action accumulates the error over time and increases the output. The I controller eliminates steady-state error and ensures the furnace reaches exactly 750°C.

When the temperature approaches 750°C, the derivative action predicts how fast the error is decreasing (rate of change of error). It reduces the heating output to prevent overshooting. The D controller damps oscillations and ensures smooth stabilization at 750°C.

36. Mention the applications of each of P, I, PI, PD, PID control action.

Ans: Here are the list:

Control Type	Primary Application	Strengths	Limitations
Proportional (P)	Simple systems where immediate response is required (e.g., thermostats, flow control in steady conditions).	- Fast response. - Simple to implement.	- Steady-state error remains. -May cause oscillations.
Integral (I)	Systems with steady-state error issues, like tank level control or pressure control in pipelines.	- Eliminates steady-state error. - Simple to add.	- Slow response to transient changes. - May cause overshoot.
Proportional + Integral (P+I)	Systems requiring quick response and steady-state accuracy, like temperature control or liquid level maintenance.	- Fast error correction. - Eliminates steady-state error.	- May cause overshoot if not tuned properly.
Proportional + Derivative (P+D)	Systems needing stability and damping, such	- Quick response. - Reduces oscillations	- Cannot eliminate steady-state error.

	as motor speed control or robotic arm positioning.	and overshoot.	- Sensitive to noise.
Proportional + Integral + Derivative (PID)	Complex systems with high accuracy requirements, like industrial process control (furnaces, compressors, chemical reactors).	- Accurate control. - Eliminates steady-state error. - Damps oscillations	- Complex tuning. - Sensitive to noise in derivative action.

37. What do you mean by tunning of PID controller? How PID controller can be tuned?

Ans: Tuning of a controller is the process of setting the parameters of a controller (e.g., K_p, K_i, and K_d for a PID controller) to achieve the desired performance of the control system. The goal of tuning is to ensure the system responds effectively to changes in the setpoint or disturbances while maintaining stability, accuracy, and speed.

For manual tuning of PID controller, initially increase K_p until the system starts oscillating, then reduce it slightly for stability. After that, gradually increase K_i to eliminate steady-state error, but stop before causing excessive overshoot or instability. Then, increase K_d to dampen oscillations and improve stability.

38. What is Ziegler-Nichols Tuning Method?

Ans: Ziegler-Nichols Tuning Method is a systematic and widely used method for PID controllers.

At first, Set $K_i=0$ and $K_d=0$, then increase K_p until the system oscillates with a constant amplitude. (this is called the ultimate gain, K_u, and the oscillation period is the ultimate period, T_u). Now, K_p, K_d, K_i can be calculated by using below formula:

Controller	K_p	K_i	K_d
P	$0.5K_u$		
PI	$0.45K_u$	$1.2(K_p/T_u)$	
PID	$0.6K_u$	$2(K_p/T_u)$	$0.125K_pT_u$

39. What would be impact on the system if K_p, K_i and K_d parameters value selected very high or very low?

Ans: Below are details results:

Impact of proportional gain (K_p):

Condition	Impact on system
Too high	- System becomes unstable. - Oscillations increase or may become uncontrollable. - High sensitivity to noise.
Too low	- Slow response to errors. - Steady-state error persists. - System may not reach the setpoint efficiently.

Impact of proportional gain (K_i):

Condition	Impact on system
Too high	- System becomes unstable. - Overshoot increases. - Integral windup occurs (excessive accumulation of past errors).
Too low	- Steady-state error persists. - System is unable to correct long-term errors caused by disturbances or load changes.

Impact of proportional gain (K_d):

Condition	Impact on system
Too high	-System becomes overly sensitive to noise (since K_d reacts to changes in error). -May slow down the response unnecessarily.
Too low	- Poor damping of oscillations. - System may overshoot and oscillate around the setpoint.

Combined Effects in a PID Controller

Gain setting	Impact
All Gains Too High	- Severe instability. - Continuous oscillations or divergence from the setpoint.
All Gains Too Low	- System responds very slowly. - May fail to reach the setpoint effectively (poor performance).
High K_p, Low K_i, Low K_d	- Fast initial response but steady-state error persists. - May overshoot due to lack of damping.
Low K_p, High K_i, Low K_d	- Eliminates steady-state error but responds sluggishly. - Potential overshoot without damping.
Low K_p, Low K_i, High K_d	- Poor initial response. - Excessive damping leads to a slow, overly cautious approach to the setpoint.

40. Explain what is 'direct action' and 'reverse action' on a controller?

Ans: In a direct acting controller, the output increases when the process measurement (variable) increases. In a reverse action controller, the output decreases when the process measurement (variable) increases.

e.g. consider two different cases where level controller maintaining level in a tank by controlling a) discharge control valve and b) inlet control valve. For case a, the controller needs to increase its signal when the level in the tank increases. And for case b, the controller needs to reduce the output when the level in the tank increases.

41. What type of controller (P, PI, PID) is preferred on the process of Pressure, Level, Flow and Temperature control loops?

Ans: For pressure control, if the load change is minimum, then a proportional controller is suitable. If a frequent load change is expected then a Proportional + Integral controller is preferred.

For Level control, normally a proportional controller is preferred. For flow control, Proportional + Integral controller is preferred and for temperature control Proportional + Integral + Derivative controller is preferred.

42. How does a pneumatic PID controller work?

Ans: A pneumatic PID controller is a control device that uses compressed air (usually 3–15 psi) to perform Proportional (P), Integral (I), and Derivative (D) control actions. It receives a pneumatic signal representing the process variable (PV), compares it to a setpoint (SP), and outputs another pneumatic signal to adjust the final control element, typically a valve.

The controller works based on the force-balance principle and uses mechanical elements like a flapper-nozzle assembly, a pivoting beam, and several bellows to perform the control actions.

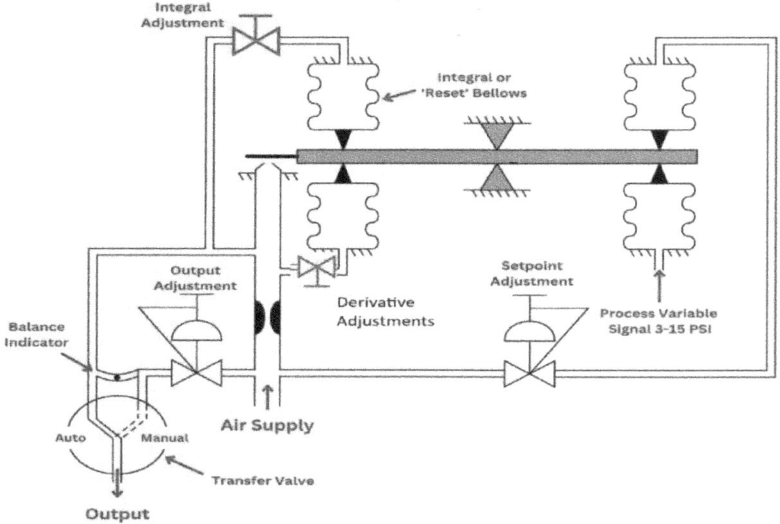

Fig 16.4 – Pneumatic PID controller

Working principle:
- The PV signal applies pressure to one of the bellows, creating a force that tilts the beam.
- This movement changes the position of the flapper relative to a nozzle, altering the backpressure and, in turn, the output pressure.
- This output pressure is also fed back to another bellow to create a balancing force, helping the system stabilize.

Control actions:
- ***Proportional action*** is adjusted by shifting the beam's fulcrum: the closer it is to the output bellows, the higher the sensitivity (gain).
- ***Integral action*** is handled by slowly building air pressure in a separate bellow over time to eliminate steady-state error. It's adjusted using an integral knob.

- **Derivative action** is tuned via another adjustment linked to the feedback bellow, helping the controller react to rapid changes.

The setpoint can also be adjusted manually by changing the air pressure in the SP bellow.

43. How does an electronic and digital PID controller work?

Ans: In an electronic PID controller, the input signals (representing the process variable and setpoint) are electrical, usually in the form of voltage or current (such as 4–20 mA). Analog circuits or operational amplifiers process these signals to produce an output that controls final control elements like valves or actuators.

In a digital PID controller, a microprocessor receives digital signals or converts analog signals into digital form using an Analog-to-Digital Converter (ADC). It then applies mathematical algorithms based on the PID formula to calculate the output. The proportional term produces an output proportional to the current error, the integral term addresses accumulated past errors, and the derivative term predicts future error based on the rate of change. After processing, the controller uses a Digital-to-Analog Converter (DAC) if needed to send an analog output signal. Digital PID controllers often provide additional features such as auto-tuning, remote communication, data logging, and more precise and flexible control compared to traditional analog systems.

44. What is PV Tracking in Control Systems?

Ans: PV Tracking is an option on many controllers. When a control loop is in MANUAL, with PV tracking turned on, the controller setpoint (SP) will follow the PV. When the loop is returned to AUTO, there is no sudden movement of the process, because the PV is already at setpoint. If PV tracking is turned off, returning to AUTO will drive the loop to its previous setpoint.

45. Why is PV Tracking Used?

Ans: The main purpose of PV tracking is to ensure a smooth transition between control states and prevent sudden or drastic changes in the controller output, which could destabilize the system or damage equipment. It avoids unnecessary oscillations or overshooting when transitioning between modes.

When PV tracking is enabled, the setpoint of the system is adjusted to the same value as the PV. For example, if a temperature controller is switched from manual to automatic mode, PV tracking ensures that the controller starts controlling from the current temperature (PV) rather than jumping to a predefined setpoint (SP).

46. What is override control functions?

Ans: Override control is a technique used in process control systems to protect equipment, ensure safety, and maintain critical process limits. In this setup, multiple controllers are involved, but only one is allowed to control the process at any given time depending on the situation.

Under normal operating conditions, the primary controller handles the process based on the desired setpoint, keeping everything running as intended. However, if a critical variable, like pressure, temperature, or level, starts approaching a dangerous limit, an override controller takes over automatically. This ensures that the system responds immediately to prevent damage or unsafe conditions. Once the critical variable returns to a safe range, control is handed back to the primary controller without disrupting the process.

For example, consider a boiler drum level control system. Normally, the drum level is controlled by adjusting the feedwater flow to maintain a steady water level. But if the level begins to rise too high or drop too low due to sudden disturbances, the override controller steps in to limit or shut off the feedwater, protecting the boiler from flooding or running dry. Once the water level returns to normal, the primary controller resumes its role.

47. What is selector control function?

Ans: A "selector" control strategy is where one signal is selected from multiple signals in a system to perform a measurement control function. This selected signal determines the controller's output. Selector control is often employed in systems where safety, process constraints, or operational efficiency require prioritization of specific variables. Examples of a selector control strategy is where we must select a process variable signal from multiple transmitters.

48. What are the various selector control function?

Ans: Following are the selector control function with example:

Type	Description	Example
High-Select Control	The controller selects the highest value among multiple inputs to maintain the critical parameter.	Temperature control in a heat exchanger where among three temperature sensors, the highest temperature is selected to ensure the cooling system responds to the worst-case scenario and prevents overheating.
Low-Select Control	The controller selects the lowest value among multiple inputs to ensure safety or process constraints.	Pressure control in a boiler system where Among multiple pressure readings, the lowest pressure is selected to avoid exceeding the maximum safe limit.

Mid-Select Control	The controller selects the middle value among multiple inputs to eliminate outliers or noise.	Reactor temperature control where Three temperature sensors are used, and the middle value is selected to eliminate outliers caused by faulty sensors.

49. What are the number of transmitters or input devices needed to be installed for redundancy of the system?

Ans: Three transmitters or input devices needed to be installed for redundancy. The problem with having two transmitters is a lack of information for accepting the value if the two transmitters happen to disagree. In a three-transmitter system, the function blocks may select the median signal value, or average the "best 2 out of 3."

50. What is single element, two element and three element boiler drum level control?

Ans: Boiler drum level control is critical in ensuring the safe and efficient operation of a boiler.

Single element control

The drum level (water level in the boiler drum) is controlled using a single input: the drum level signal. A feedback control loop adjusts the feedwater flow based solely on the drum level. The controller compares the measured drum level (process variable) to the desired level (setpoint). If the drum level deviates from the setpoint, the controller adjusts the feedwater flow to correct the level.

This control strategy is best for small boilers with steady steam demand. And it is ineffective for boilers with rapid load changes.

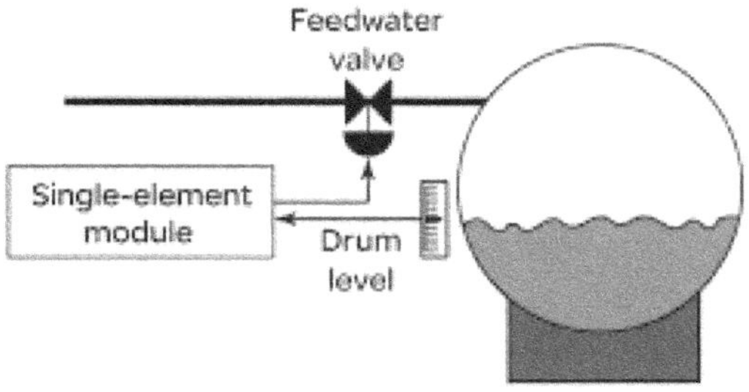

Fig 16.5 – Single element control

Two element control

It uses two inputs: Drum level signal for feedback control and Steam flow signal for feedforward control. Feedwater flow is adjusted based on both the drum level and the steam flow rate. The controller adjusts the feedwater flow based on the steam flow signal (anticipating changes in demand) while simultaneously correcting for errors in drum level. Best For Medium-sized boilers with moderate load variations.

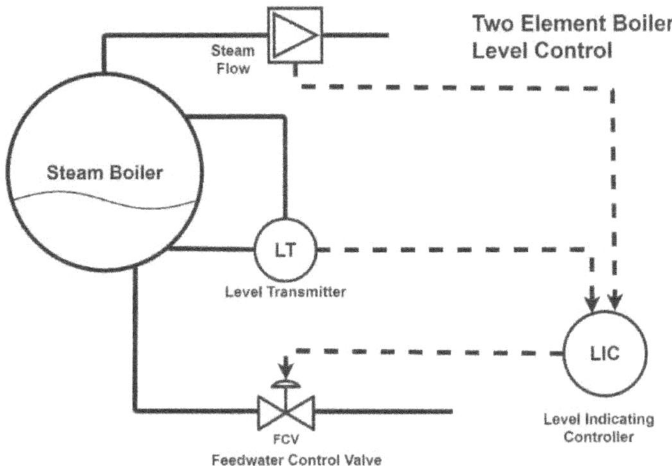

Fig 16.6 – Two element control

Three element control

It uses three inputs: Drum level signal for feedback control, Steam flow signal and Feedwater flow signal for feedforward control. Steam Flow: Monitors the rate at which steam is being drawn from the boiler. This information helps in understanding the demand for steam.

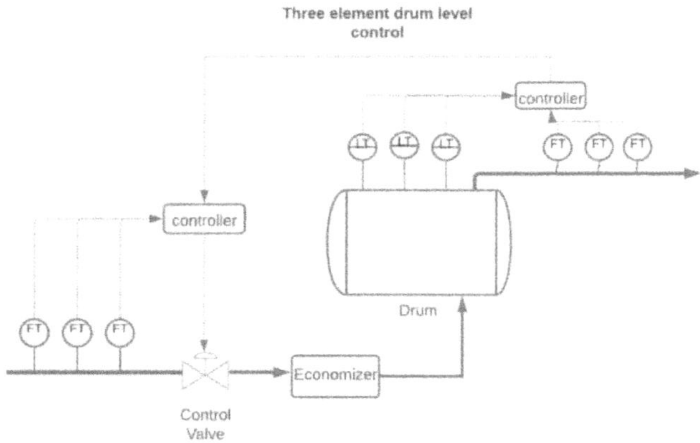

Fig 16.7 – Three element control

Feedwater Flow: Monitors the rate at which water is fed into the boiler. This provides information about the input of water to compensate for the steam being produced.

Drum Level: Monitors the actual water level in the boiler drum.

By considering the interactions between these three elements, the control system can adjust the feedwater flow to maintain a stable water level in the boiler drum. It is best for large boilers with significant load variations and dynamic operating conditions.

51. What is split range control loop?

Ans: A Split Range Control Loop is a type of control strategy in which a single controller output is divided between two or more final control elements (e.g., valves, dampers, or actuators), each responsible for a specific part of the process. Split Range Control Loop is used, where there are several manipulated variables, but a single output variable. The controller output is divided to operate multiple actuators, typically in different directions or ranges.

For e.g. Maintain boiler temperature at a desired setpoint. If the temperature is too high, the cooling water valve (say A) opens from 0 – 100% for controller output 0 -50% range. And if the temperature is too low, the steam valve opens (say B) from 0- 100% for controller output 50- 100% range. The control valve operates for the controller output above 50%.

Chapter: 17

Industrial Communication

1. What are the functions of Analog to Digital converter (ADC) and Digital to Analog Converter (DAC) in Instrumentation system?

Ans: In an instrumentation system, Analog-to-Digital Converters (ADC) and Digital-to-Analog Converters (DAC) play crucial roles in signal processing and control.

ADC converts analog signals (such as temperature, pressure, flow, or voltage) into digital signals for processing by microcontrollers, PLCs. DAC converts digital signals from controllers or processors back into analog signals for controlling actuators, motors, and other analog devices. ADC and DAC are essential for bridging the gap between the analog physical world and digital control systems.

2. What is an Operational Amplifier?

Ans: An Operational Amplifier (Op-Amp) is a high-gain, direct-coupled electronic voltage amplifier with differential inputs and a single-ended output. It has two input terminals, inverting (-) and non-inverting (+), for differential signal processing. It performs addition, subtraction, integration, and differentiation in analog computing.

3. What is an Instrumentation Amplifier?

Ans: An Instrumentation Amplifier (In-Amp) is a specialized differential amplifier designed for precise, low-noise signal amplification, commonly used in measurement and sensor applications. It offers high input impedance, excellent common-mode rejection (CMRR), and stable gain, making it ideal for amplifying weak signals while rejecting unwanted noise and interference. Typically built using three operational amplifiers, it ensures accurate differential signal processing with adjustable gain using external resistors. Instrumentation amplifiers are widely used in biomedical devices (ECG, EEG), industrial process control, and data acquisition systems, where precise and stable signal amplification is crucial.

4. What is CMRR (Common-Mode Rejection Ratio)?

Ans: Common-Mode Rejection Ratio (CMRR) is a key performance parameter of differential and instrumentation amplifiers that measures their ability to reject common-mode signals (signals that appear simultaneously on both input terminals) while amplifying the desired differential signal (the difference between the two input voltages).

Higher CMRR means better noise rejection, making the amplifier more effective in rejecting interference and unwanted signals. It is crucial in instrumentation amplifiers, where small sensor signals must be amplified without distortion.

5. What is a Digital Multiplexer and Demultiplexer?

Ans: A Multiplexer (MUX) is a combinational circuit that selects one of many input signals and forwards it to a single output line. It acts as a data selector, allowing multiple data sources to share a single transmission channel, reducing hardware complexity. Example: A 4-to-1 MUX has 4 input lines, 1 output line, and 2 selection bits to choose the active input.

A Demultiplexer (DEMUX) is the reverse of a multiplexer. It takes a single input signal and distributes it to one of many output lines based on control inputs. It is used when a single data source needs to be sent to multiple destinations. Example: A 1-to-4 DEMUX has 1 input, 4 output lines, and 2 selection bits to choose the active output.

6. What is a Data Acquisition System (DAS)?

Ans: A Data Acquisition System (DAS) is an electronic system used to collect, process, and store data from various sensors and instruments. The components of DAS are:

- ***Sensors and transducers***: It measure physical parameters like temperature, pressure, or vibration and convert to electrical form.
- ***Signal Conditioning***: It consists of amplifiers and filters, that converts signals to a suitable form for processing.
- ***Analog-to-Digital Converter (ADC):*** It converts analog signal to the digital signal.
- ***Processing & Storage Unit:*** It consists of PLC, microprocessor, which process the signal for necessary action and as well as stores the data.
- ***User Interface & Software***: It basically displays and analyzes data using software.

7. How does digital technology improve industrial instrumentation?

Ans: Digital technology allows multiple variables to be communicated over a single channel, increasing efficiency and reducing wiring costs. Whereas, each analog signal requires a dedicated wire pair, making communication costly and inefficient compared to digital networks. With digital signalling, a single pair of wires or coaxial cable is able to convey a theoretically unlimited number of data points.

8. What is a Bus in a Communication System?

Ans: A bus in a communication system is a data transmission pathway that allows multiple devices (such as sensors, controllers, actuators, and computers) to communicate over a shared medium.

9. What is a serial communication and parallel communication?

Ans: Serial communication is a data transfer method where data is sent bit by bit sequentially over a single data line. It is slower for short distances but efficient for long-distance communication due to reduced interference and lower signal degradation. Example: Communication between microcontrollers and sensors, USB (Universal Serial Bus) for data transfer.

Parallel communication is a data transfer method where multiple bits are transmitted simultaneously using multiple data lines. It is faster for short distances but suffers from signal degradation and crosstalk over long distances. It requires more hardware and wiring, making it more complex. Example: Communication between CPU and RAM.

10. What is baud rate and bit rate?

Ans: Both Bit rate and Baud rate are generally used in data communication to measure the speed of data. Baud rate is defined to be the number of signal changes or symbols sent per second over a communication channel. This decides the extent to which a transmission medium, such as a wire or a wireless spectrum, is capable of changing its state in one second.

Bit rate refers to the number of bits transmitted per second and is, therefore, a measure of the rapidity at which data is being transmitted over a communication channel. It is normally expressed in Kbps, Mbps, or Gbps.

Bit Rate = Baud Rate × No. of Bits per Baud

11. What is Bandwidth in Communication Systems?

Ans: In a communication system, Bandwidth refers to the range of frequencies that a communication channel, medium, or system can transmit. It is the difference between the highest and lowest frequency components in a signal or channel. Bandwidth determines the data-carrying capacity or transmission speed of the system.

12. What is simplex and duplex communication network?

Ans: Simplex and Duplex communication networks describe how data flows between two devices or points in a communication system. In a Simplex communication network, data flows in one direction only from the sender to the receiver. The receiver cannot send data back. Example: Radio Broadcasting (FM/AM radio), Fire Alarms and Public Address Systems.

Duplex communication allows two-way data flow between devices. It is further divided into: Half-Duplex Communication and Full-Duplex Communication. In half duplex communication, data flows in both directions, but only one direction at a time. Example: Walkie-Talkie. In full-Duplex Communication, data flows in both directions simultaneously, allowing simultaneous sending and receiving. Example: Mobile Networks.

13. What is MAC (Media Access Control) address? What is the difference between MAC address and IP address?

Ans: A MAC (Media Access Control) address is a unique identifier assigned to network devices for communication within a Local Area Network (LAN). Every device that connects to a network, including computers, routers, smartphones, and IoT devices has a unique MAC address. The length of MAC address is 48 bits and represented in a hexadecimal notation.

The difference between MAC address and IP address are:

Feature	*MAV Address*	*IP Address*
Purpose	Identifies hardware on a local network.	Identifies location on a global network.
Format	Hexadecimal (e.g., 00:1A:2B:3C:4D:5E)	Dotted decimal (e.g., 192.168.1.1)
Uniqueness	Globally unique (assigned by the manufacturer)	Can change (assigned by DHCP or manually)

Scope	Works only within the local network (LAN)	Can route across multiple networks (Internet)
Permanence	Permanent (can be spoofed)	Dynamic or Static (can be reassigned)

14. What is Channel Arbitration?

Ans: Channel Arbitration is a technique used in communication networks to resolve conflicts when multiple devices attempt to access a shared communication channel simultaneously. It ensures that only one device transmits at a time, preventing data collisions and maintaining orderly communication. Arbitration is crucial in networks where bandwidth is shared, such as buses, Ethernet.

15. What is Master-Slave Communication Method?

Ans: The Master-Slave Communication Method is a hierarchical communication protocol where one device (Master) controls the communication by initiating, managing, and coordinating the data exchange with one or more subordinate devices (Slaves). In this model, slaves cannot communicate directly with each other; they can only respond when requested by the master. Example: PLCs (Programmable Logic Controllers) using Modbus.

16. What is a Communication Protocol?

Ans: A Communication Protocol is a set of rules, standards, and procedures that define how data is formatted, transmitted, received, and interpreted between two or more devices in a communication system. These protocols ensure that devices from different manufacturers or systems can communicate seamlessly by adhering to common guidelines.

Types of communication protocol:

- **Network Communication Protocols**: Used for network communication between devices. Example: - Ethernet

- ***Serial Communication Protocols***: Transmits data bit by bit over a single channel. Example: - UART (Universal Asynchronous Receiver-Transmitter): Serial communication in microcontrollers, RS-232: Used in serial ports.
- ***Parallel Communication Protocols***: Transmits multiple bits simultaneously over multiple channels. Example: - Centronics: Used in older printers.
- ***Industrial Communication Protocols***: Used in automation and industrial control systems. Example: - Modbus, Profibus, CAN (Controller Area Network).

17. What is network topology?

Ans: Network topology refers to the arrangement or layout of devices (nodes) and connections (links) in a communication network. It defines how devices such as computers, switches, routers, and sensors are interconnected and how data flows between them.

Types of network topologies:

- ***Bus topology:*** All devices are connected to a single shared cable. The main drawback is if the common cable fails, then the whole system will crash down. Example: Old Ethernet networks.
- ***Star Topology***: All devices are connected to a central hub or switch. In this case, Hub or switch is a single point of failure. Example: Modern Ethernet LANs.
- ***Ring Topology***: Each node connects to exactly two other nodes, forming a ring.
- ***Mesh Topology***: Nodes on a network are interconnected to one or more nodes directly, forming a mesh-like structure. It's highly reliable but expensive due to many connections.
- ***Tree (Hierarchical) Topology***: It is a combination of star and bus topology in a hierarchical structure.

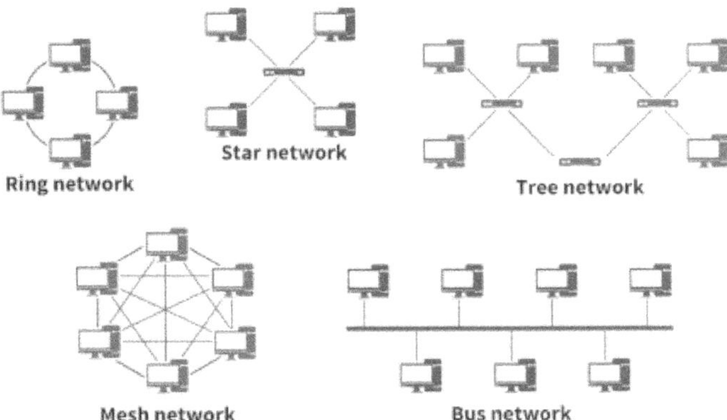

Fig 17.1 – Network topology

18. What is DTE and DCE devices?

Ans: DTE (Data Terminal Equipment) devices are the end devices or source/destination of the data. They are responsible for generating or receiving information. Example: Computer, Printers, PLC.

DCE (Data Communication Equipment) devices act as intermediaries that facilitate communication between two DTE devices by transmitting, receiving, and converting data signals. Example: Modem, router, switch.

19. What is the OSI Model?

Ans: The OSI (Open Systems Interconnection) model is a conceptual framework developed by ISO (International Organization for Standardization) to standardize the functions of a communication system. It divides the process of communication between two devices into seven distinct layers, each with specific responsibilities.

- ***Physical Layer (Layer1):*** It deals with hardware, electrical signals, and bit transmission. Example: Twisted-pair cables (RS-485), Fiber optics, Ethernet cables.
- ***Data Link Later (Layer 2);*** It manages physical addressing, error detection, and frame transmission. It manages physical addressing, error detection, and frame transmission. Example: Modbus RTU, Profibus DP,

Ethernet/IP, MAC Addresses.

- ***Network Layer (Layer 3***): IT handles logical addressing and routing of packets. Example: IP Addressing, Routing, Modbus TCP/IP.

- ***Transport Layer (Layer 4***): It ensures reliable data transfer, error correction, and flow control. Example: TCP/IP (for reliability), UDP (for speed).

- ***Session Layer (Layer 5):*** Manages session establishment, maintenance, and termination. Example: SCADA-HMI communication sessions.

- ***Presentation Layer (Layer 6):*** It ensures data formatting, encryption, and compression. Example: Data conversion from sensors to human-readable values (temperature, pressure).

- ***Application Layer (Layer 7):*** It Provides user interface and network services. Example: SCADA Systems, HMI (Human-Machine Interface).

20. What is a gateway device in communication system?

Ans: A gateway is a protocol converter. A gateway potentially operates in all seven layers of the OSI model. A gateway by itself can accept a packet formatted for one protocol & convert it to a pocket formatted for another protocol before forwarding it. Example: RS232 to USB converter.

21. What is timeout in communication protocol?

Ans: A transmitter will send a message and the receiver will receive it. In return, the receiver will send an acknowledgment to the transmitter that it has received the message. The transmitter waits for this acknowledgement and it understands that the message has been communicated properly. For this purpose, there is a waiting time for getting this acknowledgment.

In this time interval, the acknowledgment should reach the transmitter. After the time elapses, if still the acknowledgment is not received, then it means the communication has not happened. This causes the transmitter to throw an exception message in the whole network, alarming about the failure in communication. This waiting time is called a timeout in communication protocols.

22. What happens when the timeout is too fast or too slow?

Ans: If the timeout is set too slow or long, then it will result in communication lag of the network. Because, if there are many devices in the network with a single master and multiple slaves, then the next slave will have to wait to give its response till the response of the first slave is over and acknowledged. Due to this, the network becomes slow and all the resources will not be utilized efficiently. Also, if other devices are added in the future, then a lot of network traffic will increase leading to increased congestion.

If the timeout is set too fast or short, then it will cause data loss or an unreliable network. This is because the slave devices will not get much time to respond to a request. If the ideal time for communication is 5 seconds, and if the time is set to 3 seconds, then communication errors will arrive every time.

23. What is EIA/TIA-232? Mention its key features.

Ans: EIA/TIA-232 (also known as RS-232) is a standard for serial communication developed by the Electronic Industries Alliance (EIA) and Telecommunications Industry Association (TIA). This standard allows point-to-point data transfer between Data Terminal Equipment (DTE) (e.g., a computer) and Data Communication Equipment (DCE) (e.g., a modem). It is the part of Physical Layer (Layer 1) of OSI model.

Key features:

- Full-Duplex: Simultaneous two-way communication is supported.

- Maximum Cable Length: Up to 15 meters (50 feet) for reliable transmission.
- Data Transfer Speed: Up to 115.2 kbps (kilobits per second).
- It uses a DB9 connector.

24. What is EIA/TIA-422 (RS-422) and EIA/TIA-485 (RS-485)?

Ans: EIA/TIA-422 and EIA/TIA-485 are serial communication standards. These standards define differential signalling for long-distance and noise-resistant data transmission. It is the part of Physical Layer (Layer 1) of OSI model.

Differences Between EIA/TIA-422 and EIA/TIA-485:

Feature	_EIA/TIA-422 (RS 422)_	_EIA/TIA-485 (RS 485)_
Communication	Point-to-multipoint	Multipoint (multi-drop)
Max Distance	1200 m (4000 ft)	1200 m (4000 ft)
Max Speed	10 Mbps (short distance)	10 Mbps (short distance)
Max Devices	1 driver, 10 receivers	32 drivers, 32 receivers
Noise Immunity	High	Very high

25. What RS stands for in RS-232 communication Protocol?

Ans: RS stands for Recommended Standard.

26. What is the difference between RS-232 and RS-485 in Cable and Connector Selection?

Ans: The difference between RS-232 and RS-485 in Cable and Connector Selection are:

Feature	RS-232	RS-485
Cable Type	Shielded/Unshielded Twisted Pair	Mostly Shielded Twisted Pair

	3 to 9 wires (TX, RX, GND, control)	2 wires for half-duplex, 4 for full-duplex
Number of Wires		
Connectors	DB-9, DB-25, RJ45	DB-9, Terminal Blocks, RJ45
Maximum Distance	15 m (50 ft) at 9600 bps	1200 m (4000 ft) at 100 kbps
Topology	Point-to-Point	Multi-Point (up to 32 devices)

27. What are crossed and Straight RS-232 cable used in Industry?

Ans: Cross cable wiring for RS232 usually happens between two DCE (data communication equipment) devices, or two DTE (Data Terminal Equipment) devices.

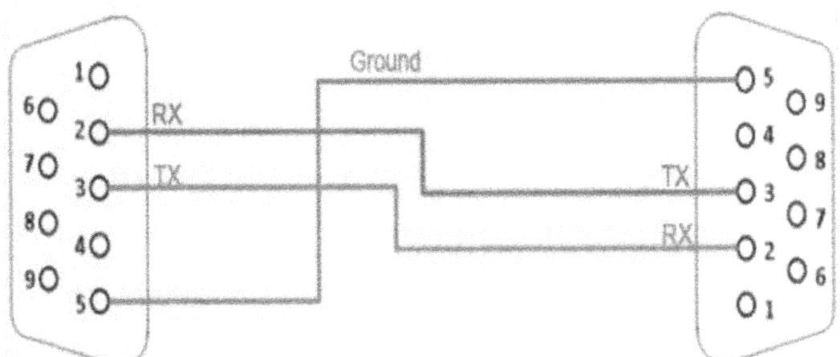

Fig 17.2 – RS-232 cross cable

Straight cable wiring for RS232 usually happens between DCE (data communication equipment) devices, and DTE (Data Terminal Equipment) devices.

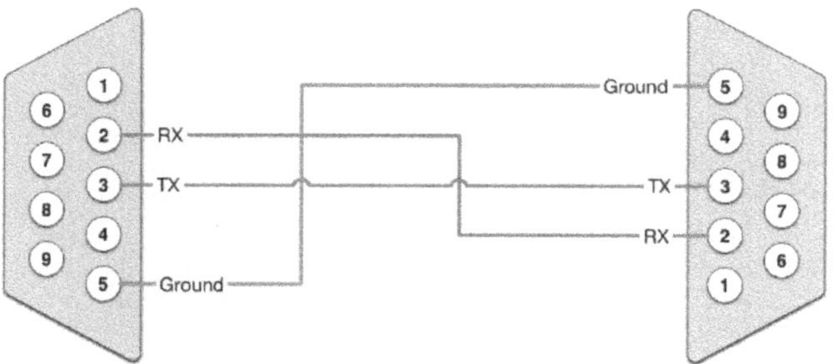

Fig 17.3 – RS-232 straight cable

28. How can RS232 or RS485 cable used in USB port?

Ans: By using RS232 to USB converter or RS485 to USB converter.

29. What is Ethernet Networking?

Ans: Ethernet is a wired networking technology protocol that enables devices to communicate within a Local Area Network (LAN). In ethernet protocol, data is broken into frames, each containing: Source MAC Address (where data is coming from), Destination MAC Address (where data is going), Data and Error Checking (CRC).

Ethernet is the most widely used LAN technology due to its speed, reliability, and ease of implementation. It continues to evolve with higher speeds (100 Gbps+), Power over Ethernet (PoE) for powering devices, and advanced security features for modern networks. In the OSI (Open Systems Interconnection) model, Ethernet operates primarily at the Physical Layer (Layer 1) and Data Link Layer (Layer 2). These layers define how data is transmitted over cables and how devices identify and communicate with each other on a local network.

30. What is a Repeater (Hub) in Ethernet Networking?

Ans: A Repeater (or Hub) is a basic network device used in Ethernet networking to regenerate and amplify signals over long distances. In Ethernet networks, signals weaken or degrade as they travel through cables due to attenuation (loss of signal strength). A repeater boosts the signal back to its original strength, ensuring reliable communication across extended distances.

31. What is an Ethernet Switch?

Ans: An Ethernet switch is a network device that connects multiple devices (such as computers, servers, printers, and routers) within a Local Area Network (LAN). It uses MAC addresses to forward data to the intended recipient, rather than broadcasting it to all devices like a hub. This makes Ethernet switches more efficient, secure, and scalable, as they significantly reduce network collisions and bandwidth congestion.

32. What is Layer 2 and Layer 3 network switch?

Ans: A Layer-2 switch is the one that operates in Data Link Layer (Layer 2) of the OSI model. In the data link layer, the MAC address of the device is defined. When a device wants to communicate, it will pass the destination MAC address to the layer-2 switch. The switch will browse the network for the destination address and send the data to it. However, a layer-2 switch cannot communicate with devices of different IP address ranges.

A Layer-3 switch is the one that operates at both the Data Link Layer (Layer 2) and the Network Layer (Layer 3). In the network layer, the IP address of the device is defined. When a device wants to communicate, it will pass the destination IP address to the layer-3 switch. The switch will browse the network for the destination address and send the data to it.

33. What is Ethernet driver?

Ans: It is a software that allows an Ethernet card in a computer to decode packets and send them to the operating system and encode data from the operating system for transmission by the Ethernet card through the network.

34. What is a media converter?

Ans: A media converter is a networking device that transparently converts Ethernet or other communication protocols from one cable type to another type, usually copper CATx/UTP to optical fibre.

35. What is the difference between Ethernet hub and Ethernet switch?

Ans: Following are the difference between Ethernet hub and Ethernet switch:

Ethernet switch	_Ethernet hub_
Switches record MAC addresses in a table to learn which devices to transmit information to.	Hubs are less intelligent devices and always send all information to all connected devices.
Switches connect devices to a singular LAN to transmit data from one device to another.	Hubs group Ethernet devices on a LAN, broadcasting all data to all devices.
Switches can operate at full duplex or half duplex, using all available bandwidth, creating faster and more efficient networks.	Hubs operate at half duplex, making them slower and forcing devices to share bandwidth equally.
Switches send information using data packets.	Hubs send information using bits.

36. What types of cable are used in ethernet networking?

Ans: In ethernet networking, unshielded, twisted pair (UTP)wiring and RJ-45 "flat" connectors are used.

37. What are Straight-Through and Crossover Ethernet Cables?

Ans: Straight-through and crossover Ethernet cables are two types of twisted-pair cables used for connecting devices in a network. They follow different wiring standards (TIA/EIA-568A and TIA/EIA-568B) that determine how the twisted pairs of wires inside the cable are arranged.

A straight-through cable has identical wiring on both ends, following the same standard- either TIA/EIA-568A or TIA/EIA-568B. This means the pinouts match on both connectors. It is used to connect different types of devices, such as: PC to Switch or Hub, Router to Switch and PC to Router.

Pin Configuration:

- Pin 1 to Pin 1 (Orange/White)
- Pin 2 to Pin 2 (Orange)
- Pin 3 to Pin 3 (Green/White)
- Pin 6 to Pin 6 (Green)
- Pin 4,5,7,8 for other purposes or remain unused in standard Ethernet.

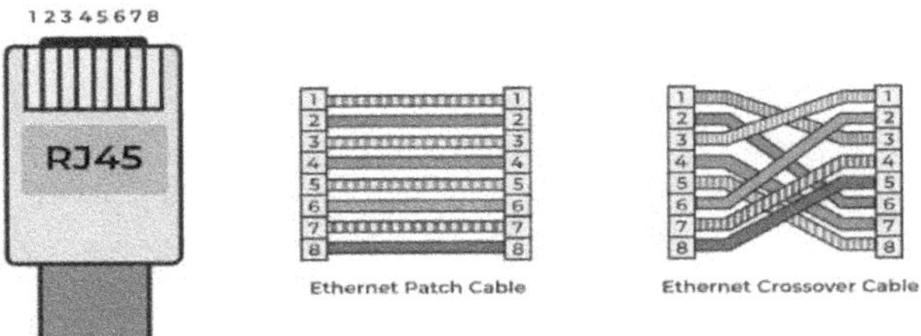

Fig 17.4 – Ethernet cable

A crossover cable has different wiring standards on each end — one end follows   TIA/EIA-568A and the other follows TIA/EIA-568B. This allows transmit (TX) and receive (RX) signals to be crossed, enabling direct communication between similar devices. It is used to connect similar types of devices, such as: PC to PC, Switch to Switch, Hub to Hub, Router to Router.

Pin Configuration:

- Pin 1 (Orange/White) → Pin 3 (Green/White)
- Pin 2 (Orange) → Pin 6 (Green)
- Pin 3 (Green/White) → Pin 1 (Orange/White)
- Pin 6 (Green) → Pin 2 (Orange)

38. What is a PoE Switch?

Ans: A PoE (Power over Ethernet) Switch is a network switch that not only provides data connectivity but also supplies electrical power to connected devices through Ethernet cables. This eliminates the need for separate power cables, simplifying network installation and reducing infrastructure costs. It is ideal for modern networks that require flexible placement of devices such as IP cameras, VoIP phones, and wireless access points.

39. What types of cable are used in Ethernet protocol?

Ans: All the CAT-type cables and fiber optic cables are used.

40. What is the function of Hub, switch and router?

Ans: Hub connects two or more Ethernet devices. Switch connect two or more LAN devices and Router usually connects at least two networks together, such as two LANs, two WANs.

41. What is Internet Protocol (IP)?

Ans: Internet Protocol (IP) is a fundamental communication protocol used for addressing, routing, and delivering data packets across networks, including the internet. It operates at the Network Layer (Layer 3) of the OSI model and defines how data is structured, addressed, transmitted, and routed between devices such as computers, servers, routers, and IoT devices. The Internet Protocol (IP) functions primarily at the Network Layer (Layer 3) of the OSI model.

In IP protocol, each device is assigned a unique IP address (IPv4 or IPv6) to identify the sender and receiver. Data is broken into smaller units called packets, each with header information containing source and destination IP addresses. IP uses routers to determine the best path for packets to travel from source to destination.

There are two types of IP address:

- IPv4 (Internet Protocol Version 4): It has 32-bit address (e.g.,

192.168.1.1)

- IPv6 (Internet Protocol Version 6): It has 128-bit address (e.g., 2001:0db8:85a3:0000:0000:8a2e:0370:7334)

42. How to check the communication status between two IP enabled devices?

Ans: Computers enabled to communicate using Internet Protocol (IP) are equipped with a utility program named ping useful for detecting the presence of other IP-enabled computers or devices connected to the same network. The format of this program is execution by typing the word "ping" at the computer's command-line interface followed by the IP address of the other device you wish to detect the presence of.

43. Which is the protocol used to map IP address and Mac Address?

Ans: Address Resolution Protocol (ARP).

44. How IP Address and MAC Address Function Together in Networking?

Ans: In a network, IP Address and MAC Address work in conjunction to ensure data reaches the correct destination.

When a device (e.g., a computer or sensor) needs to send data, it creates packets with IP addresses for the sender and receiver. Before sending the packet on the local network, the sender uses Address Resolution Protocol (ARP) to find the MAC address corresponding to the receiver's IP address. The IP packet is encapsulated into an Ethernet frame, with the MAC address in the frame header and the IP address inside the packet. The Ethernet frame travels over the LAN using MAC addressing to reach the destination device. At the destination network, the final router resolves the destination IP to a MAC address, ensuring the frame reaches the correct device.

Example: Consider a DCS control system having Pressure Sensor (Field Instrument): 192.168.1.10, DCS Controller: 192.168.1.20 and HMI (Human-Machine Interface): 192.168.1.30.   The pressure sensor collects real-time pressure data and needs to send it to the DCS controller. The data is packed into IP packets with Source IP (192.168.1.10) and Destination IP (192.168.1.20). The sensor uses ARP (Address Resolution Protocol) to resolve the MAC address of the DCS controller. The data is encapsulated into Ethernet frames with the MAC addresses and the switch delivers the frame to the correct destination device. The DCS controller extracts the data from the received frames and processes it.

45. What is the FDT Technology?

Ans: FDT Technology standardizes the communication interface between field devices and control systems or engineering and asset management tools. Key features are its independence from the communication protocol and the software environment of either the device or the host system. FDT Technology allows any device to be accessed from any host through any protocol.

46. What is a HART communication protocol?

Ans: The HART (Highway Addressable Remote Transducer) communication protocol is a hybrid industrial automation protocol that enables two-way digital communication over the existing 4-20 mA analog signal. It is widely used in process control industries to communicate with field devices such as transmitters, valves, and actuators.

The HART communication protocol is based on the Bell 202 telephone communication standard and operates using the frequency shift keying (FSK) principle. The digital signal is made up of two frequencies— 1,200 Hz and 2,200 Hz representing bits 1 and 0, respectively. Sine waves of these two frequencies are superimposed on the direct current (dc) analog signal cables to provide simultaneous analog and digital communications. Because the average value of the FSK signal is always zero, the 4–20 mA analog signal is not affected.

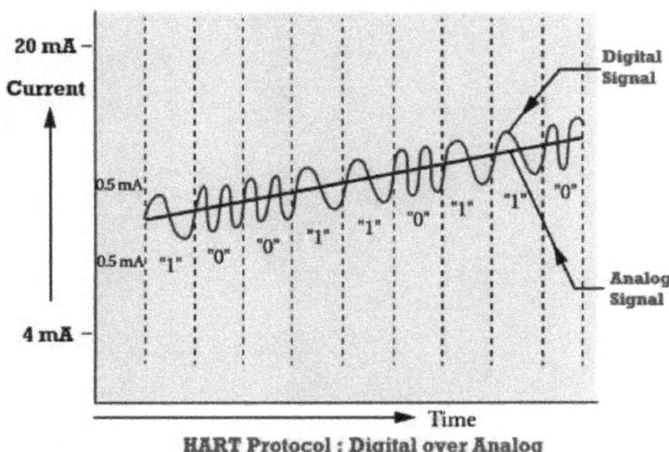

Fig 17.5 – HART protocol

The HART Protocol communicates at 1200 bps without interrupting the 4-20mA signal and allows a host application (master) to get two or more digital updates per second from a smart field device. As the digital FSK signal is phase continuous, there is no interference with the 4-20mA signal.

47. What is a HART communicator? What are its key functions?

Ans: A HART (Highway Addressable Remote Transducer) Communicator is a handheld device used to configure, calibrate, troubleshoot, and monitor field instruments that operate using the HART communication protocol.

Key features:

- It is used to configure device to Set range, span, and zero values of field instruments.
- It is used to perform sensor zeroing and calibration checks.
- It is used to Retrieve error codes and status reports for

troubleshooting.

- It is used to read real-time process variables like pressure, flow.
- It is used to test signal strength and loop connectivity in the 4-20 mA loop.

Fig 17.6 – Hart communicator

48. How is HART communicator connected in loop?

Ans: HART can be connected in any set of points in the circuit electrically parallel to the transmitter's terminals.

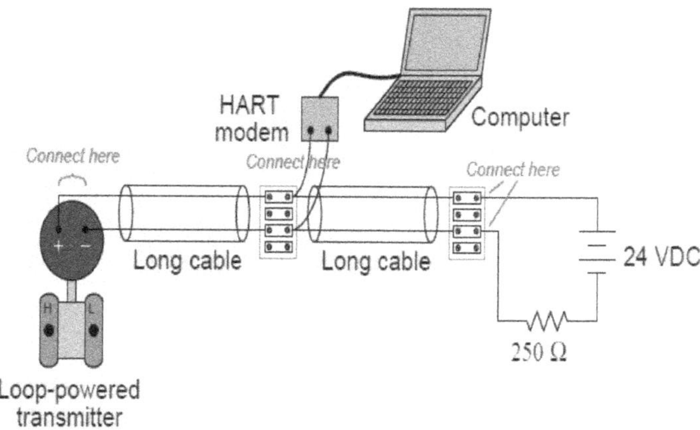

Fig 17.7 – Hart communicator connection

49. What value of resistance required in loop for HART communication?

Ans: Minimum 250 Ohm. The impedance is needed to get the amplitude of the frequency pulses high enough to be read.

50. What is HART multi-variable transmitters?

Ans: A HART Multi-Variable Transmitter is a type of field device that can measure and transmit multiple process variables simultaneously over a single 4-20 mA loop using the HART communication protocol. Unlike traditional transmitters where a single pair of wires can only convey one 4-20 mA analog signal, but in HART multi-variable transmitters, that same pair of wires may convey multiple digital signals using HART protocol. Example of this is Coriolis-effect flowmeters, which by their very nature simultaneously measure the density, flow rate, and temperature of the fluid passing through them.

51. What is Modbus protocol?

Ans: MODBUS is a serial communication protocol that enables communication between field devices (like sensors, actuators, and PLCs) and control systems (like DCS or SCADA). It is developed by Modicon published by Modicon in 1979 for use with its programmable logic controllers (PLCs). MODBUS is popular due to its simplicity, robustness, and ability to work over multiple physical layers like RS-232, RS-485, and Ethernet (TCP/IP).

MODBUS is based on a master-slave architecture where The Master initiates queries (e.g., PLC or DCS) and the Slave devices (e.g., sensors or actuators) respond with the requested data. Only one master is allowed, but multiple slaves can be connected. Modbus works by using standard digital codes to read from or write to devices. Any Modbus-compatible device is programmed to understand and respond to these codes correctly.

The Modbus functions primarily at the Physical layer (Layer1), Data link layer (layer2) and application layer (Layer 7) of the OSI model.

52. How many slave devices can be connected to master device in Modbus?

Ans: 247

53. What types of cable are used for Modbus communication?

Ans: The choice of cable for MODBUS communication depends on the physical layer being used: RS-232, RS-485, or MODBUS TCP/IP (Ethernet).

For Modbus RTU RS-485 with Shielded Twisted Pair (120Ω impedance) cable are used. Twisted pairs help reduce noise by canceling electromagnetic interference, and the shielding further protects the signal over long distances. For short-distance and point-to-point communication RS-232 is used and standard serial communication cables like DB9 or DB25 connector cables are sufficient, typically using simple unshielded multi-core cables. And for MODBUS TCP/IP over networks CAT5e/CAT6 Ethernet cables are used.

54. How Modbus transmit data between the devices?

Ans: The Modbus communication standard defines a set of commands for reading (receiving) and writing (transmitting) data between a master device and one or more slave devices connected to the network. Each of these commands consists of frame of messages that includes: Device address, Function code, 8 bit data types, error checking.

Two different formats are specified in the Modbus standard: ASCII and RTU. In Modbus ASCII mode, all slave device addresses, function codes, and data are represented in the form of ASCII characters (7 bits each), which may be read directly by any terminal program intercepting the serial data stream. This makes troubleshooting easier; to be able to directly view the Modbus data frames in human readable form. In Modbus RTU mode, all slave device addresses, function codes, and data are expressed in raw binary form. The number of bits as RTU frames, making Modbus ASCII slower than Modbus RTU for any given data.

A Modbus network relies on IDs of individual slave devices. Master device request data from specific ID and the slave device of that ID responds accordingly. Since the Modbus master is the only device to send requests to the slaves, they are not assigned any ID. The communication does not exist between the slaves.

55. What is function code used in Modbus message structure?

Ans: Function codes are one-byte numerical identifiers that represent specific operations in Modbus communication.

Common Modbus function codes

Code	Description
01	Read coil status
02	Read input status
03	Read holding registers
04	Read input registers
05	Force single coil
06	Preset single register
07	Read exception status
15	Force multiple coils
16	Preset multiple registers
17	Report slave ID

These codes instruct the device on actions to take such as reading the status of coils, retrieving values from registers, or writing new data. Modbus has nine number of such function codes.

In Modbus language, a coil is a discrete output value. Modbus function 01 can be used to read the status of such an output. It is only possible to query one device at a time. When receiving a Modbus query message with function 01, the slave collects the necessary output values and constructs an answer message.

Function 01 query structure

Byte	Value	Description
1	1...247	Slave device address
2	1	Function code
3	0...255	Starting address, high byte
4	0...255	Starting address, low byte
5	0...255	Number of coils, high byte
6	0...255	Number of coils, low byte
7(...8)	LRC/CRC	Error check value

Similarly for function code 03, internal values in a Modbus device are stored in holding registers. These registers are two bytes wide and can be used for various purposes. Some registers contain configuration parameters where others are used to return measured values (temperatures etc.) to a host. Modbus function 03 is used to request one or more holding register values from a device. Only one slave device can be addressed in a single query. After processing the query, the Modbus slave returns the 16-bit values of the requested holding registers.

56. How to build a 2 wire (half duplex) Modbus network using RS-485?

Ans: In half duplex Modbus communication, two wires are required for each signal. These wires create a half-duplex solution, where the signal can travel in only one direction at a time. Each device should have an 'A' and a 'B' wire connected, forming a half-duplex communication channel. The A- wire connects to A-, and the B+ wire connects to B+. Together, A- and B+ create the signal.

A logic value of 1 is transmitted when line A is low, and line B is high. Conversely, a value of 0 is transmitted when line A is high, and line B is low. The number of wires needed is proportional to the number of simultaneous signals. For example, transmitting four signals requires eight wires.

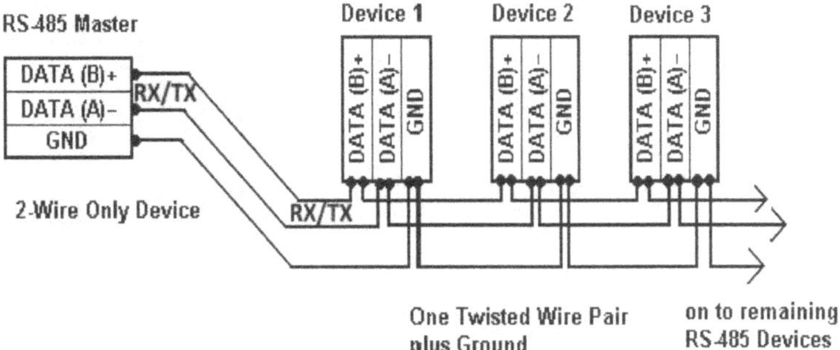

Fig 17.8- 2 wire duplex modbus

An RS485 system consists of a single linear cable (with no branches) and 120-ohm resistors connected across the two wires at each end of the cable.

57. How to build a 4 wire (full duplex) Modbus network using RS-485?

Ans:

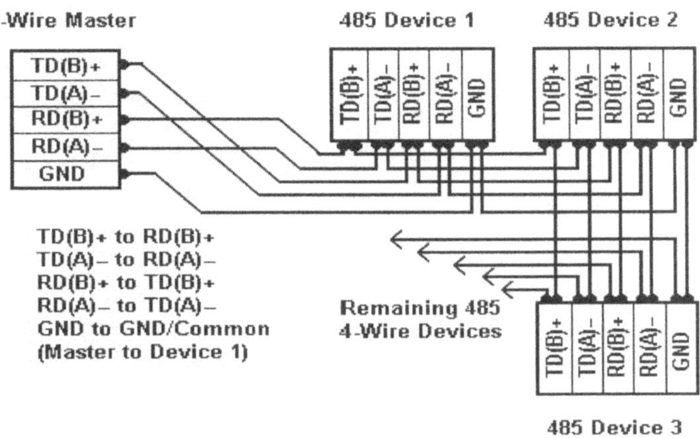

Fig 17.9- 4 wire duplex modbus

Full Duplex means that data can pass simultaneously both directions. This requires 4 wires - one pair to Transmit and one pair to Receive. The advantage of the 4-wire connection is that all devices only see commands from the Master, and no Device sees the responses from other devices.

58. How can RS232/RS485 Modbus devices communicate over Modbus TCP/IP?

Ans: Modbus TCP/IP is simply Modbus protocol with a TCP wrapper, it is very simple for existing Modbus devices to communicate over Modbus TCP/IP. A gateway device is required to convert from the current physical layer (RS232, RS485 or others) to Ethernet and to convert Modbus protocol to Modbus TCP/IP.

59. What is the significance of baud rate in Modbus communication?

Ans: Baud rate should be the same in both the master and slave devices. It is not like one device will be set to 19200 and another at 9600. Otherwise, communication will not happen.

60. What is DNP3 Protocol?

Ans: DNP3 (Distributed Network Protocol) is an open-source communication protocol primarily used in SCADA (Supervisory Control and Data Acquisition) systems for industrial automation, developed by GE in 1990. It facilitates reliable data transmission between master stations, Remote Terminal Units (RTUs), and Intelligent Electronic Devices (IEDs) in environments where long distances and noise interference are common.

DNP3 uses 27 basic function codes to exchange data between Masters and Remotes. Some of those function codes enable a Master to request and receive status info from a Remote. Other function codes enable a Master to change a Remote's settings.

The DNP3 functions primarily at the Physical layer (Layer1), Data link layer (layer2) and application layer (Layer 7) of the OSI model.

61. What is the difference between Modbus and DNP3?

Ans: Following are the differences between Modbus and DNP3:

Feature	DNP3 Protocol	Modbus Protocol
Architecture	Event-driven protocol (transmits only changes).	Polling-based (Master continuously polls slaves).
Communication Type	Multi-master and multi-slave.	Single master, multiple slaves.
Speed	Slower but more reliable (ideal for critical systems).	Faster but less efficient (suitable for simpler networks).
Data Structure	Complex, supports binary, analog, and counter data.	Simple, uses registers, coils, and bits.
Scalability	Supports large networks with multi-layered architecture.	Works better in small to medium networks.
Network Type	Works with Ethernet, RS-232, RS-485, TCP/IP.	Mainly RS-232, RS-485, or TCP/IP.

62. How to choose between Modus and DNP3 protocol?

Ans: It is preferable to use DNP3 if:

- The system requires time synchronization, event logging, and advanced error handling.
- The system operates over long distances with potential noise interference.
- The system dealing with critical infrastructure like power utilities.

It is preferable to use Modbus if:

- The system is simple and lightweight protocol for local

communication.

- The application is in manufacturing or industrial automation with fewer devices.
- High speed is more important than detailed event logging.

63. What is Actuator Sensor Interface (ASi) Protocol?

Ans: In earlier PLC systems, sensor and actuator connections were made exclusively through hardwiring. As the number of input and output devices increased, the corresponding wiring also grew, leading to increased system complexity.

To address this issue, the Actuator-Sensor Interface (ASi) protocol was developed. ASi is a simple and cost-effective interface system that connects sensors and actuators using only two wires, significantly reducing wiring requirements and system complexity.

The ASi protocol operates in a master-slave configuration. An ASi master module can communicate with up to 62 slave I/O modules, with each slave supporting up to eight inputs and eight outputs simultaneously. This enables the master module to efficiently handle a total of 992 I/O points (496 inputs and 496 outputs).

64. What do you mean by fieldbus?

Ans: Fieldbus is a digital, two-way communication network used for connecting field devices (such as sensors, actuators, transmitters, and controllers) to a central control system in industrial automation. Unlike traditional point-to-point wiring, where each device needs separate cabling, Fieldbus allows multiple devices to be connected on a single cable, drastically reducing wiring complexity and cost. In a Fieldbus system, devices can communicate with each other and with the control system in real-time, sharing information like process values, status, and diagnostic data. Fieldbus networks use a master-slave or peer-to-peer communication model, depending on the protocol. Fieldbus not only transmits measured values but also supports device configuration, remote calibration, and diagnostic functions, improving maintenance and system efficiency.

65. What is Profibus communication protocol?

Ans: PROFIBUS (Process Field BUS) is a high-speed, industrial communication protocol used in automation and control systems. It has two variants: Profibus DP (Decentralized Periphery) and Profibus PA (Plant automation).

Profibus DP is a type of fieldbus protocol that allows communication between a "master" controller device and a number of "slave" field sensors. It operates on the physical layer RS-485, the same physical layer as Modbus but it has a specialized token ring protocol that enables multiple master devices to exist on the same network, differentiating it from other bus networks. A "token" is passed between masters, and whichever master is holding the token has the exclusive ability to communicate with slave devices on the network.

The term "decentralized periphery" is derived from the structure of a PROFIBUS DP system. Instead of having every single field device in a system connected to the programmable logic controller (PLC) directly via extensive cabling, PROFIBUS DP decentralizes the I/O connections and brings them near to the sensors. This shortens the length of cable needed to connect field devices to the I/Os, and only a single (RS-485) cable is needed to connect the I/Os and PLC.

Profibus PA further enhances efficiency by eliminating I/O units and extra cables. It uses a single Profibus-PA bus to connect all sensors. And requires a segment coupler to convert Profibus-PA signals into Profibus-DP signals, since most PLCs don't support Profibus-PA directly.

66. Which tools do you need for troubleshooting a running PROFIBUS installation?

Ans: There are two basic tools which required: a bus analyzer to verify the protocol quality and an oscilloscope to verify the signal quality.

67. What is the difference between Profibus and Profinet?

Ans: Profibus and Profinet both are industrial communication protocol. The difference between them is mentioned below:

Feature	Profibus	Profinet
Technology Base	A serial-based protocol	Ethernet-based protocol, Integration with IT
Physical Connection	Uses a DB-9 serial connector a	Uses an RJ-45 Ethernet jack
Speed & Performance	Operates at speeds from 9.6 kbps to 12 Mbps	Operates at 100 Mbps with a response time of less than 1 millisecond

68. What is CAN bus technology?

Ans: CAN bus (Controller Area Network) is a robust, high-speed communication protocol originally developed by Bosch in the 1980s. CAN bus allows multiple microcontrollers and devices to communicate with each other without needing a host computer. It uses a multi-master architecture, meaning that any device can send a message when the bus is free, and collision detection is built into the system. CAN bus transmits data over a two-wire twisted pair cable (CAN High and CAN Low) and uses differential signaling to make it highly resistant to electrical noise, making it ideal for harsh environments. CAN bus supports error checking and automatic retransmission if a communication error occurs, ensuring reliability. Typical data speeds are up to 1 Mbps for short distances, with lower speeds used for longer cable runs. In industrial systems, CAN forms the basis for higher-level protocols like DeviceNet, CANopen.

69. What is the DeviceNet communication protocol?

Ans: DeviceNet is an industrial communication protocol developed by Allen-Bradley (Rockwell Automation) based on the Controller Area Network (CAN) bus technology. It is designed to connect and communicate between industrial devices such as sensors, actuators, variable frequency drives (VFDs), and PLCs over a simple and robust network. DeviceNet supports both data communication and power supply (typically 24V DC) over a single 5-wire cable (two wires for communication, two for power, and one for shielding/ground). It operates at data rates of 125 kbps, 250 kbps, or 500 kbps, depending on the network length, with a maximum of 64 devices (nodes) per network. DeviceNet follows the Common Industrial Protocol (CIP) standard, allowing devices from different manufacturers to interoperate. It uses cyclic (scheduled), change-of-state, and polled messaging to efficiently manage real-time and non-real-time data.

70. What is the ControlNet communication protocol?

Ans: ControlNet is an industrial communication protocol developed by Allen-Bradley (Rockwell Automation) for high-speed, real-time control applications. It is specifically designed to handle both time-critical control data (such as I/O updates) and non-time-critical messaging data (such as configuration and programming information) over the same network without interference. ControlNet uses a coaxial cable (RG-6 quad-shielded) or fiber optic cable and operates at a fixed data rate of 5 Mbps. One of its key features is the way it organizes communication: it separates messages into scheduled and unscheduled traffic. Scheduled communication happens at precise intervals to ensure time-sensitive data is delivered on time, while non-urgent messages are sent in between these scheduled slots. It is based on a token passing bus control network. ControlNet does not supply power & signal in a single cable unlike DeviceNet.

71. What are the difference between DeviceNet and Modbus communication protocol?

Ans: Following are the differences:

DeviceNet	_Modbus_
DeviceNet is one type of network protocol.	Modbus is one type of serial communication protocol.
This protocol is used to connect control devices for the exchange of data within the automation industry.	This protocol is used for communication purposes between PLCs

72. What are the difference between DeviceNet and ControlNet?

Ans: Following are the differences:

DeviceNet	_ControlNet_
DeviceNet is a device-level network.	ControlNet is a scheduled network.
DeviceNet is used to connect & serve as a communication network between industrial controllers & I/O devices for providing a cost-effective network to users for managing & distributing simple devices with the architecture.	ControlNet is used to provide consistent, high-speed control & I/O data transfer with programming that sets the logic to particular timing on the network.
The devices allowed by Devicenet are up to 64 on a single node.	The devices allowed by ControlNet are up to 99 per node.
The data transfer rates of DeviceNet are 125, 250, or 500 Kilobits/sec.	The data transfer rate of ControlNet is 5 Mbps.
Devicenet supplies power & signal in a single cable.	ControlNet does not supply power & signal in a single cable.

73. What is the DDE Protocol?

Ans: DDE, or Dynamic Data Exchange, is a communication method developed by Microsoft that allows two programs running on the same computer to share data in real time. It works on a client-server model, where one application (the server) supplies data and the other (the client) receives and updates it.

In earlier Windows systems, DDE was commonly used to link software like Microsoft Excel or Word with external systems such as SCADA or databases. For example, a cell in Excel could automatically update with live data coming from a SCADA system, using a DDE link. While DDE was useful in its time, it's now considered outdated. It's relatively slow, lacks modern security features, and has been replaced by more advanced technologies like OPC and OPC UA, which are more reliable and secure for industrial and automation applications.

74. What is the OPC server?

Ans: An OPC Server is a software application that acts as a bridge between industrial hardware (like PLCs, DCS systems, sensors, and controllers) and client applications (like SCADA, HMI, or historian systems). The OPC Server communicates directly with the hardware devices using their native protocols (such as Modbus, Profibus, DeviceNet, etc.), collects data from them, and then standardizes that data into a common OPC format. Client applications can then access the data using OPC standards. The Following are some of the OPC specifications that are used in Industries.

- ***OPC AE (Alarms and Events)*** – OPC AE servers are used to accept and exchange process alarms and events.
- ***OPC-HDA (Historical Data Access)*** – This is used to retrieve historical process data for analysis. This data is typically stored in files, databases, or remote telemetry systems.
- ***OPC-DA (Data Access)*** – Provides access to real-time data.

75. What are the different types of network connector used in Industrial networking?

Ans: Following are the network connectors:

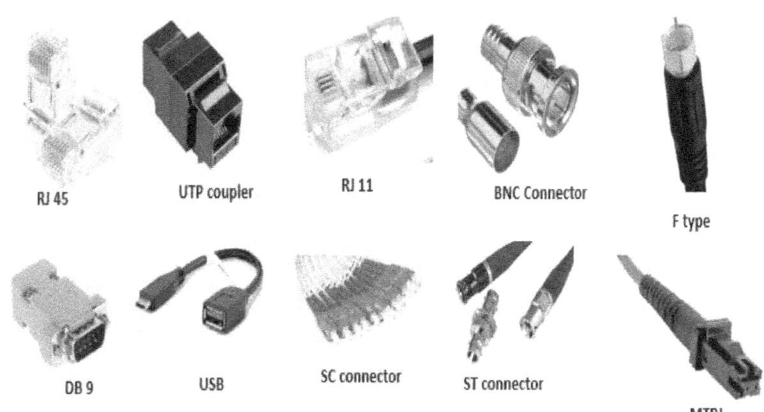

Fig 17.10 – Network connector

- **RJ45** - RJ45 consists of an 8-pin metal connector which is then connected to a twisted unshielded cable by means of crimping.

- **UTP coupler**- UTP stands for unshielded twisted pair UTP coupler is used in cases when the Ethernet cable is too short to run.

- **RJ 11** - The RJ-11 connector looks similar to the RJ45 connector, but it has only 4 pins. RJ11 is used extensively for telephonic network connections.

- **BNC Connector** - BNC stands for Bayonet Neill-Concelman. BNC connector is a traditional coaxial cable connector. BNC connector is mostly used for video and audio network transmissions

- **F -type connector** - The F-type connector is another type of connector used for coaxial cables. The F-type connector is smaller in size as compared to BNC connectors.

- **_DB 9 (RS 232_**) - The DB9 is a serial-type connector, used only for serial line communication. It is specifically designed for the RS232 protocol.
- **_USB connector_** - The USB is used in almost every device, be it a small pen drive or a complex PLC programming port. One main advantage of USB is that it is available in versatile versions, like USB to RJ45, USB to DB232.
- **_SC connector_** - The SC connector is also called as standard or square connector comes under an optical fiber connection. The SC connector is a push-pull type.
- **_ST connector_** - The ST connector is called a straight-tip connector and comes under an optical fiber connection. The ST connector is a metallic locking assembly.
- **_MTRJ connector_** - MRTJ stands for mechanical transfer register jack. The MTRJ connector is an extension of the SC connector.

Fiber optics

76. What is total internal reflection?

Ans: Total Internal Reflection (TIR) is a phenomenon that occurs when a light ray traveling from a denser medium to a rarer medium hit the boundary at an angle greater than the critical angle, causing the light to be completely reflected back into the denser medium instead of refracting into the second medium.

77. What is refractive index?

Ans: The refractive index (also known as the index of refraction) of a medium is a measure of how much the speed of light is reduced when it passes through that medium, compared to the speed of light in a vacuum.

78. What is the composition of the fibre optic cable?

Ans: A fiber optic cable is composed of the following main components:

- Core: It is the central part of the fibre which serves as a waveguide for the light. It is made of ultra-pure glass or plastic with a high refractive index.
- Cladding: It surrounds the core and has a lower refractive index. It ensures that light reflects back into the core by total internal reflection.

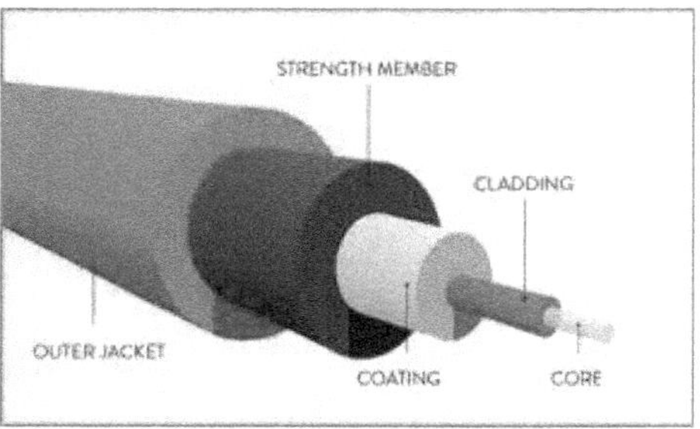

Fig 17.11 – Fiber optic composition

- Primary & Secondary Coating: Primary Coating is a protective polymer layer that directly coated on the cladding to provides cushioning and protects the fibre from physical damage. Secondary Coating is an additional layer that offer mechanical protection and strength.
- Strength Members: Materials such as aramid yarn (e.g., Kevlar) or fiberglass rods is used to provide tensile strength and protect the fibre during installation and handling.
- Outer Jacket (Sheath): The outermost protective layer made of PVC, polyethylene, or other durable materials. It Shields the cable from moisture, chemicals, abrasion, and environmental conditions.

79. How is signal transmitted through fiber optic?

Ans: In a fiber optic cable, signals are transmitted in the form of light pulses generated by a light source such as a laser diode or LED. The process of signal transmission involves the following steps:

- **_Conversion of Electrical Signal to Light_**: The input electrical signal (such as voice, video, or data) is first converted into a modulated light signal by a transmitter (such as LED).

- **_Transmission Through the Core_**: The light travels through the core of the optical fibre. Due to the difference in refractive index between the core and the cladding, total internal reflection keeps the light confined within the core.

- **_Propagation of Light Pulses_**: The light pulses travel through the fibre over long distances with minimal attenuation and distortion.

- **_Reception and Conversion Back to Electrical Signal_**: At the receiving end, a photodetector (such as a photodiode) converts the light pulses back into electrical signals for further processing or output.

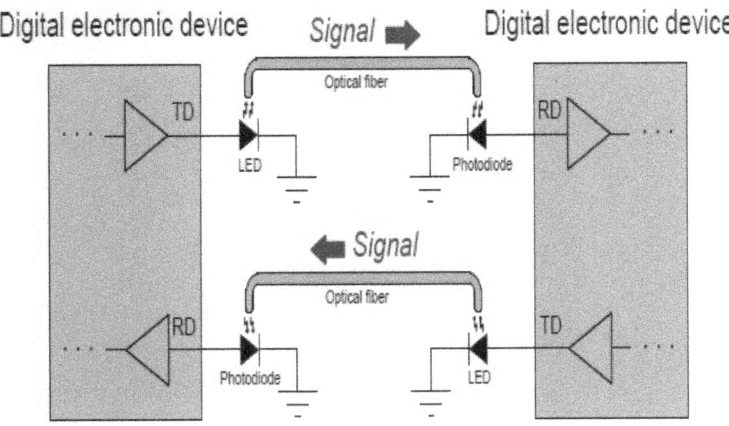

Fig 17.12 – Fiber optic signal transmissions

80. How is light propagated through fiber optic?

Ans: Light propagates through a fiber optic cable by the principle of total internal reflection.

Light from a source enters the core of the fiber at a specific angle. The core has a higher refractive index than the cladding surrounding it and hence core acts a denser medium w.r.t cladding. When the light ray strikes the core-cladding boundary at an angle greater than the critical angle, it reflects back into the core instead of passing into the cladding. This internal reflection continues repeatedly along the length of the fibre, allowing the light to travel long distances with minimal loss.

81. What is single-mode and multi-mode optical fiber?

Ans: In single mode optical fiber, light travels in a straight path through a very narrow core. Single-mode fiber cores typically range from 4 to 10 microns in diameter. It is suitable for long-distance communication (tens to hundreds of kilometers).

In multi-mode fibre, light reflects at multiple angles, allowing more paths but with greater dispersion. Optical fibers with core diameters of 50 microns or more are referred to as multi-mode fibers. It is suitable for short-distance communication (up to a few kilometers).

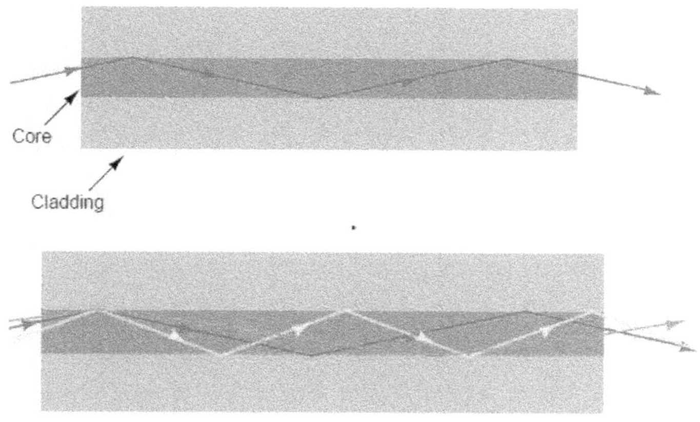

Fig 17.13 – Single & multi-mode fiber cable

82. Why is fiber optic cable always in pairs?

Ans: Fiber optic cables are typically installed in pairs to support bidirectional communication — that is one cable is to transmit data while the other is used to receive data.

83. What precautions are to be taken while laying fiber optic cable in cable tray?

Ans: When installing fiber optic cables in a cable tray, one of the most important precautions is to avoid bending the cable too sharply. Every fiber optic cable has a minimum bend radius specified by the manufacturer, and it's crucial to follow that. If the cable is bent too tightly, it can cause the light traveling through the fiber to leak out of the core and into the cladding. This happens because the angle of the light changes and may no longer meet the condition for total internal reflection, the principle that keeps light contained within the fiber. As a result, the signal can degrade or be lost entirely.

To prevent this, junction boxes and cable management panels often include smooth plastic guides or forms that ensure any coiled or excess cable is looped gently, staying within the safe bend radius. Following these practices helps maintain signal quality and ensures the long-term reliability of the fiber optic connection.

84. What are the types of connectors used in optical fiber?

Ans: There are four types of connectors used — FC (Ferrule Connector), LC (Lucent Connector), SC (Subscriber Connector), and ST (Straight Tip).

- FC connector is Push-pull snap-in connector.
- LC connector is Push-pull type with latch.
- SC connector is a plastic molded body of square shape, with a push-pull locking technique. Instead of a latch, it uses a lock method for a secure connection to the port.
- ST connector has round ceramic ferrules and bayonet locking

features. It has to rotate until tight and rotate reverse to remove it. It comes with a spring-loaded sheath that holds the fiber in place.

85. What is splicing of fiber optic cable?

Ans: Splicing is a process that permanently joins two optical fibers end-to-end, creating a continuous optical path. The goal is to ensure that the light passing through the fibers continues with as little loss or reflection as possible. There are two types of splicing:

- *Fusion Splicing*: This involves using an electric arc or laser to melt the ends of the optical fibers together. It provides a very low-loss connection, and when done correctly, the splice may be almost as strong as the original fiber.
- *Mechanical Splicing*: This involves aligning the fiber ends and holding them together using an adhesive or mechanical clamp. It is generally quicker but may have a higher loss and less mechanical strength compared to fusion splicing.

86. Why is fiber optic cable spliced rather than terminated?

Ans: Termination is commonly used in copper cable systems where conductors are joined using connectors. If the termination method is used in fiber optics, it typically involves higher loss compared to splicing, as the fibers are not fused together and there may be a small air gap or mismatch between the fibers. This leads to reflection and scattering of the light signal and leads to signal loss.

87. How is fiber optic cable tested?

Ans: Two basic types of optical fiber tests are: Optical power loss testing and Optical time domain reflectometer (OTDR).

In optical power loss testing, a known light source is connected at one end of the fiber, and a power meter is connected at the other end. The power meter reads the received optical power, and the difference between the transmitted and received power indicates the optical loss in the fiber. Lesser the optical power loss better the quality of the fibre. This method is common in field testing and certification.

An OTDR sends a short pulse of laser light into the fiber and monitors the reflected light that returns due to scattering and reflections within the fiber. By analyzing the timing and intensity of the returning light, the OTDR generates a graphical trace showing: Total length of the fiber, Connector losses and break locations or faults. OTDR is especially useful for long-distance fiber runs.

88. What are the advantages of optical fibre over conventional cable?

Ans: Following are the advantages of optical fibre over conventional cable:

- Optical fibres support much higher data transmission rates, making them suitable for high-speed internet and communication systems.
- Optical fibres can transmit data over longer distances without significant signal loss, unlike copper cables which require signal boosters.
- Optical fibers has complete immunity to external "noise" sources.
- Since optical fibers are manufactured from glass which is electrically non-conductive, it is possible to route optical fibers alongside high-voltage power lines.
- The low power levels associated with optical fiber signals also makes this technology completely safe in areas where explosive compounds in the atmosphere might otherwise be ignited by faults in electrical communications cable.

89. What are the different types of standards for optical fibre cable?

Ans: The types of standard optical fiber cables are as below:

- ➢ ***100 Base FX*** (Fast Ethernet at 100 Mbps): up to distance of 2 Km.
- ➢ ***1000 Base SX*** (Gigabit Ethernet at 1000 Mbps; SX means short reach): up to distance of 275 m.
- ➢ ***1000 Base LX*** (Gigabit Ethernet at 1000 Mbps; LX means long reach): up to distance of 10 km.
- ➢ ***1000 Base BX*** (Gigabit Ethernet at 1000 Mbps; BX means bidirectional transmission): up to distance of 40 Km.
- ➢ ***1000 Base EX*** (Gigabit Ethernet at 1000 Mbps; EX means extend reach): up to distance of 80 Km.

Chapter:18

Industrial Control system, Foundation Fieldbus and Cyber Security

Industrial Control system

1. What is the role of control system in Process Industry?

Ans: Following are the key functions of control system in Industries:

- ***Automation*** – It automates operations, reducing manual intervention and improving consistency in production.
- ***Safety & Reliability*** – It ensures safe operation by detecting faults, triggering alarms, and initiating emergency shutdowns when needed.
- ***Energy Efficiency*** – By maintaining optimal process conditions, it reduces energy consumption and operating costs.
- ***Quality Control*** – It ensures products meet required specifications by maintaining precise process parameters like pressure, temperature etc.
- ***Remote Monitoring & Control*** – Modern control systems enable remote supervision and troubleshooting, improving operational efficiency.
- ***Data Logging & Analysis*** – It collects and analyzes process data for continuous improvement and predictive maintenance.

2. How do control system works?

Ans: Field instruments measure physical parameters such as pressure and temperature and transmit the data to the control room via cables in electrical form. The control system converts the analog signals into digital form for processing by the control unit or processor. The processor analyzes the data based on a predefined program and takes the necessary actions. It then converts the processed digital signals back into analog form and transmits them via cables to actuators.

For example, in boiler drum level control, sensors measure the drum level and transmit the data to the control system. Based on this data, the control unit determines whether to open or close the valve to maintain the desired drum level setpoint.

3. What are the five levels in industrial automation

Ans: the five levels in Industrial automation are:

- ***Level 0 (Sensors and Signals):*** This is the first and lowest level of industrial automation. It consists of field devices like sensors, actuators, instruments, motors, valves, actuators, switches, and other equipment. These devices send and receive data with respect to the next level.
- ***Level 1 (Manipulation and Control):*** In this level automation and execution of control logic takes place. It includes PLC, DCS.
- ***Level 2 (Supervisory Control):*** It includes real time monitoring, data visualization, and operator control. This is done in HMI or SCADA.
- ***Level 3 (Planning and Operations):*** It includes production management, scheduling, and performance analysis. This is done by analysis historians data
- ***Level 4 (Enterprise Level):*** Its function is business and corporate decision-making. It uses ERP (Enterprise Resource Planning) for finance, supply chain management.

4. What is a centralized and decentralised control system?

Ans: A centralized control system is one where all the processes are controlled by a single master unit. All decision-making and data processing occurs in a single main controller. If the main controller fails, the entire system stops. For example: In a thermal power plant, different stages occur like fuel handling, boiler control, turbine control. If all these operations are executed by a single controller than it is called centralized control system.

A decentralized control system distributes control functions across multiple controllers, allowing independent processing at different levels. Each controller operates autonomously but can communicate with others. Failure of one controller does not affect the entire system. For Example: In a thermal power plant, if fuel handling, boiler control, and turbine control are each managed by individual controllers, rather than a single controller handling all stages, it is called a decentralized control system.

5.   What is HMI (Human Machine Interface)?

Ans: HMI, or Human Machine Interface, is the system that allows humans to interact with a machine or process, typically through a computer-based control system. It provides operators with a visual interface to monitor, control, and analyze the status and performance of equipment or an entire plant.

Through the HMI, users can view real-time data, adjust setpoints, log historical data, analyze trends, and respond to alarms. It often includes graphical displays like process flow diagrams (mimic diagrams), system overviews, and alarm panels that show alerts and their status. In short, HMI serves as the bridge between human operators and automated systems, making complex industrial processes easier to manage and understand.

6.   What is a Historian or Data Logger?

Ans: A historian or data logger is a software or hardware system used to continuously record, store, and retrieve process data over time from industrial systems like DCS, PLC.

7.   How are relay-based control system functions?

Ans: A relay-based control system is an electromechanical system that uses relays to control and automate processes. It operates by switching circuits on and off in response to input signals from sensors, switches, or other control devices.

Sensors, switches, or push buttons detect process conditions and send electrical signals. The input signal energizes a relay coil, creating a magnetic field that pulls or releases relay contacts. The relay contacts switch ON or OFF the connected electrical circuit, controlling devices such as motors, solenoids, or alarms.

Example: In a pump control system, a float switch detects water level. When the level is low, the relay energizes and switches ON the pump motor. Once the water reaches the desired level, the relay de-energizes, turning OFF the pump.

8. What is an interposing relay?

Ans: An interposing relay is an electrical relay used as an interface between two circuits that operate at different voltage levels, current ratings, or signal types. It acts as a buffer to ensure compatibility between control systems and field devices.

In a PLC-based control system, the PLC may output a 24V DC signal, but the field actuator (e.g., a motor contactor) requires a 110V AC signal. An interposing relay is used to bridge this voltage difference, allowing the PLC to control the actuator safely.

9. What is a PLC (Programmable Logic Controller)?

Ans: A Programmable Logic Controller (PLC) is an industrial digital computer designed to automate, monitor, and control machinery and processes in industrial environments. It replaces traditional relay-based control systems with a more flexible and programmable solution.

10. What are the components of PLC?

Ans: Following are the components of PLC:

- ***Input Modules***: The input module of a Programmable Logic

Controller (PLC) is responsible for receiving signals from field devices (such as sensors, switches, and push buttons) and converting them into a standardized form that the PLC's processor can understand. It electrically isolates high-voltage signals from the PLC's internal circuit to protect against voltage spikes or noise.

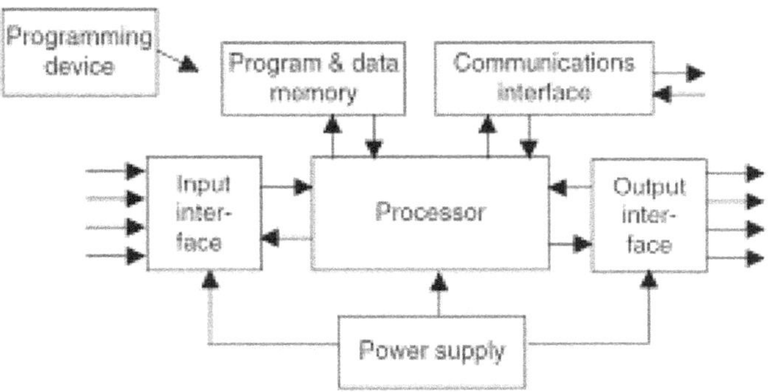

Fig 18.1 – PLC components

- **_Output Modules:_** The output module of a Programmable Logic Controller (PLC) is responsible for sending control signals from the PLC's processor to external devices such as motors, solenoids, relays, and indicators. It converts the processed digital signals from the CPU into appropriate electrical signals required to operate the connected field devices.

- **_Central Processing unit_**: The central processing unit perform the tasks necessary to fulfill the PLC function such as Scanning of I/O bus, program execution, peripheral and external device communication and self-diagnostics.

- **_Memory unit:_** It is the library where the application program is stored. It is also where the PLC's executive program is stored. An executive program functions as the operating system of PLC. It is the program that interprets, manages and executes the user's application program.

- ***Communication Ports***: It enables networking with HMI and other systems.

11. What types of I/O modules are commonly used in PLC systems?
Ans: I/O (Input/Output) modules in a Programmable Logic Controller (PLC) serve as the interface between the PLC processor and field devices such as sensors, switches, motors, and actuators. They can be categorized into digital, analog, and special-purpose modules based on the type of signals they handle.

- ***Digital I/O Module (Discrete I/O)***: In digital Input module, it receive signals from devices that provide discrete (ON/OFF) outputs such as Push buttom, Limit switch. And in digital output module, it send ON/OFF control signals to field devices. The ouput devces such as Relay, solenoids.
- ***Analog I/O Module***: Analog input module receive variable signals (4-20 mA, 0-10V) from sensors (e.g., pressuretransmiter etc). And analog output module send variable control signals (4-20mA) to field devices like control valve, VFD etc.
- ***Special Purpose I/O Modules***: These modules provide advanced functionality for specific industrial applications. It includes Temperature Input Modules (used for direct connection with RTDs and thermocouples to measure temperature), Communication Modules (enable PLCs to communicate with other devices via industrial communication protocols), High-Speed Counter (HSC) Modules (Used for fast pulse counting from encoders, flow meters, or rotary encoders).

12. What is Ladder Logic in PLC programming?

Ans: Ladder Logic is a graphical programming language that resembles electrical relay circuits. It consists of rungs with input conditions on the left and output actions on the right.

13. What are different types of PLC programming languages?

Ans: Followings are the different types of PLC programming languages:

- Ladder Logic (LAD) – Uses relay-style logic.
- Function Block Diagram (FBD) – Uses graphical blocks.
- Structured Text (ST) – Uses high-level language similar to C/Pascal.
- Sequential Function Chart (SFC) – Uses flowchart-based logic.
- Instruction List (IL) – Uses assembly-like instructions.

14. What is a scan cycle in PLC?

Ans: A PLC scan cycle consists of Reading Inputs → Executing Logic → Updating Outputs. It repeats continuously to ensure real-time process control. The ideal scan time depends on the application requirements, but generally:

- Fast processes (high-speed control, motion control, robotics): <1 ms to 10 ms
- General industrial automation (motor control, conveyors, pumps): 10 ms to 50 ms

15. What is a watchdog timer in PLC?

Ans: A watchdog timer monitors the PLC scan cycle. If the cycle exceeds a set time limit due to a program error, it triggers a system reset or fault alarm.

16. What is redundancy in PLC systems?

Ans: PLC redundancy means using backup CPUs, power supplies, or networks to ensure system reliability in case of failure. It is used in critical applications like power plants.

17. How do you connect multiple PLCs in a network?

Ans: By using Modbus protocol or any other communication protocol available at the respective PLC.

18. What is a Distributed Control System (DCS)?

Ans: A DCS (Distributed Control System) is an automated control system used in industrial processes where control functions are distributed across multiple controllers. It consists of field devices, controllers, operator workstations, and a communication network to manage large-scale industrial operations.

19. How does a DCS differ from a PLC?

Ans: Followings are the difference between DCS and PLC:

Feature	*DCS*	*PLC*
Architecture	Decentralized (Distributed)	Centralized
Application	Large, continuous processes (oil & gas, power)	Discrete Manufacturing
Scalability	High	Limited
Redundancy	Built-in	Requires additional components
Response Time	Slower, optimized for process control	Faster for real-time operations

20. What are the main components of a DCS?

Ans: Following are the main components of DCS:

- Field Instruments – Sensors, transmitters, and actuators.
- Controllers – Processors that execute control logic.
- I/O Modules – Interface between field devices and controllers.

- Engineering Workstation – Used for programming and configuration.
- Operator Workstations (HMI/SCADA) – Provide visualization and control.
- Communication Network – Ethernet, Profibus, Modbus, or Fieldbus for data transfer.

21. How does a DCS handle redundancy?

Ans: A DCS uses redundancy mechanisms such as:

- Dual CPUs – Ensures continuous operation if one fails.
- Redundant I/O Modules – Prevents data loss in case of a module failure.
- Redundant Networks – Backup communication paths for uninterrupted data transfer.
- Hot Swappable Components – Faulty modules can be replaced without shutting down the system.

22. What is a hot standby system in DCS?

Ans: A hot standby system provides redundancy by keeping a backup controller online. If the primary controller fails, the standby system takes over immediately without disrupting operations.

23. How does DCS integrate with a PLC system?

Ans: DCS and PLCs communicate via: Modbus or OPC UA/DA.

24. How is DCS communicates with other devices (HMI, Printers, etc) in the network?

Ans: Each device on the network keeps a table that associates an IP address with a MAC address. This table is built at run time as the devices come onto the network. As each device is powered up it broadcasts its IP address to inform the other devices to update their tables. If a station wants to send out a packet to an IP address that is not in its table, it will broadcast an ARP (address resolution protocol) to locate the associated MAC address. The station with that IP address responds to the broadcast with a response message.

25. How is a DCS Designed for Scalability?

Ans: A Distributed Control System (DCS) is built with scalability in mind, using a modular architecture that makes it easy to expand as the plant or process grows. Components like controllers, I/O modules, and HMIs can be added or removed depending on changing requirements.

If a new section of the plant is introduced, additional controllers can be installed and connected to the existing network without disrupting current operations. Similarly, as more field instruments are added, extra input/output (I/O) modules, whether analog or digital can be integrated into the system to accommodate them.

26. What types of programming generally used in DCS?

Ans: DCS use a graphical programming language that uses function blocks to represent control functions such as logic gates, mathematical functions, and control algorithms. Each block has built in features and are connected in graphics to create a complex control loop via computer software. Example: PID block, SR block etc.

27. How does a DCS interface with actuators?

Ans: DCS output modules consist of analog output (AO) and digital output (DO) cards. For continuous actuators (e.g., control valves), the DCS processing unit sends a 4-20 mA signal to the actuator through the analog output card. For discrete actuators (e.g., solenoid valves), the processing unit provides an ON/OFF digital signal via the digital output card, which is transmitted through an interposing relay and auxiliary power supply.

28. How can you operate a 230V AC solenoid from DCS Digital output card?

Ans: A 230V AC solenoid can be operated from a DCS Digital Output (DO) card by using an auxiliary relay and external 24V DC and 230V AC supplies. When an ON command is initiated from the DCS, the corresponding channel of the DO card activates the auxiliary relay using the 24V DC supply. Upon energization, the relay's contacts change state, allowing the 230V AC supply to pass through the relay contacts to the solenoid, thus energizing and operating the solenoid.

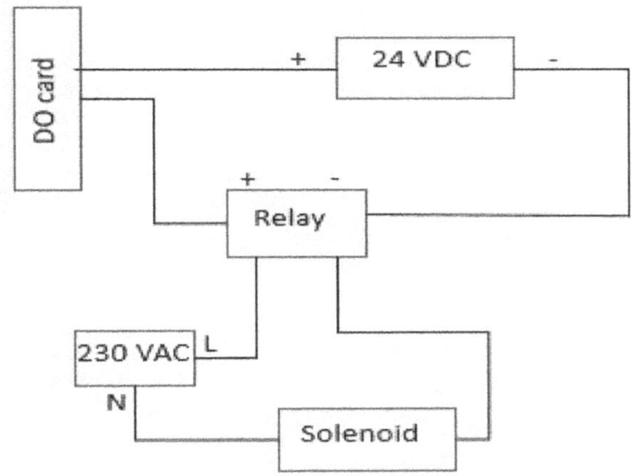

Fig 18.2 – DCS output circuit

29. What is logic and interlocks in control system?

Ans: Logic refers to the set of programmed rules and conditions used to control a process based on input signals. It determines how a system responds to various conditions using logical operations. Types of logic:

- Combinational Logic – Uses AND, OR, NOT gates to determine process outcomes
- Sequential Logic – Involves timing, counting, and memory-based operations.

An interlock is a safety mechanism that prevents unsafe operations by restricting process conditions. It ensures that equipment operates only when predefined conditions are met. Types of interlocks:

- Process Interlocks – Prevent unsafe process conditions (e.g., stopping a heater if airflow is lost).
- Safety Interlocks – Ensure personnel and equipment protection (e.g., preventing a pump from starting if suction valve is not open).
- Startup/Shutdown Interlocks – Ensure the correct sequence of operations (e.g., a compressor cannot start unless lubrication oil pressure is normal).

30. What is 2/3 logic? How an it be implemented in DCS?

Ans: 2/3 logic (also called two-out-of-three voting logic) is a redundant decision-making system commonly used in process control, industrial automation, and emergency shutdown systems. In a 2/3 logic system, three independent sensors (or inputs) monitor the same condition or process parameter, and a decision (such as a shutdown or alarm) is triggered only if at least two out of the three sensors agree that action is necessary.

In DCS 2/3 logic can be implemented by using AND gate and OR gate.

31. What is Fastout and Permit in automation system?

Ans: A Fastout is a forced or emergency shutdown command that immediately stops or isolates a process or equipment when a critical condition is detected. For example: In a gas compressor system, if high vibration is detected beyond a safe threshold, a Fastout signal is triggered to shut down the compressor immediately, preventing damage.

A Permit is a pre-condition that must be met before a system or equipment can operate. It ensures that all required safety and operational conditions are satisfied before starting or continuing a process. For example: In In a boiler startup sequence, the system requires: Water level within safe limits and fuel pressure in range. Only if all conditions are met, a Permit signal is issued, allowing the burner ignition sequence to proceed.

32. What is the Difference Between SOE and Alarms?

Ans: SOE (sequence of events) is a record of events, captured with high time resolution (typically in milliseconds). It is primarily used for diagnostics and root cause analysis, especially in the event of a system trip or shutdown. SOE helps identify the exact sequence in which signals changed state, allowing operators or engineers to determine the origin or cause of the trip by identifying the first signal in the sequence.

Alarms are used to warn operators about deviations in process conditions that may need corrective actions. They are typically displayed on Human-Machine Interface (HMI) systems and are prioritized based on severity.

33. What are the advantages of DCS over PLC?

Ans: Following are the advantages of DCS over PLC:

- DCS is ideal for large-scale, continuous, complex processes for industries like oil and gas, power generation, and chemical processing whereas PLC, on the other hand, is more suitable for discrete control systems (e.g., assembly lines, automated machinery) and smaller-scale applications where simpler control logic is sufficient.
- DCS has advanced control features like PID control, cascade control, feedforward control, etc. whereas PLC require additional hardware and software to execute this function.
- DCS is designed with high redundancy in both hardware and communication to ensure zero downtime.
- DCS has decentralized controller and I/O module making it more convenient than PLC. Thus, failure of any control unit doesn't affect the plant operation unlike PLC.

- DCS has RTD and thermocouple input module to read the raw value from RTD and TC and thereby eliminates the need of temperature transmitter.

34. What is Alarm Prioritization?

Ans: An alarm indicates an abnormal situation or developing abnormal situations. So, the control room operator has to acknowledge the alarm and has to take preventive actions in order to keep the plant safe and to avoid any sort of process disturbances. The alarm usually triggers in a plant in an audio-visual format i.e. the alarm will be displayed on an operator screen (HMI) and there will be an audible horn also. There are three types of Alarm:

- ➢ **High priority alarm**: Utmost importance has to be given to high priority alarms as it has the capacity to cause serious damage to human or equipment. Example: Activation of gas detection installed at gas station.
- ➢ **Medium priority alarm**: Next importance has to be given to medium priority alarm, these are not as critical as high priority alarms, but still, if left unattended can cause damage to the equipment. Example: A low-pressure alarm at the suction of a centrifugal pump is a medium priority alarm. It will not cause any damage to site personnel or the local community, neither can it affect the environment, but it can cause wear & tear of the pump components decreasing the life span of the pump.
- ➢ **Low priority alarm**: These are the least priority alarms among all if left unattended can cause minor or no loss to the equipment. Example: Not receiving the feedback of control valve.

35. What is the importance of earthing system in DCS/PLC?

Ans: The control system has a ground bus bar inside the panel located at an appropriate place to which all internal grounding connection is returned. Once the final ground bus bar is connected to an actual-earth pit or earth grid that the system finally earthed.

Improper earthing or grounding of Distributed Control System (DCS) or Programmable Logic Controller (PLC) may result in either mal-operation of the control system or a controller or failure of electronic cards or sometimes even embedded software gets erased.

36. How is cumulative flow calculated from flow rate in a DCS?

Ans: In a DCS, the cumulative flow is calculated by summing the instantaneous flow rate over discrete time intervals. This process involves sampling the flow rate at regular intervals (eighter in minutes or seconds), integrating or summing the values, and then updating the cumulative flow value. The flow rate is measured by flow meters, and the DCS performs the necessary calculations, providing a real-time accumulation of total flow over time.

37. What are level compensation and flow compensation, and how are they implemented in a DCS?

Ans: Level compensation and flow compensation is correcting the level and flow measurement based on process conditions like pressure, temperature, density or tank shape.

For level compensation, DCS read raw value from differential pressure transmitter and applies mathematical calculation gas pressure effect (especially in closed tanks) and liquid density variation (due to temperature or composition).

For flow compensation, DCS receives the raw DP signal from the flow transmitter and uses live pressure and temperature inputs to correct the flow measurement by using typical Formula for compensated flow.

38. How can the ON/OFF control logic for a motor or pump be implemented in a DCS?

Ans: The ON/OFF control logic for a motor or pump can be implemented in a DCS using an SR flip-flop. In an SR flip-flop, the output changes state based on which input (Set or Reset) is activated, and the output remains in that state even after the input signal is removed. When the motor start command is triggered, the flip-flop sets the output, which remains active even after the start command is released. The output will stay in the ON state until a stop command is triggered, which resets the flip-flop and turns the motor OFF.

39. What are the Data Types Used in DCS/PLC Systems?

Ans: Following are the data types used:

- Boolean data type: It represent two states — ON/OFF, TRUE/FALSE, 1/0. It is used for start stop signal, alarm status (High/Low), Limit switches etc.
- Integer data type: It handles whole number and is used in counters, run hours etc.
- Float data type: It handles decimal number and used in process value (flow, pressure etc) representations.
- String data type: It handles text data and used for operator message, alarm descriptions.
- Time data type: It represents time value.

40. What are Mark IV, Mark V, and Mark VI Control Systems?

Ans: Mark IV, Mark V, and Mark VI are industrial control systems developed by GE (General Electric) for controlling gas turbines, steam turbines, and sometimes compressors in power plants. It is based on triple modular redundancy (TMR) concept where three separate CPUs/processors doing the same job for high reliability. It uses programmable logic and functional block for programming through a tool called Toolbox. IV , V, VI indicates the version of the control system.

41. What is SCADA?

Ans: SCADA (Supervisory Control and Data Acquisition) is a computer-based system used to monitor, control, and collect data from industrial processes that may be distributed over a large geographic area.

Sensors installed at various locations measure important process parameters. Remote Terminal Units (RTUs) or Programmable Logic Controllers (PLCs) located at these sites collect data from the sensors. The RTUs or PLCs then transmit this data to the SCADA Master Station using communication protocols such as Modbus or Ethernet. The SCADA software displays the collected data on operator screens (HMIs) and stores it in a historical database (historian) for analysis and record-keeping. Operators can supervise the entire system and perform remote control of equipment as needed.

Example: In a water treatment plant spread over 50 kilometres, the SCADA system monitors pump stations, water storage tanks, and chlorine dosing units. If a pump failure occurs, SCADA immediately generates an alarm on the operator's screen. The operator can then remotely restart the pump without physically visiting the location.

Electric grid consisting of transmission line and sub stations is monitored and operated by SCADA.

42. What are the differences between DCS and SCADA?

Ans: Following are the differences:

DCS	*SCADA*
Real-time process control and automation	Monitoring and supervisory control over large areas
Closed-loop control with continuous feedback	Open-loop supervisory control with operator interventions

Localized within a single plant or facility	Application in wide-area systems like utilities, pipelines, and transportation network
Very fast and critical for process stability	Slightly slower, acceptable for monitoring and remote actions
Manages complex and continuous process control strategies	Supervises and controls simple, widely spread operations

43. What is the license key for PLC/DCS?

Ans: In PLC and DCS systems, a license key is a software authorization code that activates and enables the use of certain engineering tools, programming software, configuration features, or system functions. Manufacturers issue license keys to protect their software products and ensure that users have legally purchased the right to use the software.

Foundation Field bus

44. what is the foundation fieldbus? What are its key features?

Ans: Foundation Fieldbus is an all-digital, two-way serial communication protocol designed for process automation networks. It serves as the "base-level" network linking field devices (transmitters, sensors, valves) with higher-level control systems.

Key Features:

- It is digital, noise-resistant communication.
- It allows multiple devices to share one cable and to exchange not just a single process value but also diagnostics, status, and configuration information.
- It has distributed control where field devices can execute local

control algorithms.

45. What are the key components of Foundation Fieldbus (FF)?

Ans: Following are the key components of FF:

- **_Fieldbus Segment (H1):_** It consists of a two-wire twisted-pair bus carrying 31.25 kbps digital signal. Each segment requires exactly two terminating resistors (one at each end) and a Fieldbus Power Supply (FPS) which conditions the power/data on the line. A single H1 segment can support dozens of devices.

- **_Host Interface Card (H1 Card):_** A fieldbus interface card installed in a controller or DCS that connects to the H1 segment.

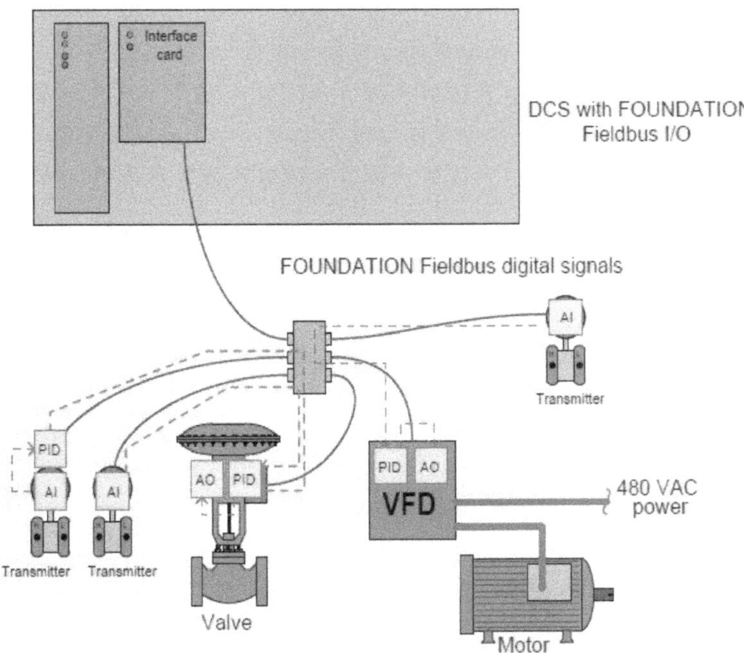

Fig 18.3- Foundation Fieldbus

- **_Fieldbus Power Supply (FPS)_** – Provides DC power and signal conditioning for the H1 segment.

- **_Linking Device_** – A junction or terminator that couples one or more H1 segments to a High-Speed Ethernet (HSE) backbone.

The linking device acts as a gateway, allowing an HSE network (100/1000 Mbps Ethernet) to interface with multiple 31.25 kbps H1 segments.

- ***Field Devices*** – Smart transmitters, sensors, actuators, and other instruments designed with Foundation Fieldbus interfaces. Each device contains function blocks (e.g. PID control, characterization) and communicates using FF messages.
- ***Host System (DCS/PLC)*** – The central control or automation system (such as a DCS or PLC) that interacts with fieldbus devices. It typically includes HSE or H1 interface modules to communicate with devices.

46. What is trunk and spur cable in FF?

Ans: The cable connecting all junctions to the main power source (where a host DCS would typically be located) is called a trunk.

The cable connecting each instrument to the nearest junction is called a spur.

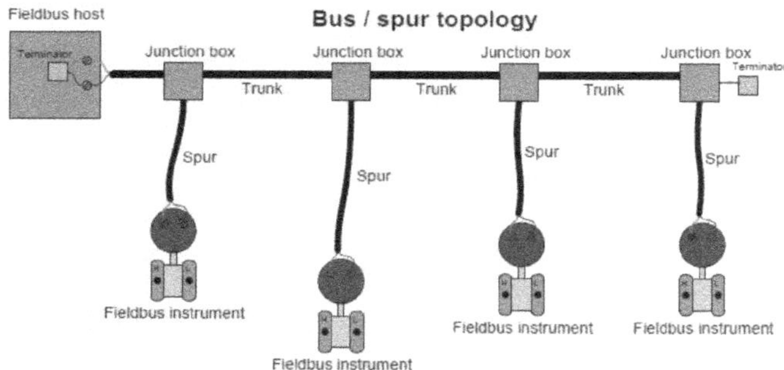

Fig 18.4- FF bus topology

47. What is a coupling device used in FF?

Ans: Coupling devices provide a convenient means of forming highly reliable connections between field instruments and the trunk cable. It also equipped with features such as short circuit protection (so that a shorted spur cable or field instrument does not cause the entire segment to stop communicating) and LED indication of spur status.

48. What is Manchester encoding?

Ans: Foundation Fieldbus H1 networks use Manchester encoding to represent bit states: a "high-to low" transition represents a logical zero (0), while a "low-to-high" transition represents a logical one (1).

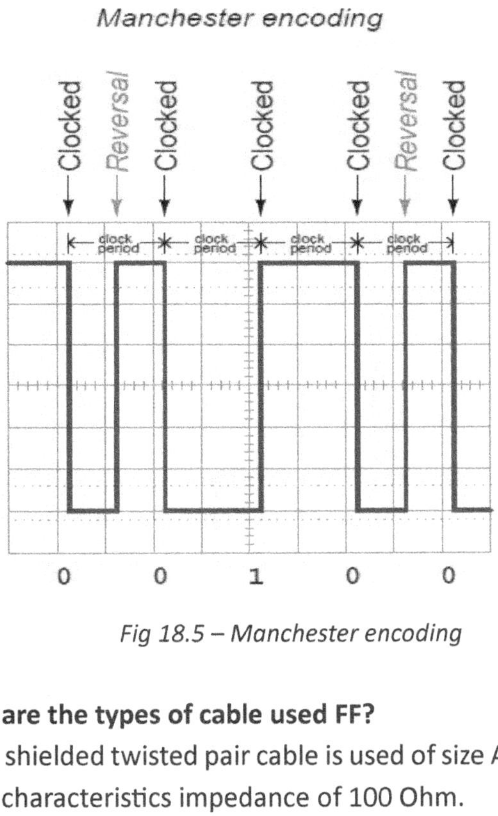

Fig 18.5 – Manchester encoding

49. What are the types of cable used FF?

Ans: In FF, shielded twisted pair cable is used of size AWG 18 to AWG 16 having characteristics impedance of 100 Ohm.

50. How are field devices communicating in FF H1 network?

Ans: In F H1 network, field devices communicate using Master/slave network behaviour for cyclic communications (i.e. one device polls the others, and the others merely respond) and delegated token network behaviour for acyclic communications (i.e. devices serially granted time to broadcast at will).

51. What is FF function blocks?

Ans: Data-processing modules within FF systems are known as function blocks. These "blocks" are not physical entities, but rather abstract software objects, they exist only as bits of data and instructions in computer memory. However, the blocks are represented on FF computer configuration displays as rectangular objects with input ports on the left-hand side and output ports on the right-hand side. The construction of a working control system comprised of FF devices consists of linking the outputs of certain function blocks with the inputs of other function blocks via configuration software and computer-based tools. This usually takes the form of using a computer to draw connecting lines between the output and input ports of different function blocks.

Example: For a control valve, controlled based on Pressure transmitter in FF segment.

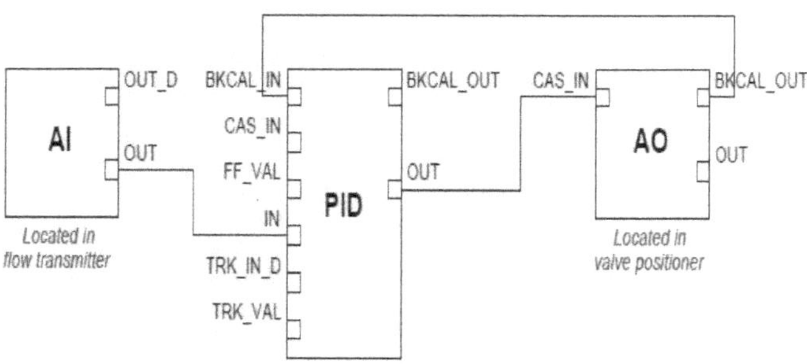

Fig 18.6 – FF functional block

In this function block program, data from the analog input (AI) block flows into the PID block. After calculating the proper output value, the PID block sends data to the analog output (AO) block where the final control element (e.g. valve, variable-speed motor) is adjusted. The AO block in turn sends a "back calculation" signal to the PID block to let it know the final control element has successfully reached the state commanded by the PID block's output. The analog input (AI) block must reside in the transmitter, because only the transmitter is able to measure the process fluid flow rate. Likewise, it should be obvious that the analog output (AO) block must reside in the control valve positioner and PID block can be placed in either transmitter or Positioner.

52. Which is the topology used in FF?

Ans: Bus, Tree and Daisy chain topology.

53. What is the ideal cable resistance, Signal strength and Electrical noise value for a healthy FF segment?

Ans: The ideal cable resistance is more than or equal to 50 Kohm. Signal strength should be 350 mV to 700 mV and Electrical noise should be equal or less than 25mV.

54. What are the advantages and disadvantages of Foundation fieldbus system?

Ans: *Following are the advantages of FF:*

- Multiple devices share a single two-wire trunk, drastically reducing cable runs, trenching, and conduits. This can cut field wiring by up to 50–70% in a fully digital plant
- Smart fieldbus devices continuously report not only process variables but also device health and diagnostics (e.g. valve position deviation, sensor drift). Access to multi-parameter data enables online calibration checks and predictive maintenance, reducing downtime.
- Function blocks in field devices allow implementation of PID control or interlocks at the device level. This reduces latency and host CPU load, and allows fast responses.

    Following are the disadvantages of FF:

- Fieldbus-enabled instruments and infrastructure (power conditioners, interface cards, linking devices) are generally more expensive upfront than simple analog sensors and junction boxes.

- Troubleshooting FF networks requires understanding of digital communication (e.g. message scheduling, link noise analysis) in addition to traditional instrument skills.

55. What is the difference between Foundation Fieldbus system and 4-20 mA analog system?

Ans: Foundation Fieldbus delivers far more information per cable run than a 4–20 mA loop. Multiple smart devices share a single twisted-pair (trunk), whereas a traditional 4–20 mA setup needs a separate pair of wires to each instrument. The digital nature of FF means one cable carries many parameters (e.g. valve position, temperature, plus device health), while analog loops carry only a single measurement. FF also supports device-level control blocks and simultaneous bidirectional messaging, features that do not exist with passive analog loops.

However, a 4–20 mA system is simpler and familiar: it requires minimal configuration, has no digital protocol to manage, and is inherently compatible with any analog input. For purely simple measurements (e.g. on/off flows) it remains cost-effective. The trade-off is that analog loops must be manually wired and calibrated, provide limited information, and can suffer from drift and noise over long distances. Foundation Fieldbus, by comparison, reduces wiring and maintenance costs in complex plants and offers higher functional capability at the expense of higher upfront investment and system complexity

56. Isn't Fieldbus too slow, 31.25 kbit/s compared to several Mbit/s for DCS?

Ans: In Fieldbus there are typically only 12 device per segment (on a pair of wires) whereas on a DCS all the device of the entire plant are indirectly connected to a single bus which therefore must be faster.

57. Is it possible to place a thermocouple or RTD directly on fieldbus?

Ans: No, transmitter electronics is required to implement the communication protocol.

58. What is the difference between Profibus and Foundation Fieldbus?

Ans: Although both Profibus and Foundation Fieldbus are digital communication, the main difference is that. Foundation Fieldbus allows field devices like transmitters or valves for controlling process by themselves whereas Profibus mainly lets a central controller (like a PLC) make all the decisions.

Industrial Cyber Security

59. What is industrial cybersecurity?

Ans: Industrial cybersecurity refers to protecting industrial control systems (ICS), such as PLC, SCADA, DCS, and field devices, against cyber threats to ensure safety, reliability, and availability of critical industrial operations.

Cybersecurity is crucial to prevent disruptions that could cause production losses, safety incidents, environmental harm, or financial damage.

60. What are the main threats to ICS (Industrial control system) networks?

Ans: Main threats include malware, ransomware, unauthorized access, insider threats, Denial of Service (DoS) attacks.

61. What is a DMZ (Demilitarized Zone) in industrial networks?

Ans: A DMZ is a network segment that separates the corporate (IT) network from the industrial (OT) network to control and limit communication between them.

62. How to Stop Cyber Attacks on PLC or DCS Systems?

Ans: To stop cyber-attacks on PLC and DCS systems, following steps can be adopted:

- ***Foster Awareness:*** Educate all employees continuously about cybersecurity threats and safe practices. Critical information like passwords should be shared only when necessary and encrypted.

- ***Employ Security Personnel:*** Appoint dedicated cybersecurity experts who regularly monitor, audit, and test the system for vulnerabilities.

- ***Utilize Effective Authentication:*** Avoid default passwords, use strong passwords, change them regularly, and do not use the same password across multiple systems.

- ***Cautiously Grant Authorization:*** Limit system access only to necessary personnel, applying the principle of "least privilege."

- ***Maintain Good Documentation:*** Keep updated records of network architecture, access lists, and configuration changes for accountability and troubleshooting.

- ***Close Unnecessary Access Pathways:*** Disable unused network ports, services, and access routes to minimize attack surfaces.

- ***Maintain Operating System Software:*** Regularly update and patch operating systems, antivirus software, and firmware to fix known vulnerabilities.

- ***Routinely Archive Critical Data***: Backup important control system data periodically to secure locations to ensure recovery after an attack.
- ***Limit Mobile Device Access***: Control the use of mobile devices like laptops and USB drives that could introduce malware into control networks.
- ***Secure All Toolkits***: Secure configuration tools, engineering stations, and programming software against unauthorized access.
- ***Advanced Authentication:*** Implement two-factor authentication and biometric verification wherever possible for higher security.
- ***Air Gaps:*** Isolate critical systems from external networks physically where possible to prevent remote cyberattacks.
- ***Network Segregation:*** Segment industrial networks from corporate IT networks using firewalls and DMZs to prevent malware spread.
- ***Read-Only System Access***: Set critical control systems to read-only mode wherever practical to prevent unauthorized changes.
- ***Control Platform Diversity***: Use a mix of hardware and software vendors to avoid single-point vulnerabilities and reduce systemic risks.

63. What is the importance of VPN in Industrial cyber security?

Ans: VPN (Virtual Private Network) is a secure communication technology that creates an encrypted tunnel between a user's device and a remote server or network over the internet. It hides the data from outsiders, protects privacy, and prevents unauthorized access. In industrial systems, VPNs allow safe remote access to control systems like PLCs and DCS without exposing them directly to public networks, reducing the risk of cyber-attacks.

If data is being required on a regular basis on cloud platforms through the SCADA, the internet will be required and thus, VPN plays another important role here. IO modules and sensors or other instruments which are IoT enabled can be easily configured remotely through VPN.

Chapter :19

Safety Instrumentation System

1. How are the hazardous types classified in different classes?

Ans: Following are the classification of hazardous types:

- *Class I* - For gases or vapours
- *Class II* - For combustible dusts
- *Class III* – For flammable fibres.

2. How are the hazardous areas classified in different divisions?

Ans: Following are the classification of hazardous areas in divisions:

- *Division 1*: Areas are those where explosive concentrations can or do exist under normal operating conditions.
- *Division 2*: Areas are those where explosive concentrations only exist infrequently or under abnormal condition.

3. How are the hazardous areas classified in different Zones?

Ans: Following are the classification of hazardous areas in Zones:

- *Zone 0*: It defines areas where explosive concentrations are continually present or normally present for long periods of time.
- *Zone 1*: It defines areas where those concentrations may be present under normal operating conditions.
- *Zone 2*: It defines areas where explosive concentrations are unlikely under normal operating conditions, and when present do not exist for substantial periods of time.

4. What do you mean by the terms maximum experimental safe gap (MESG) and the minimum ignition current ratio (MICR)?

Ans: The Maximum Experimental Safe Gap (MESG) is a key

parameter used in classifying explosion-proof enclosures for hazardous areas. It is defined as the maximum width of a gap (in millimeters) through which a gas or vapor explosion cannot propagate from one compartment to another under specified test conditions.

MESG helps determine the safety level of flameproof enclosures (Ex d) and is used to classify gases into explosion groups. Higher MESG values indicate that a gas requires a larger gap to ignite an explosion, meaning it is less dangerous compared to gases with lower MESG values. Example: Methane (CH_4): High MESG (less hazardous), Hydrogen (H_2): Low MESG (more hazardous).

The Minimum Ignition Current Ratio (MICR) is the ratio of the minimum ignition current of an air/fuel mixture to the minimum ignition current of methane when tested under identical conditions. It indicates the ease of igniting a gas using an electrical spark.

If MICR < 1: The gas is more easily ignitable than methane and if MICR > 1: The gas is less easily ignitable than methane. MICR is used in electrical classification to define intrinsic safety (Ex i) requirements for hazardous areas.

Both MESG and MICR are important for designing explosion-proof equipment in industries to prevent ignition hazards.

5. What do you mean by hermetically sealed device?

Ans: A hermetically sealed device is an enclosure or component that is completely sealed to prevent the entry of air, or hazardous gas. This sealing is achieved using materials like glass, metal, or special adhesives to ensure an airtight and gas-tight environment.

6. What do you mean by the term intrinsically safe?

Ans: Intrinsically Safe (IS) refers to a design approach for electrical and electronic equipment used in hazardous areas, ensuring that the equipment cannot generate enough energy (electrical or thermal) to ignite flammable gases, vapors, or dust.

Electrical circuits are designed to operate below the ignition energy of the flammable substances present. Safety barriers (Zener barriers or galvanic isolators) limit energy transfer from power sources. Most modern 4 to 20 mA analog signal instruments may be used as part of intrinsically safe circuits so long as they are connected to control equipment through suitable safety barrier interfaces, the purpose of which is to limit the amount of voltage and current available at the field device to low enough levels that an explosion-triggering spark is impossible even under fault conditions.

7. How intrinsic safety barrier works?

Ans: Two types of safety barrier used: Zener barrier and Galvanic isolators.

Zener Barrier: In normal operation, the 4-20 mA field instrument possesses insufficient terminal voltage and insufficient loop current to pose any threat of hazardous atmosphere ignition. This is the purpose of the intrinsic safety barrier circuit: to serve as a safeguard in the event of unforeseen wiring and/or component faults so that there is no possible way for enough voltage or current to develop to trigger an explosion.

If a short-circuit develops in the field instrument, the series resistance of the barrier circuit will limit fault current to a value low enough not to pose a threat in the hazardous area. If something fails in the receiving instrument to cause a much greater power supply voltage to develop at its terminals, the zener diode inside the barrier will break down and provide a shunt path for fault current that bypasses the field instrument (and may possibly blow the fuse in the barrier). Thus, the intrinsic safety barrier circuit provides protection against overcurrent and overvoltage faults, so that neither type of fault will result in enough electrical energy available at the field device to ignite an explosive atmosphere.

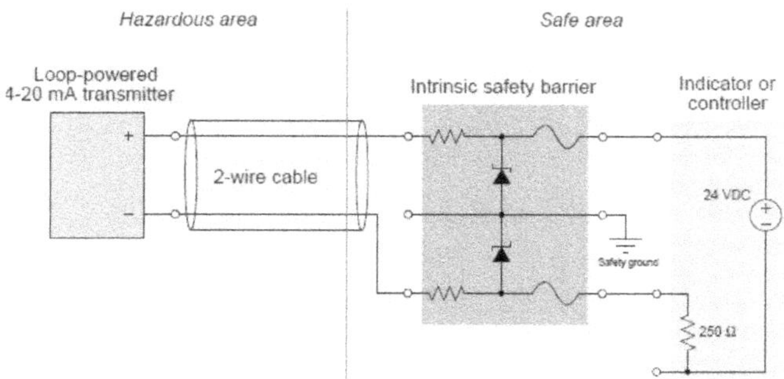

Fig 19.1- Zener barrier

Galvanic isolators: A Galvanic Isolator is a type of Intrinsic Safety (IS) barrier that electrically isolates circuits in hazardous areas from those in safe areas without a direct electrical connection. It achieves this by transmitting signals and power through isolation techniques such as transformers, optocouplers, or capacitive coupling.

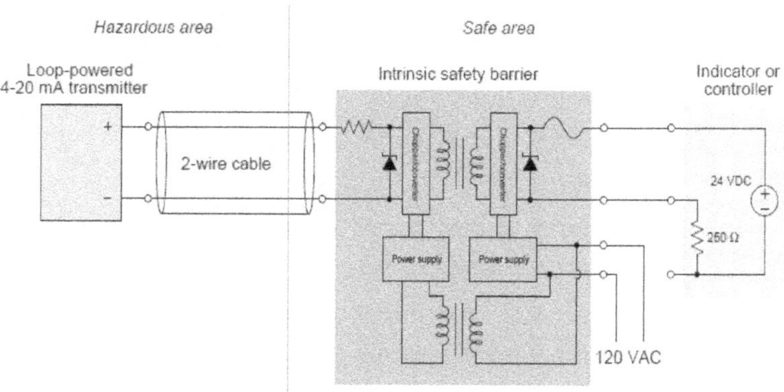

Fig 19.2 – Galvanic barrier

8. What is Ex-i intrinsic safety?

Ans: Ex i Intrinsic Safety is a protection method used in hazardous areas, where the electrical energy within a circuit or device is restricted to a level insufficient to cause ignition of a surrounding explosive atmosphere. This also ensures that the surface temperature of the equipment remains below the ignition temperature of the hazardous environment.

Intrinsic safety works by limiting the energy (voltage and current) in both normal and fault conditions, preventing sparks or heat that could ignite flammable gases or dust. There are two sub-categories under the Ex i protection concept:

- ***Ex-ia***: Provides the highest level of protection. It is designed to remain safe even with two independent faults occurring. Suitable for Zone 0 (an area where an explosive atmosphere is continuously present or present for long periods).
- ***Ex-ib***: Offers a slightly lower level of protection, remaining safe with one fault condition. It is suitable for Zone 1 (an area where an explosive atmosphere is likely to occur during normal operation).

9. What is Ex d flameproof protection?

Ans: Ex d Flameproof protection is a method used to ensure safety in hazardous areas where explosive atmospheres may be present. In this protection concept, any component or equipment capable of igniting an explosive mixture is housed within a robust enclosure. The enclosure is constructed to withstand the pressure generated by an internal explosion and to cool escaping gases below the ignition temperature before they reach the outside. Additionally, the enclosure is designed to prevent the ingress of explosive atmosphere, reducing the chance of ignition.

10. What is Ex m encapsulation protection?

Ans: Ex m Encapsulation is a type of explosion protection method used in hazardous areas. In this concept, components or parts of electrical equipment that could potentially cause ignition are fully encapsulated in a protective compound or resin. This prevents the explosive atmosphere from coming into contact with any energized parts that might generate sparks or heat. The encapsulating material also serves to limit the surface temperature of the equipment during normal operation, ensuring it stays below the ignition temperature of the surrounding atmosphere.

Ex m protection is commonly used for small electronic devices, sensors, and circuit components.

11. What is Ex e increases safety protection?

Ans: Ex e Increased Safety is a protection concept used in hazardous areas to prevent the possibility of ignition by ensuring that electrical equipment operates without generating arcs, sparks, or excessive surface temperatures under both normal and specified abnormal conditions. This method involves applying additional design and construction precautions such as improved insulation, secure wiring, reinforced connections, and enhanced enclosure integrity to increase the safety of the equipment.

Importantly, equipment that normally produces arcs or sparks, such as contactors or switches, is not permitted under Ex e protection.

12. What is Ex p pressurised protection?

Ans: Ex p Pressurized Protection is a method used to protect electrical equipment in hazardous areas by maintaining a higher pressure inside an enclosure than the surrounding atmosphere. This prevents the ingress of flammable gases, vapours, dust, or fibres, thereby eliminating the risk of ignition within the enclosure. There are two key approaches in this protection concept:

- *Pressurization:* The enclosure is initially purged with clean air or an inert gas, and then maintained at a positive pressure relative to the external environment. This ensures that flammable substances cannot enter the enclosure.
- *Continuous Flow (or Purging)***:** A constant flow of protective gas (air or inert gas) is supplied into the enclosure to dilute and remove any potentially explosive atmosphere that may enter or be present inside.

13. What is Ex o Oil Immersion protection?

Ans: Ex o Oil Immersion is a type of explosion protection in which electrical equipment that may produce arcs, sparks, or high temperatures is completely immersed in a protective liquid, typically oil or another insulating liquid. This protective liquid acts as a barrier, preventing any flammable gas, vapor, or dust in the external hazardous atmosphere from coming into contact with the energized parts that could cause ignition. The oil also serves as a coolant and insulator, helping to dissipate heat and further reduce the risk of ignition.

Ex o protection is generally used for transformers, reactors, and other electrical equipment.

14. What is Ex q Powder Filling Protection?

Ans: Ex q Powder Filling is a type of explosion protection in which electrical components that may produce arcs, sparks, or high temperatures are enclosed within a housing that is completely filled with a fine granular material, typically quartz or glass powder. The powder surrounds and insulates the live components, effectively suppressing the ignition of any explosive atmosphere by absorbing and dissipating heat, preventing the formation of an ignitable mixture, and restricting the free movement of gases within the enclosure.

This method is primarily used for electronic devices and small power components.

15. What is Ex n Non-Sparking Protection?

Ans: Ex n (non-sparking) is a protection technique used for electrical equipment in Zone 2 hazardous areas, where explosive atmospheres are not likely to occur frequently. In this method, the equipment is designed and constructed in such a way that under normal operating conditions, it does not produce arcs, sparks, or excessive temperatures that could ignite an explosive atmosphere. The Ex n protection concept is divided into several subtypes:

- **Ex nA (Non-Sparking Equipment):** Equipment is constructed using components and wiring that do not produce sparks or hot surfaces during normal operation.
- **Ex nC (Non-Incendive Equipment):** Equipment may produce small arcs or sparks, but they are not capable of igniting a flammable atmosphere under normal conditions.
- **Ex nR (Restricted Breathing Enclosure):** The enclosure is sealed to limit the ingress of flammable gases and vapors, preventing them from reaching internal components.
- **Ex nL (Energy-Limited Equipment):** Internal circuits are designed to limit energy below the ignition threshold of explosive atmospheres.

16. What is Ex s Special Protection?

Ans: Ex s (Special Protection) is a method of explosion protection that does not conform to the standard parameters or construction requirements defined by other protection techniques (such as Ex d, Ex e, Ex i, etc.). Instead, Ex s is used for custom-designed equipment or systems where a specific safety concept is developed and formally assessed to ensure that it prevents ignition in a hazardous environment.

The equipment must undergo a detailed risk assessment and evaluation by a certified testing body to verify that it meets the required safety standards for use in explosive atmospheres. Ex s is typically used in situations where no other standardized method is applicable, but a high level of explosion protection is still required.

17. What is 'simple apparatus' in the context of intrinsic safety?

Ans: Simple apparatus refers to devices that do not appreciably affect intrinsic safety, such as switches, thermocouples, RTDs, and junction boxes.

18. In intrinsic safety, how is energy storage in cables accounted for?

Ans: During system analysis, energy storage due to cable capacitance and inductance is calculated to ensure it does not exceed safe limits.

19. What is ingress protection (IP Code)?

Ans: Ingress Protection (IP) refers to the degree of protection provided by an enclosure against the intrusion of solid foreign objects (such as dust or tools) and water. It is an important consideration for equipment installed in both hazardous and non-hazardous areas, ensuring reliable and safe operation under various environmental conditions.

The level of protection is defined by the IP Code, also known as the Ingress Protection Rating, which is standardized under IEC 60529. The IP Code consists of two digits: The first digit indicates the level of protection against solid objects and dust and the second digit indicates the level of protection against water ingress.

For example, IP66 means the equipment is dust-tight and protected against powerful water jets.

20. What are IEC and NEMA Standards?

Ans: The IEC is a global organization that prepares and publishes international standards for electrical, electronic, and related technologies. IEC standards ensure uniformity and safety in electrical products and systems across countries. In instrumentation and automation, IEC standards define: Electrical enclosure classifications (e.g., IEC 60529 for IP ratings), Instrumentation symbols and design.

NEMA is a U.S.-based organization that defines standards for electrical enclosures, motors, controls, and other electrical equipment. NEMA standards are focused on product performance, safety, and reliability, especially in industrial and commercial environments.

IEC standards are international, while NEMA is primarily used in North America.

21. What is ATEX standards?

Ans: ATEX stands for "**ATmosphères EXplosibles**", and it refers to a set of European Union directives for equipment and protective systems intended for use in explosive atmospheres.

The ATEX standards are designed to ensure that electrical and mechanical equipment used in hazardous areas do not cause explosions due to sparks, hot surfaces, or other sources of ignition.

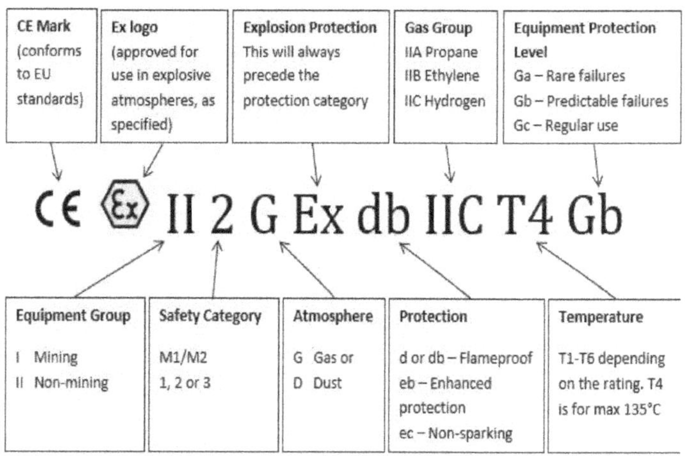

Fig 19.3 – ATEX standards

22. How do you Know if a Product Complies with ATEX?

Ans: A product complies with ATEX has the following markings:

- The **CE Mark**, indicating compliance with EU directives.
- The **Ex Mark**, denoting suitability for use in explosive atmospheres under ATEX.

23. What is the operational temperature in hazardous area?

Ans: All equipment used within hazardous areas has an operational temperature band or limit. This is the upper and lower ambient temperatures of which the equipment is approved for use in.

As defined in IEC 60079-0 the standard limits are – 20℃ to +40℃. Where the operation temperatures of the equipment fall between these parameters no additional marking is required.

24. What do you mean by redundancy in Instrumentation system?

Ans: In instrumentation systems, redundancy means having duplicate or backup components or systems to ensure continuous operation and maintain system reliability in case of failure of a primary component.

Different types of redundancy:

- *Hardware redundancy*: It can be achieved by using two or more sensors to measure the same process variable, so if one fails, the other can provide the measurement. Having multiple power supplies to ensure that if one fails, the system can continue operating using the backup power supply. Having backup controllers for DCS or PLC that can take over the control functions of the primary controller if it fails.

- *Network redundancy*: Having multiple communication paths or networks to ensure that if one fails, the system can still communicate.

- *Software redundancy*: Having backup software programs or algorithms to take over in case of failure.

- *Functional redundancy*: Instead of duplicating hardware, this redundancy ensures that different sensors or algorithms can perform the same function. For example, A temperature monitoring system using both RTD sensors and thermocouples to ensure readings remain accurate even if one sensor type fails.

25. What is Triple Modular Redundant (TMR) System?

Ans: A Triple Modular Redundant (TMR) System is a fault-tolerant system that uses three identical subsystems (such as sensors, controllers, or processors) to improve reliability, safety, and availability. It employs voting logic, where the system compares outputs from all three modules and selects the majority (at least 2 out of 3) as the correct output.

26. What is cold standby, warm standby and hot standby?

Ans: Cold standby, warm standby and hot standby are the types of controller redundancy of DCS or PLC.

Cold standby: The backup system is powered off and activated only when the primary system fails.

Warm standby: The backup system runs in standby mode and takes over with minimal delay.

Hot standby: Both systems run simultaneously, and the backup takes over instantly if the primary fails.

27. What are the different types of overpressure protection devices?

Ans: The different types of overpressure protection devices are: Rupture disk, Pressure relief valve and Pressure regulating valve.

Rupture disk is a thin sheet of material (usually alloy steel) designed to rupture in the event of an overpressure condition. The amount of force applied to this thin metal sheet is given by the formula F = P * A (force equals pressure times area). The thin metal sheet is designed to rupture at a certain threshold of force equivalent to the burst pressure. Once the disk ruptures, the fluid vents through new-formed path, thus relieving pressure. Like an electrical fuse, a rupture disk is a one-time device which must be replaced after it has "blown."

Pressure Relief Valves (PRVs) and Pressure Safety Valves (PSVs) are special types of valves designed to open up in order to relieve excess pressure from inside a process vessel or piping system. Unlike regular control valves, PRVs and PSVs are actuated by the process fluid pressure itself rather than by some external pressure or force.

A relief valve opens in direct proportion to the amount of overpressure it experiences in the process piping. That is, a PRV will open slightly for slight overpressures, and open more for greater overpressures. Pressure Relief Valves are commonly used in liquid services.

A safety valve opens fully whenever it experiences a sufficient overpressure condition, not closing until the process fluid pressure falls significantly below that "lift" pressure value.

Pressure Safety Valves are commonly used in gas and vapor services, such as compressed air systems and steam systems.

28. What is energize to safe and de-energize to safe loop philosophy? Which is the safest option?

Ans: In industrial safety and control systems, Energize-to-Safe and De-Energize-to-Safe philosophies define how safety loops behave in response to faults or hazardous conditions. These philosophies determine whether a device requires power to remain in a safe state or if removing power ensures safety.

In energize to safe loop, the final element (e.g., a valve, pump, or actuator) is designed to move to its safe state when the system is energized. This approach is typically used in situations where uninterrupted operation is a priority and unwanted shutdowns need to be avoided. For example: A fire suppression system that sprays water when activated. It needs power to open the valve and release water.

In de-energize to safe loop, the final element is designed to move to its safe state when the system is de-energized. The system or device must be powered (energized) in normal operation and automatically moves to a safe state when power is lost. This philosophy is often used when safety is the primary concern, and a failure or loss of power could lead to a dangerous condition. For example: Emergency Shutdown Valve (ESDV), it remains open when energized, but in case of a failure (loss of power or air pressure), it closes automatically.

Between the Energize-to-Safe and De-Energize-to-Safe loop philosophies, the De-Energize-to-Safe loop is considered the safest option. This is because, in an Energize-to-Safe loop, if there is an unintended instrument cable disconnection or an electrical blackout, the final element would not be energized to move to the safe state.

29. What is the difference between Process shutdown (PSD) and Emergency shutdown (ESD)?

Ans: Emergency Shutdown (ESD) and Process Shutdown (PSD) are both safety mechanisms in industrial systems, but they serve different purposes and operate under different conditions.

ESD is a high-priority safety system designed to immediately shut down critical equipment or the entire plant in response to hazardous events such as fire, gas leaks, or extreme overpressure, preventing catastrophic failures. It is typically controlled by a Safety Instrumented System (SIS) and follows strict safety integrity levels (SIL 2 or SIL 3), ensuring rapid and fail-safe operation.

PSD is a lower-priority system that performs a controlled and safe shutdown of specific process units due to non-emergency conditions like equipment malfunctions, process deviations, or sensor failures.

Unlike ESD, PSD does not require immediate shutdown and instead allows for a gradual stop to avoid damage to equipment while maintaining operational flexibility.

30. What is safety instrumented function and system?

Ans: A Safety Instrumented Function (SIF) is a specific safety function designed to detect hazardous conditions and take corrective action to bring the system to a safe state.

A Safety Instrumented System (SIS) is a set of multiple SIFs working together to monitor, control, and mitigate hazards. It is an independent system designed to prevent accidents, explosions, or environmental damage.

SIS consists of:

- Sensors – Detect unsafe conditions (e.g., high pressure, high temperature)
- Logic Solver (PLC/DCS/SIS Controller) – Processes sensor signals and decides the necessary action.
- Final Control Elements (Valves, Relays, Shutdown Systems) – Execute corrective actions, such as closing a valve or stopping a machine.

31. What is safety integrity level?

Ans: Safety Integrity Level (SIL) is a measure of the reliability and performance of a Safety Instrumented Function (SIF) or Safety Instrumented System (SIS) in reducing risk. SIL ratings are defined by the IEC 61508 and IEC 61511 standards and determine how well a system can prevent hazardous failures.

SIL levels range from SIL 1 to SIL 4, with SIL 4 offering the highest level of safety and risk reduction. SIL 3 and SIL 4 are used in high-risk industries (e.g., nuclear, oil & gas).

32. What is Process Hazard Analysis (PHA) & Layer of Protection Analysis (LOPA)?

Ans: Process Hazard Analysis (PHA) and Layer of Protection Analysis (LOPA) are the methodologies used in industries to identify, assess, and mitigate risks in process operations.

Process Hazard Analysis (PHA) is a systematic risk assessment method used to identify potential hazards, failures, and consequences in a process system.

Key features of PHA:

- **Identifies Hazards**: Recognizes potential risks in process design and operation.
- **Evaluates Consequences**: Assesses the impact of failures.
- **Recommends Safeguards**: Suggests safety measures to prevent or mitigate hazards.

Layer of Protection Analysis (LOPA) is a semi-quantitative risk assessment method used to evaluate whether existing safety layers are sufficient to reduce risk to an acceptable level.

Key features of LOPA:

- **Focuses on Risk Reduction**: Determines if additional safety layers (e.g., alarms, shutdowns) are needed.
- **Uses Risk Tolerability Criteria**: Compares risk levels against industry-accepted safety limits.
- **Identifies Independent Protection Layers (IPLs)**: Evaluates barriers that work independently to prevent failures.

33. What do you mean by the terms Availability, reliability, MTBF, Failure rate, PFD?

Ans:

Availability: It refers to the percentage of time a system is operational and capable of performing its function when needed.

Availability(A)=MTBF /(MTBF +MTTR)

where:

MTBF (Mean Time Between Failures) = Average time between failures

MTTR (Mean Time to Repair) = Average time taken to repair the system

For Example: If a gas compressor has an MTBF of 1,000 hours and an MTTR of 10 hours, then:

A=1000 /(1000+10) = 0.99 = 99%

This means the compressor is available 99% of the time.

Reliability: It is the probability that a system will perform its intended function without failure for a specific period under given conditions.

$$R(t)=e^{-\lambda t}$$

Where:

λ (Failure Rate) = 1 / MTBF

t = Operating time

For Example: A system with an MTBF of 500 hours has a failure rate of 1/500=0.0021/500 = 0.002 failures per hour. If we want to find the probability of the system surviving for 100 hours:

$R(100) = e^{-0.002*10} = e^{-0.2} = 0.818$

This means the system has an 81.8% chance of operating without failure for 100 hours.

Mean Time between Failure (MTBF): MTBF is the average time a system operates before failing. It is a key measure of system reliability.

Failure Rate: It is the number of failures per unit time (usually expressed in failures per hour).

$$\lambda = 1/MTBF$$

For example: A motor with an MTBF of 5,000 hours has a failure rate of:

$$\lambda=1/5000=0.0002 \text{ failures per hour}$$

Probability of failure on demand (PFD): It is a measure of how likely a safety system or safety function is to fail when it is required to act in response to a hazardous event. A lower PFD value means higher reliability, and a higher PFD value indicates a higher risk of failure.

$$PFD = (\lambda * T)/2$$

where:

λ = failure rate

T = proof test interval (time between maintenance checks)

For example: A shutdown valve with a failure rate of 0.0001 failures per hour and a test interval of 1 year (8760 hours) has:

$$PFD = (0.0001 * 8760)/2 = 0.438$$

This means there is a 43.8% chance that the valve will fail when required if not tested regularly.

Chapter: 20
Gas & Fire Detection System

1. What is a gas detector?

Ans: A gas detector is a device that detects the presence of gases in an area, often as part of a safety system. This type of equipment is used to detect a gas leak or other emissions and can interface with a control system so a process can be automatically shut down.

2. What are the different types of gas detectors used in industry?

Ans: Electrochemical Gas Detectors, Catalytic (Pellistor) Gas Detectors, Infrared (IR) Gas Detectors, Photoionization Detectors, Open Path Gas Detectors.

3. Explain the working of Electrochemical Gas Detectors and its applications.

Ans: Electrochemical gas detectors are commonly used to measure toxic gases, and they work by using a chemical reaction to generate an electrical signal. Inside the detector, there is an electrochemical cell that contains electrodes and an electrolyte. When the target gas enters the detector, it passes through a gas-permeable membrane and reaches the working electrode. Here, the gas reacts chemically with the electrolyte.

This reaction produces an electrical current, and the strength of this current depends on how much gas is present. In other words, the higher the concentration of gas, the stronger the electrical signal that is generated. The detector then measures this current and converts it into a readable value, usually displayed in parts per million (ppm) or as a percentage of the gas in the air.

Applications: to detect toxic gases like carbon monoxide (CO), hydrogen sulfide (H_2S).

4. Explain the working of Catalytic (Pellistor) Gas Detectors and its applications.

Ans: Catalytic gas detectors, are widely used to detect the presence of flammable gases. These detectors work on the principle of combustion. When a flammable gas enters the detector, it diffuses into a chamber that contains a small sensing element, typically a bead coated with a catalyst such as platinum or palladium. This bead is kept at a heated state.

As the target gas comes into contact with the hot bead, it begins to oxidize, or in other words, it burns on the catalyst-coated surface. The oxidation reaction releases heat, which increases the temperature of the bead. This rise in temperature causes a change in the bead's electrical resistance. The sensing element is part of a Wheatstone bridge circuit, and the change in resistance causes an imbalance in the circuit. This imbalance generates an electrical signal that is directly proportional to the concentration of the flammable gas in the surrounding atmosphere.

Applications: Suitable for detecting hydrocarbons like methane and propane in refineries

5. Explain the working of Infrared (IR) Gas Detectors and its applications.

Ans: Infrared (IR) gas detectors are based on the principle that gases absorb infrared light at specific wavelengths. When a gas is present in the detection area, it absorbs a portion of the IR radiation that passes through it. This absorption is unique to each type of gas.

The detector works by emitting infrared light from an IR source, which then travels through a chamber or sampling area containing the air or gas mixture. If the target gas is present, it will absorb some of the infrared light at its characteristic wavelengths. On the other end, a photodetector measures the intensity of the light that has passed through the chamber. By comparing the amount of light emitted with the amount received, the detector can determine how much light was absorbed by the gas.This difference in light intensity directly relates to the concentration of the gas in the sample. The detector then processes this information and provides a gas concentration reading, usually shown on a display.

Applications: Used for flammable gases (e.g., hydrocarbons)

6. **Explain the working of Photoionization Detectors**

Ans: Photoionization Detectors are used to detect low concentrations of volatile organic compounds and certain toxic gases. They work on the principle of photoionization, which involves using ultraviolet (UV) light to ionize gas molecules.

Inside the detector, a UV lamp emits high-energy photons that are directed at the gas sample. When the energy of the UV light is higher than the ionization potential of a gas molecule, the molecule absorbs that energy and becomes ionized. This means it loses an electron, forming a positively charged ion. Once ionized, the gas molecules and free electrons are attracted to a pair of electrodes inside the sensor. As these charged particles move, they create a small electric current. The strength of this current depends on how many gas molecules were ionized—which directly reflects the concentration of the gas in the sample. The detector measures this current and converts it into a gas concentration reading.

7. **What do you mean by the term LEL and UEL.**

Ans: *LEL*- Lower Explosive Limit. The minimum concentration of a combustible gas or vapor in air which will ignite if a source of ignition is present. Below the LEL, the mixture is too "lean" (not enough fuel) to ignite.

UEL: Upper Explosive Limit. Most combustible gases have an upper explosive limit which is the maximum concentration in air which will support combustion. Above the UEL, the mixture is too "rich" (not enough oxygen) to ignite.

8. What are TWA and STEL?

Ans: TWA stands for Time Weight Average. This in reference to dosages of toxic gas you may encounter in the work place. It is based on an 8-hour day/ 40-hour work week.

STEL stands for Short Term Exposure Limit. This is the average amount of gas you can be exposed to in a 15-minute period with no long-term health effects.

9. What are the common units of measuring gas concentration?

Ans*: %(percent*)- This unit expresses concentration in parts per hundred (percentage) of a substance in 100mL of a medium such as air.

Ppm (parts per million)- This unit that expresses concentration in parts per million is measured as the volume (denoted in litres [L]) of a substance found in 1L of a medium such as air.

mg/L (milligram per litre)- This unit expresses the concentration in one litre of air (1000mL) of a substance in terms of its mass (measured in milligrams).

10. What is test gas used to calibrate a gas monitor?

Ans: *Methane.*

11. Why gas or fire detectors are 3 wires instead of 2 wires?

Ans: In a 2-wire system, the device gets its power from the loop itself. It's advantageous because it simplifies wiring and reduces installation costs. However, the power available to the device is limited by the loop voltage and resistance. Therefore, if the fire and gas detector requires more power to operate correctly (for example, for heaters in certain gas detectors, or for advanced diagnostic capabilities), a 2-wire system may not be adequate.

In a 3-wire system, the device has a separate power supply, which means it's not limited by the loop voltage and can, therefore, handle more power-intensive operations. This can be advantageous for devices that need additional power, beyond what the 4-20 mA loop can provide, to function correctly or for additional features.

12. What is fire triangle?

Ans: The Fire Triangle illustrates the three essential elements required for a fire to ignite and sustain: *heat, fuel*, and *oxygen*. Heat provides the energy needed to raise the fuel's temperature to its ignition point, while the fuel serves as the combustible material, which can be a solid, liquid, or gas. Oxygen, typically supplied by air, supports the combustion process by reacting with the fuel. If any one of these elements is removed, by cooling to eliminate heat, cutting off the fuel supply, or smothering the fire to deprive it of oxygen, the fire will extinguish. That's why the fire triangle is often used in fire prevention and firefighting: it shows that disrupting just one side of the triangle is enough to stop a fire.

13. What are the different types of detectors used in industrial firefighting system?

Ans: Heat Detector, Smoke Detector, Beam Detector.

14. What is the working principle of Heat detector?

Ans: Heat detectors in fire-fighting systems work based on the principle of detecting a rapid increase in temperature or a temperature exceeding a pre-set threshold. Uses two metals with different thermal expansion rates bonded together. When heated, the strip bends and completes an electrical circuit, triggering the alarm.

15. What is the working principle of Smoke detector?

Ans: Smoke detectors work on the principle of detecting smoke particles in the air, which are indicative of a fire. They use a small amount of radioactive material (commonly Americium-241) to ionize the air in a sensing chamber. The radioactive material emits alpha particles that collide with air molecules, creating ions. The ions allow a small, steady electric current to flow between two electrodes. When smoke particles enter the chamber, they disrupt the flow of ions, reducing the current. This drop in current triggers the alarm.

16. What is the working principle of beam detector?

Ans: A beam detector is a type of smoke detection system commonly used in large, open areas like warehouses, auditoriums, or industrial places where installing multiple smoke detectors might be impractical.

It works by sending a narrow beam of infrared or visible light from a transmitter across the room to a reflector on the opposite side. The reflector bounces the beam back to the detector. Under normal, smoke-free conditions, the beam travels freely between the two ends. But when smoke enters the path of the beam, it scatters or blocks part of the light. This reduction in light intensity is monitored by the detector. If the loss of light goes beyond a certain threshold, the system takes it as a sign of smoke in the area and triggers an alarm.

This method allows the detector to cover a wide area with just a single device, making it efficient and cost-effective for large spaces.

17. What is Manual Call Point (MCP)?

Ans: A Manual Call Point (MCP) is a device used in fire alarm systems to manually trigger an alarm in case of a fire. Once activated, the MCP completes an electrical circuit, sending a signal to the fire alarm control panel.

18. What is addressable fire alarm system? What are its advantages over conventional system?

Ans: An addressable fire alarm system is a type of fire detection and alarm system where every device (e.g., smoke detectors, heat detectors, manual call points) has a unique identifier or "address." This allows the fire alarm control panel to identify the exact location of an activated device, making it easier to pinpoint the source of a potential fire or fault.

These systems offer several key advantages over conventional ones. First of all, they are able to monitor the status of each detector. As a detector becomes dirty, the microprocessor recognizes a decreased capability, and provides a maintenance alert.

19. What is End of Line resistor in fire protection system? What are its uses?

Ans: An End-of-Line Resistor (EOLR) in a fire alarm system is a component used to monitor the integrity of a circuit. It is typically installed at the end of the wiring in conventional fire alarm systems.

By adding a specific resistance to the circuit, the fire control panel can differentiate between normal operation, an alarm condition, and a fault condition. The FACP sends a small current through the fire detection circuit to check its resistance. Based on the measured resistance, the panel determines the circuit's status:

- ***Normal Condition***: Resistance matches the EOL resistor value.
- ***Open Circuit Fault***: Infinite resistance (circuit broken or disconnected).
- ***Short Circuit Fault***: Very low resistance (wires shorted together).
- ***Alarm Condition***: Resistance changes (e.g., when a detector or call point is activated).

20. Why EOL resistor not used in addressable fire protection system?

Ans: EOL resistors are generally not used because addressable systems continuously monitor each device individually.

Chapter: 21

Analyzers

1. What are the different types of analysers used in process Industry?

Ans: The different types of analysers used are: Silica Analyser, Oxygen Analyser, pH Analyser, Conductivity Analyser, SPM Analyser, Sodium Analyser.

2. What is the working principle of Silica Analyser?

Ans: A silica analyzer is used to measure how much silica (SiO_2) is present in water, commonly in power plants and water treatment systems. It works on a colorimetric principle, where the amount of colour formed in a chemical reaction tells how much silica is in the sample.

A water sample is first filtered to remove any solid particles. Then, a chemical called ammonium molybdate is added. This reacts with any silica in the water to form a yellow compound. Next, a reducing agent, like ascorbic acid or oxalic acid is added, turning the yellow compound blue.

The analyzer then uses a light sensor (photometer or colorimeter) to measure how deep the blue colour is, usually at a wavelength of 815 nm. The darker the blue, the more silica is present. The device then converts this colour intensity into a readable value (in ppb or ppm) using a pre-set calibration, and the result can be shown on a display or sent to a control system.

3. What is the working principle of Oxygen Analyser?

Ans: An oxygen analyzer is used to measure the concentration of oxygen (O_2) in gases or liquids. The working principle depends on the type of oxygen analyzer used, which includes electrochemical, zirconia, paramagnetic, and tunable diode laser analyzers.

347

Electrochemical Oxygen Analyzer (Galvanic or Fuel Cell): An Electrochemical Oxygen Analyzer, often referred to as a "galvanic" or "fuel cell" oxygen sensor, is a device that measures oxygen concentration by utilizing an electrochemical reaction where oxygen acts as the oxidant, generating a measurable electrical current directly proportional to the amount of oxygen present.

Oxygen diffuses through a permeable membrane and reaches a cathode where it is reduced, accepting electrons from an anode which is simultaneously oxidized, producing a current that is proportional to the oxygen concentration.

Zirconia Oxygen Analyzer: A zirconia cell with a thin layer of platinum electrodes is heated to about 600–800°C. Oxygen ions move through the zirconia membrane from the high O_2 concentration side (typically ambient air) to the low O_2 concentration side (sample gas). This movement generates a voltage (Nernst equation), which is proportional to the oxygen concentration. The analyzer converts the voltage into an oxygen percentage and displays it.

Paramagnetic Oxygen Analyzer: It is based on oxygen's paramagnetic properties (oxygen is attracted to magnetic fields). A gas sample is placed in a magnetic field. Oxygen molecules align with the magnetic field, creating a force. This force is measured and converted into an oxygen concentration.

Tunable Diode Laser (TDL) Oxygen Analyzer: It uses infrared laser absorption spectroscopy. A laser beam is transmitted through the gas sample. Oxygen molecules absorb specific wavelengths of light. The reduction in laser intensity is analyzed to determine oxygen concentration.

4.   What is the working principle of pH Analyser?

Ans: A pH analyzer is an instrument used to measure how acidic or alkaline a solution is, which it does by determining the concentration of hydrogen ions (H^+) present in the liquid. It works based on an electrochemical principle using two main components: a glass electrode and a reference electrode.

The glass electrode has a special membrane that is sensitive to hydrogen ions. When it's placed in a solution, it responds to the activity of those ions by generating a small electrical voltage. Alongside it, the reference electrode, usually made from silver/silver chloride or calomel, provides a stable, known voltage for comparison.

When both electrodes are immersed in the sample, a potential difference is created between them. This difference is related to the hydrogen ion concentration and follows the Nernst equation, which allows the analyzer to calculate the pH. The voltage typically ranges from about +414 millivolts at pH 0 (very acidic) to -414 millivolts at pH 14 (very alkaline). The analyzer measures this voltage and converts it into a readable pH value on a scale from 0 to 14. Since the pH reading can be affected by temperature, the system also includes a temperature sensor, usually an RTD or thermistor to automatically adjust and compensate for temperature variations, ensuring accurate and stable measurements.

5. What is the working principle of Conductivity Analyser?

Ans: A conductivity analyzer measures how well a solution can conduct electricity, which depends on the amount of dissolved ions in it, such as sodium (Na^+), chloride (Cl^-), or sulfate (SO_4^{2-}). The more ions present, the better the solution conducts electricity. To measure this, the analyzer applies a small alternating voltage across two electrodes that are placed in the solution. As current flows between the electrodes, the analyzer measures the strength of that current. Since the current is directly related to the number of ions, it gives a good indication of the solution's conductivity.

The measurement is based on Ohm's Law, where conductance (G) is calculated as the current (I) divided by the voltage (V). Conductance is simply the inverse of resistance. Because conductivity changes with temperature, most analyzers are equipped with automatic temperature compensation (ATC) to adjust the reading to a standard reference temperature, usually 25°C.

There are two main types of conductivity sensors used depending on the application. Contacting or electrode-based sensors are commonly used for low to moderate conductivity solutions, like pure or treated water. For solutions with higher conductivity, such as industrial wastewater, inductive or toroidal sensors are preferred. These work without direct contact by using electromagnetic induction. Conductivity is typically expressed in Siemens per centimeter (S/cm).

6. What is a SPM analyser?

Ans: An SPM analyzer is an instrument used to measure the concentration of suspended particulate matter (SPM) in the air or a gas stream. These particles, which include dust, smoke, soot, and aerosols, are typically classified based on their size, such as PM10 (particles ≤10 μm) and PM2.5 (particles ≤2.5 μm). SPM analyzers are widely used in air quality monitoring, industrial emissions control, and environmental compliance.

7. What is the working principle of Sodium Analyser?

Ans: A sodium analyzer is used to measure very small amounts of sodium (Na^+) in water, especially in places like power plants or industries that need ultra-pure water. Even tiny traces of sodium can cause problems like corrosion in boilers and turbines, so it's important to monitor it.

The analyzer takes a water sample and adjusts its pH using a buffer to make sure all sodium is in the right ionic form for measurement. Then, it uses a special sodium-sensitive electrode that reacts only to sodium ions. When sodium ions touch the electrode, they create a small voltage. This voltage is compared to a reference electrode, and the difference tells how much sodium is present.

Because temperature can affect the reading, the analyzer also has a temperature sensor to correct for that. After calibration with known standards, it gives the sodium concentration—usually in parts per billion (ppb) or parts per million (ppm).

8. What is SWAS?

Ans: A Steam and Water Analysis System (SWAS) is a specialized system used in power plants, refineries, and industrial boilers to continuously monitor the quality of steam and water. It ensures the early detection of contaminants like silica, sodium, chloride, dissolved oxygen, and pH deviations that can cause corrosion, scaling, or deposition in boilers, turbines, and heat exchangers.

9. What is CEMS?

Ans: A Continuous Emission Monitoring System (CEMS) is an automated system used to continuously measure and record the emissions of pollutants from industrial sources such as power plants, refineries, cement plants, and chemical industries. It ensures compliance with environmental regulations by monitoring emissions like SO_2 (Sulfur Dioxide), NO_x (Nitrogen Oxides), CO (Carbon Monoxide), CO_2 (Carbon Dioxide), O_2 (Oxygen), PM (Particulate Matter), and VOCs (Volatile Organic Compounds).

10. What is a Gas chromatography?

Ans: Gas Chromatography (GC) is a powerful analytical method used to separate, identify, and measure the amounts of different substances in a sample, especially when those substances are volatile. It's commonly used in fields like environmental monitoring, pharmaceuticals, petrochemicals, and chemical research to analyze complex mixtures.

The process starts when a small amount of the sample, either a gas or a liquid is injected into the system. If it's a liquid, it's first heated and vaporized in an injector. From there, an inert carrier gas (such as helium, nitrogen, or hydrogen) moves the vaporized sample through a narrow tube called the chromatography column.

This column is coated on the inside with a stationary phase, usually a thin film of liquid or polymer. As the sample moves through the column, each compound in the mixture interacts with the stationary phase in its own way. Some compounds move quickly through the column because they don't interact much, while others move more slowly because they stick to the stationary phase for longer. This difference in travel time causes the compounds to separate from each other.

Once they exit the column, the separated compounds pass through a detector, which measures their presence and generates an electrical signal.

Common detectors include:

- **Flame Ionization Detector (FID):** Detects hydrocarbons.
- **Thermal Conductivity Detector (TCD):** Measures gas mixtures.
- **Mass Spectrometer (GC-MS):** Identifies unknown compounds by their molecular structure.

The detector sends signals to a computer or chromatographic software. The software generates a chromatogram, where:

- Each peak represents a compound in the sample.
- The retention time (Rt) is the time taken for a compound to travel through the column.
- The peak area is proportional to the compound's concentration.

11. What is the working principle of SOx and NOx Analyser?

Ans: SOx (Sulfur Oxides) and NOx (Nitrogen Oxides) analyzers are used to monitor emissions of sulfur dioxide (SO_2) and nitrogen oxides (NO, NO_2) from industrial sources power plants, refineries.

SO_2 is commonly measured using Ultraviolet (UV) Fluorescence method. The sample gas is drawn into the analyzer and exposed to UV light. SO_2 absorbs the UV energy and emits fluorescence (light) at a specific wavelength. A photomultiplier tube (PMT) detects the fluorescence intensity, which is proportional to the SO_2 concentration.

NOx analyzers use Chemiluminescence Detection (CLD) method. The sample gas is mixed with ozone (O_3) inside a reaction chamber. NO reacts with ozone to form NO_2 and emits light (chemiluminescence reaction). The emitted light is detected by a photomultiplier tube (PMT), and its intensity is proportional to the NO concentration. To measure NO_2, the sample is first passed through a converter that reduces NO_2 to NO, allowing total NOx (NO + NO_2) measurement.

Chapter: 22

Miscellaneous Industrial

Instruments

LVDT (Linear Voltage Differential Transformer)

1. What is LVDT?

Ans: The LVDT stands for Linear Variable Differential Transformer. It converts the Linear motion into an electrical signal using an inductive transducer.

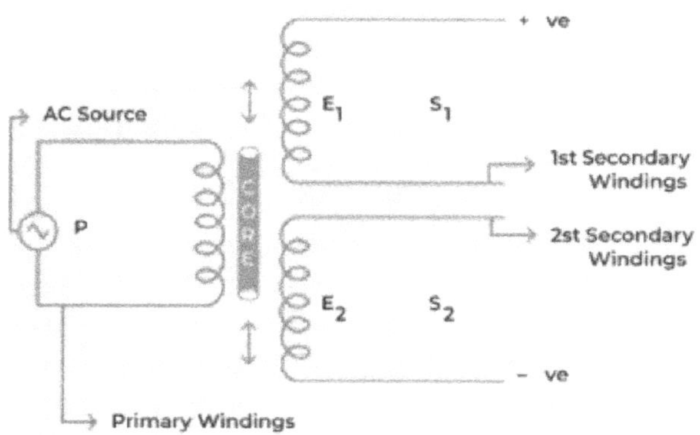

Fig 22.1- LVDT

The transformer and LVDT share a similar construction. It consists of one primary winding(P) and two secondary windings (S1 & S2). The primary and secondary windings are bounded by a hollow cylinder, known as the former. The primary winding is at the center and the secondary windings are present on both sides of the primary winding at an equal distance from the center. Both the secondary windings have an equal no. of terms and they are linked with each other in series opposition, i.e. they are wounded in opposite directions, but are connected in series with each other.

2. Explain the working of LVDT.

Ans: The working of LVDT is based on Faraday's law of electromagnetic induction, which states that "the electrical power in the network induction circuit is proportional to the rate of change of magnetic flux in the circuit."

As the primary winding of LVDT is connected to the AC power supply, The alternating magnetic field is produced in the primary winding, which results in the induced EMF of secondary windings.

Let's assume that the induced voltages in the secondary windings S1 & S2 are E1 & E2 respectively. Now according to using the rate of change of magnetic flux i.e. $d\Phi/dt$ is directly proportional to the magnitude of induced EMF i.e E1 and E2.

When the core of LVDT moves towards the second winding S1 then the flux linkage S will be more as compared to S2. The EMF induced in S1 will be more than the EMF of S2. Hence E1 is greater than E & net differential voltage Eo(E1-E2) will be +ve.

When the core is at a null position then the flux generated in both the secondary windings will be the same. The induced EMF E1 & E2, and both the windings will be the same. Hence the net differential output voltage Eo will be 0. It shows 0 displacement of the core.

When the core of LVDT moves towards secondary winding S2 then the flux linkage with S2 will be more than S1. It means the EMF induced in S2 will be more than the induced EMF of S1. Hence E2 is greater than E1 & net differential voltage Eo (E1-E2) will be negative.

The output of a Linear Variable Differential Transformer (LVDT) is an AC voltage that is proportional to the displacement or position of its core.

3. What are the applications of LVDT?

Ans: LVDT are used to detect the motion and displacement of the object. It can also be used as secondary transducer to measure pressure.

If an LVDT is installed on a valve, it can precisely measure the position of the valve stem, allowing accurate feedback for process control systems.

4. Why LVDT's secondary winding are connected in series opposition?

Ans: It is connected in series opposition for polarity-based direction detection. The polarity of the output voltage indicates the direction of the core's movement. For positive output, core moves in one direction and for negative output, core moves in opposite direction.

5. What is Residual Voltage of an LVDT?

Ans: Residual voltage in an LVDT (Linear Variable Differential Transformer) is the small voltage output that remains even when the core is exactly at the null (zero) position—that is, when it's cantered between the two secondary coils and theoretically should produce zero output.

Ideally, at the null position, the induced voltages in both secondary coils are equal and opposite, so they cancel each other out, and the differential output is zero. However, in real-world conditions, a small non-zero voltage (called residual voltage) appears due to:
- Imperfect coil winding symmetry
- Core misalignment
- Magnetic hysteresis
- Internal electrical noise or interference
- Manufacturing tolerances

6. What is LVDT excitation voltage?

Ans: An LVDT (Linear Variable Differential Transformer) requires an

AC excitation voltage to operate. This excitation is applied to the primary winding of the transformer to generate an alternating magnetic field, which is then coupled to the secondary windings through a movable magnetic core.

It is in the range of 5 – 12 VAC.

7. Is an LVDT Linear?

Ans: LVDT (Linear Variable Differential Transformer) is highly linear within a specific range of core movement. Beyond that range output of LVDT is nonlinear.

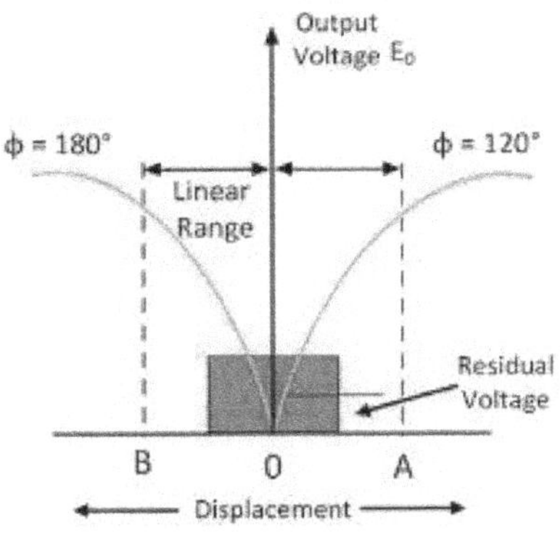

Fig 22.2- LVDT curve

Displacement measurement

8. Which instrument is used in the measurement of displacement?

Ans: Strain Gauge, LVDT and Capacitive transducer.

9. How strain gauge is used in the measurement of displacement?

Ans: Strain gauge is positive type resistance transducer which converts a mechanical displacement into a change of resistance. The strain gauge is basically a fine wire which changes its resistance when mechanically strained, due to physical effects. Its length and cross-sectional area vary and change of electrical resistivity also occurs. The strain gauge is mounted to the measured surface so that it elongates or contracts with that surface. This deformation of the sensing materials causes it to undergo a change in resistance.

The resistance change of the strain gauge is usually converted into voltage by connecting one, two or four similar gauges as arms of a wheat-stone bridge and applying excitation to the bridge. The bridge output voltage is then measure of the strain, which is calibrated to measure displacement.

10. How mechanical force can be measured?

Ans: Force measurement can be done by electric means in which the force is first converted into a displacement at an elastic element and then the displacement is measured. This displacement can be measured by LVDT or strain gauge.

11. What is load cell and how it works?

Ans: A load cell is a transducer that converts force (usually weight or load) into an electrical signal. It is widely used in industrial applications such as weighing scales, force measurement.

A load cell has a mechanical body that supports the force applied to it. The body contains a strain gauge, which is an internal sensor that deforms when force is applied. The deformation of the strain gauge changes its electrical resistance. The change in electrical resistance is measured and converted into an electrical signal.

12. What is excitation voltage in strain gauge load cells?

Ans: The strain gauge load cell is an active transducer. Active transducers can be excited by a controlled current or voltage source. A constant-voltage excitation is used for strain sensors.

Speed Measurement

13. What is tachometer?

Ans: Tachometer is an instrument used to measure speed of any rotating body.

14. Explain the working of eddy current tachometer and its applications.

Ans: In an eddy current tachometer, a small permanent magnet is attached to the rotating shaft whose speed we want to measure. As the shaft spins, the magnet also rotates. Close to this magnet is a metal disk—usually made of a non-magnetic material like aluminium—that doesn't touch the magnet.

When the magnet rotates, it generates eddy currents in the nearby metal disk. These currents create their own magnetic field, which pushes against the magnet's field. This interaction causes a drag force on the disk, trying to make it spin.

The disk is connected to a pointer through a spring. The faster the shaft spins, the stronger the eddy currents, and the more the disk (and pointer) gets pulled. The pointer moves over a calibrated scale to show the RPM (revolutions per minute).

Eddy current tachometers are commonly used in vehicles to measure engine or wheel speed.

15. What is magnetic pickup sensor and how it works?

Ans: A magnetic pickup sensor is a non-contact sensor used to measure the speed of rotating machinery, such as engines, turbines, and gas compressors.

The sensor has a permanent magnet and a coil of wire wound around it. It is positioned close to a rotating gear, toothed wheel, or any ferromagnetic target. As the gear teeth pass by the sensor, they disturb the magnetic field. This change in magnetic flux induces a voltage pulse in the coil. The sensor outputs a series of AC voltage pulses, where the frequency of the pulses is proportional to the rotational speed (RPM).

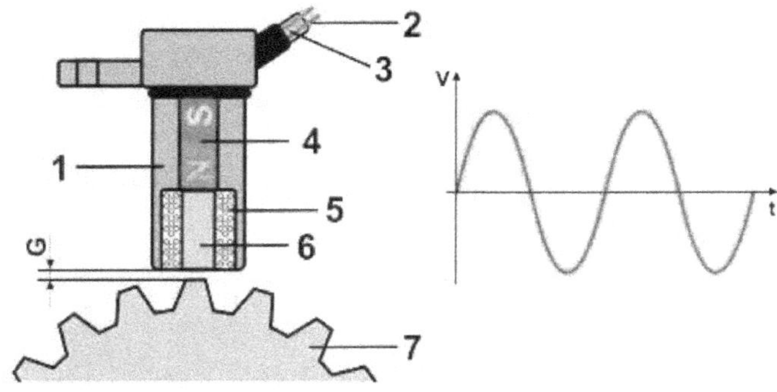

Fig 22.3- Speed pick up sensor

16. How magnetic pick-up sensor installed for speed measurement?

Ans: Following are the steps of installation of magnetic pick-up sensors:

- At first ensure the healthiness of the probe by measuring resistance of the coil. The value of resistance should be in the range of 100 ohm to 500 ohm.
- Insert the probe in the hall provided for installation. Measure the air gap between sensor tip and the trigger wheel by the gauge filler. The value should be: $G \approx 0.8 - 1.5$ mm.
- When the gap is set, tighten the check nut securely against the housing or bracket so the pickup cannot turn in or out.

17. Explain stroboscopic method of speed measurement.

Ans: The stroboscopic method is a non-contact optical technique used to measure the rotational speed (RPM) of a moving object, such as a rotating shaft, fan, or motor.

A stroboscope emits brief pulses of light at an adjustable frequency. The user directs the light toward the rotating object.

When the flash rate matches the rotational speed (or a multiple of it), the object appears stationary or slow-moving due to the persistence of vision. The strobe frequency (flashes per second) is adjusted until the object appears stationary. The RPM is then calculated as:

RPM=Strobe Flash Frequency (Hz)×60

Miscellaneous Instruments

18. What is Flame scanner and how it works?

Ans: Flame detector is an instrument used to detect flame in the combustion chamber of gas turbine and gas or coal fired boiler.

Flame scanners detect the ultraviolet (UV), infrared (IR), or visible light radiation emitted by a flame. The flame scanner converts the detected radiation into an electrical signal.

19. What is spark plug and how it works?

Ans: Spark is a component that ignites the air-fuel mixture within the combustion chamber of gas turbine or gas engines.

Ignition system consists of spark plug and ignition transformer. The ignition transformer generates a high voltage, typically between 10,000 and 50,000 volts. This voltage is supplied to the spark plug. The high voltage creates a strong electric field across the spark gap. When the voltage exceeds the dielectric strength of the air in the gap, the air becomes ionized, turning it into a conductor. The ionized air allows current to flow between the central and ground electrodes. This sudden discharge produces a spark that ignites the air-fuel mixture in the combustion chamber.

20. What is hall effect sensor? Explain its working principle.

Ans: A Hall Effect sensor is a device that detects the presence of a magnetic field and converts it into an electrical signal. It is widely used for speed sensing, position detection.

The sensor consists of a thin semiconductor layer through which a constant current flows. When a magnetic field is applied perpendicular to the semiconductor, it disturbs the movement of charge carriers. This disturbance creates a voltage difference across the semiconductor, called the Hall Voltage (V_H). The magnitude of V_H is proportional to the strength of the magnetic field. The Hall voltage is amplified and processed to generate an analog or digital signal, which can be used to detect speed, position.

21. What is proximity sensor?

Ans: A proximity sensor is a non-contact sensing device used to detect the presence or absence of an object within a specific range.

22. What are the different types of proximity sensor?

Ans: The different types of proximity sensor are: -

- **_Inductive Proximity Sensor:_** It detects metal objects using electromagnetic induction. When a metal object comes near the sensor, it changes the inductive field, generating an output signal.

- **_Capacitive Proximity Sensor:_** It detects both metal and non-metal objects (plastic, wood, liquid, etc.). Works by sensing changes in the electric field when an object is nearby.

- **_Optical (Photoelectric) Proximity Sensor:_** It uses a light beam (infrared or laser) to detect objects.

- **_Ultrasonic Proximity Sensor:_** It uses sound waves (ultrasound) to detect objects and measure distances.

23. What is a MEMS sensor?

Ans: MEMS stands for Micro-Electro-Mechanical Systems. A MEMS sensor is a small device that integrates mechanical elements, sensors, actuators, and electronics on a single chip to detect and measure various physical quantities like pressure, temperature, acceleration.

Example, Accelerometers: Measure acceleration and motion, used in smartphones for orientation and gaming. Temperature Sensors: Measure temperature, used in DCS PLC cards.

24. What is RVDT?

Ans: RVDT (Rotary Variable Differential Transformer) is an electro-mechanical transducer that provides a variable AC output voltage that is proportional to the angular displacement of its input shaft. RVDT is an electro-mechanical inductive transducer that converts angular displacement into the corresponding electrical signal. It is the most widely used inductive sensor due to its high accuracy level. Since the coil of RVDT is designed to measure an angular position, it is also known as an angular position sensor.

LVDT uses the soft iron core to measure the linear displacement whereas RVDT uses the Cam-shaped core (Rotating core) for measuring the angular displacement.

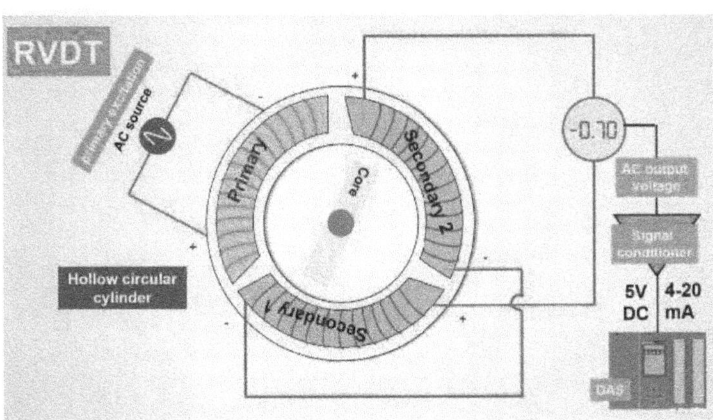

Fig 22.4- RVDT

25. What is an Inductive and Capacitive Transducer? What are their Applications in Industry?

Ans: An inductive transducer works on the principle that the inductance of a coil changes with the position or movement of a magnetic material. When displacement, pressure, or force changes the distance or area between magnetic parts, the inductance varies, producing a measurable signal.

Applications: LVDT (Linear Variable Differential Transformer) for displacement measurement, Proximity sensors for metal detection, Pressure and vibration measurement in heavy machinery.

A capacitive transducer operates based on changes in capacitance caused by the variation in distance, area, or dielectric constant between two conductive plates. Changes in physical parameters like displacement or pressure alter the capacitance, which is then measured.

Applications: Level measurement of liquids and solids, Proximity and position sensing, Pressure sensing in clean environments (e.g., semiconductor or pharmaceutical industries)

Table of Contents

1. Units and Measurement 1–4
2. Fundamentals of Instrumentation 5–16
3. Basics of Electrical Engineering 17–24
4. Tubes and Fittings 25–31
5. Instrumentation Cable and Connectors......................32–46
6. Analog Instrumentation Signals................................47–60
7. Pressure Measurement 61–81
8. Temperature Measurements 82–106
9. Level Measurements 107–118
10. Flow Measurements 119–143
11. Vibration Measurements 144–157
12. Discrete Process Measurements (Switches) 158–164
13. Instrumentation Documents 165–172
14. Pneumatic System 173–182
15. Valves and Actuators 183–224
16. Process Control..225–251
17. Industrial Communication System..........................252–294
18. Industrial Control System 295–322
19. Safety Instrumentation 323–339
20. Gas & Fire Detection System 340–346
21. Analysers 347–353
22. Miscellaneous Industrial Instruments 354–364

Preface

The book titled ***Mastering in Instrumentation: Questions and Answers*** is designed to serve as a comprehensive resource for instrumentation engineering interviews. It covers a wide spectrum of topics relevant to the field of industrial instrumentation, providing detailed explanations supported by necessary figures and illustrations.

The content ranges from conventional pneumatic systems to the latest Foundation Fieldbus technology, ensuring readers gain a thorough understanding of both traditional and modern instrumentation concepts. The book is written in clear and simple language, making it accessible to a broad audienc

Instrumentation engineering is a multidisciplinary field that draws upon fundamentals from mechanical, electrical, electronics, and information technology. Recognizing this, the book includes essential basics from all these domains to provide a well-rounded foundation.

This book is intended not only for fresh graduates and job seekers preparing for interviews but also for experienced professionals seeking a handy reference. Additionally, it can serve as a practical handbook for working engineers and students alike.

I hope this book aids readers in mastering instrumentation concepts and helps them confidently face interviews and professional challenges in this dynamic field.

Acknowledgments

- Lessons In Industrial Instrumentation by Tony R. Kuphaldt
- Measurement and Instrumentation Principles by Alan S. Morris
- Instrumentation Reference Book by Walt Boyes
- Industrial Instrumentation and control by S.K. singh
- instrumentationtools.com
- control.com